A DETAILED HISTORY OF

# RAF MANSTON

1945-1999

# A DETAILED HISTORY OF RAF MANSTON 1945-1999

JOE BAMFORD, JOHN WILLIAMS,
AND PETER GALLAGHER

FONTHILL

*This book is dedicated to*
*the memory of author John Williams, who died just as this book was going to final editing on Saturday 19 October 2019. John was a renowned historian and archivist, especially on subject matter concerning Kent and Thanet. Having been involved with a number of organisations over the years, such as the Manston History Club and Margate Historical Society, John's knowledge and experience will be very much missed by all those who knew him.*

Fonthill Media Language Policy

Fonthill Media publishes in the international English language market. One language edition is published worldwide. As there are minor differences in spelling and presentation, especially with regard to American English and British English, a policy is necessary to define which form of English to use. The Fonthill Policy is to use the form of English native to the author. Joe Bamford, John Williams, and Peter Gallagher were born and educated in the UK; therefore British English has been adopted in this publication.

Fonthill Media Limited
Fonthill Media LLC
www.fonthillmedia.com
office@fonthillmedia.com

First published in the United Kingdom and the United States of America 2020

British Library Cataloguing in Publication Data:
A catalogue record for this book is available from the British Library



ISBN 978-1-78155-764-8



Typeset in 10pt on 13pt Sabon
Printed and bound in England

FOREWORD

# Mighty Manston

Royal Air Force Manston has a long, distinguished history and its place in the annals of RAF History is secure.

Most people know the airfield for its role during the critical phase of the Battle of Britain. However, it fulfilled a variety of key functions throughout the war in an area of South East England that came to be known as 'Hell Fire Corner', which was well justified. Crews of damaged bombers found Manston's runway the most welcome sight, and FIDO allowed aircraft to land when the only other option was abandonment; finally, the V-1 threat brought Manston to the front of the fight yet again as the first operational jet fighter base in the RAF.

Less well known is Manston's pre-war role, and this is well detailed in Joe Bamford's fourth volume of his detailed history of the airfield.

RAF Manston played an important role in the Cold War both as a US strategic bomber and fighter base and a key V-bomber dispersal unit. Additionally, the airfield, with its long and welcoming runways, retained a key diversion status while SAR helicopters rescued hundreds from the sea and surrounding coast. No. 1 Air Experience Flight and 617 Voluntary Gliding School gave 'first flights' to thousands of cadets. Laterally, the airfield's civil role increased significantly, and Girdier Aviation became a renowned flying school, which has made the airfield's demise all the more disappointing. The arrival of the Fire Training School brought a new important role to the station.

As a former station commander of RAF Manston, it is a special place for me and my wife. The area is steeped in military history and it was an honour to be involved with the veterans' groups and clubs in the area, which all relished their contact with the RAF through 'their station'. The local community, including the Cinque Ports, know the value of the service and the services. We met many brave airmen—Les Colquhoun, DFC, GM, DFM (who brought the hovercraft to Thanet), and Jack Peppiatt (Operations Oyster and jubilee) to name just two—and I had the privilege of welcoming Tom Gleave, perhaps the most distinguished of our station commanders, back to RAF Manston for the seventy-fifth anniversary of the RAF, and, poignantly, of attending a dinner of the Guinea Pig Club at nearby East Grinstead.

RAF Manston may have gone, but there is much to see. I urge you to take the time to visit the Spitfire and Hurricane Memorial Museum and the display at the adjacent History Club. When you visit, take a moment to look across the airfield, over the wide grass expanse of grass to beyond the main runway towards the Channel in the distance. You may not see many aircraft, but you will be in the presence of history—and you may just see or sense a ghost or two. Manston has indeed Arisen and is Protected.

Grp Capt. Alastair Montgomery, OBE, MA, RAF (Ret'd)

# Acknowledgements

First of all, we must thank Grp Capt. Alastair Montgomery for writing the Foreword to this book. As a former CO of RAF Manston, he is extremely knowledgeable about events at the station and we have really appreciated his help and support.

Without the valuable help of our researcher at The National Archives, Peter Gallagher, it would have been very difficult to access the Operational Records Books for RAF Manston. Thanks go to him and fellow author John Williams, who has spent many hours checking the local newspapers for snippets of information of those incidents and events that were either not recorded in the ORB or when the ORBs were not available (as mentioned below).

We must also thank Elizabeth Halls who allowed us to use information and from her book *Flying Blind* (Fonthill Media), which is the story about her father, former Flt Lt Bryan Wild. During Bryan's wartime career, he trained and worked alongside two men who would later go on to become the COs of RAF Manston. One of them was Wg Cdr Bernard Wills, whose son, Nigel, has also contributed a photo of his father. Elizabeth's book is a wonderful account of men such as her late father who never became household names but played a great part in the struggle for victory.

Former newspaper photographer Collin Wilson has donated a number of the photographs to this series, including the ones that appeared on the front cover of Volume 1. He had also kindly donated some photos for this book, including the dramatic shot of G-ANCG's crash landing at Manston.

Due to the lack of information from official sources, we must also acknowledge that we have drawn upon Rocky Stockman's *The History of RAF Manston*, third edition, 1986. That book, which is now out of print, was published to celebrate seventy years of RAF Manston and was one of the first to cover the history of the station.

Finally, we must thank Mr David Otteson, the manager of the Holiday Inn Express Ramsgate–Minster for allowing us to use the hotel to launch our book on the premises. Previously known as the Prospect Inn, the building has long associations with RAF personnel who, for many years, used it as a local pub. We think it is fitting that we have maintained the connection with the hotel, which is now a listed building.

# CONTENTS

# Introduction

This is the fourth and final book in the series that covers the history of RAF Manston for the period from May 1945 until the RAF withdrew at the end of March 1999. Volume 3, which covered the years 1941–1945, was called, '*Arise to Protect*', but the coat of arms bearing that motto was not awarded to RAF Manston until November 1948, the period covered in this book.

After the Second World War, RAF Manston continued as an active station, but in 1950, it was occupied by the USAF. Various American fighter-bomber units were stationed at Manston until 1958, when the station was handed back to the Air Ministry.

There was a brief period when the airfield was closed and kept on a care and maintenance programme, but in 1959, it was reactivated and once more occupied by the RAF. Civil aviation played a great part in the growth of Manston and the first regular flights to the Middle East were operated from the airfield by Skyways using the Avro York. During the early 1960s, Air Ferry, Silver City Airways, and Invicta Airways also used Manston as a base for their operations, and the very first trooping flights were flown from the airfield.

Having been classified by the Air Ministry as a 'Master Diversion' airfield, RAF Manston was, for many years, open twenty-four hours a day and available to both civil and military aircraft 365 days a year. It was also later equipped with the Pyrene Foam System, which both civil and military aircraft could use when they had problems with their undercarriage, and there is no doubt that the facility's decision to lay down a foam carpet saved many lives. The most spectacular occasion that it was used was on 20 April 1967 when a British Eagle Britannia made a complete wheels-up landing on it.

It is claimed that Manston was the only station to serve in every command of the RAF, and until its closure in 1999, it probably dealt with more diverse types of aircraft than any other station. During its eighty-three years as a Royal Naval/RAF airfield, it played host to the Sopwith Camel, the Spitfire, Me 109, He 111, B-29, B-47, Tu-104, F-84, and Concorde, plus many other types that are too numerous to mention. We doubt that any other airfield has ever handled so many different types!

1

# The Czech Invasion

On 14 May 1945, the Operational Record Book (ORB) of RAF Manston noted that a 'Milestone' had been reached in the station's history: the change over from a wartime routine to that of a peace time regime. Headquarters of 11 Group Fighter Command had stipulated that the new working hours were to be from 8.30 a.m. to 5.30 p.m. On Wednesday afternoons, airmen were encouraged to participate in sport and organised games; Saturday afternoons and Sundays were classified as free time.

On the same day, it was noted that there had been thirteen operational visitors to Manston and that the Mosquitos of 29 Squadron, which had arrived on 11 May had carried out six night-flying tests. No. 310 Squadron's Spitfires had carried out a single test flight, while those of 312 and 313 Squadrons remained inactive. The three Czech squadrons had arrived at Manston on 27 February.

The Station Commander, Grp Capt. Murray, was visited by the Senior Account's Officer on 15 May and he was deeply concerned about the Pay Accounts Section, which was short of staff and, as a result, was being overworked. They both knew that there was no point in requesting an increase in staff, but something had to be done immediately and so they agreed to discontinue casual pay parades. This was a practice whereby an airman could request and collect his pay before the official pay day, which was normally on a Thursday. By abandoning this practice, it was assumed that it would give Pay Accounts staff more time to get on with other everyday work.

A novel concept at Manston was that the runway had its own CO in the form of an officer who actually commanded the 'Emergency Runway Party'. This was Fg Off. B. C. Wells, but he was posted out to Bradwell Bay on 15 May. Fg Off. L. E. Wade, who was described as Manston's 'Venerable' Flying Control Officer, was also posted out to 46 Group HQ on the 17th.

Over the next few days, 29, 312 (Czech), and 313 (Czech) Squadrons were increasingly active and they spent a number of sorties practising formation flying. No. 310 (Czech) Squadron was similarly engaged but carried out a number of

'Taxi' flights, including ferrying the CO, the Czech wing leader, and Wg Cdr Hlado to Hornchurch.

On Sunday 27 May, the first post-war church parade was held in the station's church and it was noted that there was an excellent turn out. The service was taken by the station *padre*, Sqn Ldr Pellet. On the same day, the Army's Territorial Unit Number 584 arrived, and its troops immediately proceeded to dig themselves into various entrenched positions around the station.

Although the war with Germany was over, the war with Japan was still continuing and RAF units continued to carry out exercises, practising tactics that might be used in the Far East. On 29 May, twelve Spitfires of 310 Squadron flew to Little Walden to carry out practice dogfights with American P-51 Mustangs. No. 312 Squadron was detailed to intercept twenty Lancasters that were being escorted by Mustangs during a simulated bombing attack on Portsmouth Dockyard. Two aircraft from 312 Squadron's 'B' Flight were detailed to carry out a weather reconnaissance over Lille.

On the first day of June, RAF Manston received a visit from Flt Lt Stirling, later of 11 Group but now working for the Air Ministry. He was accompanied by a warrant officer and two senior NCOs, and their task was to see how the amount of paperwork could be reduced, especially that involving 'Returns'. Their visit was seen by some as a sign that demobilisation would soon take place, but airmen had been warned that there was no indication of an early release for anyone.

Three members of the ground crew from 29 Squadron were taken on what was described as a 'Tour of the Continent' on 4 June in an Airspeed Oxford. There is no mention of exactly where they were going, but it is quite likely they were taken to see the bomb damage caused by Bomber Command or those targets that had been attacked by the unit's Mosquitos.

On the same day, seven Spitfires from 310 Squadron were engaged in carrying out a 'practice transport escort' when they accompanied two Oxfords from Christchurch to Sandown. The Oxfords were simulating the role of a couple of Dakotas that would carry the king, the queen, and the Royal Family to the Channel Islands on 7 June. Among the pilots involved was Sqn Ldr Hartman who landed at Northolt to attend a briefing about the escort duty before returning to Manston.

Later that same day, the same practice escort was carried out by both 312 and 313 Squadrons. At 8.30 a.m. on the 7th, pilots were briefed, and at 1.10 p.m., thirteen Spitfires, under the command of Wg Cdr Hlado, DFC, took-off on what was described as 'transport escort 143'. There was a spare aircraft in case of technical failure, but it was not required, and it returned to Manston at 2 p.m. The two Dakotas carrying the Royal Party had been late in taking-off from Northolt, and the Spitfires had to circle Jersey for fifty minutes before they could proceed any further. Once the Dakotas had landed safely on Guernsey, the aircraft flew to Warmwell to refuel before returning to Manston later.

No. 29 Squadron was kept busy on 9 June arranging and practising for a mass flypast at SHAEF HQ in Frankfurt the next day, for the benefit of Russian Army Commander General Georgy Zhukov. Wg Cdr Allan and his navigator Fg Off. Martin, and Sqn Ldr Bradwell and Flt Lt Schroder were among those that took part, but the latter crew had to land at Wiesbaden with engine trouble.

Also on the 9th, a large-scale annual sports day was held, which attracted a lot of competitors and a number of important guests, including Air Cdre Russell, the Senior Air Staff Officer of 11 Group, and Maj.-Gen. Kippenberger from the General Staff of New Zealand. It was noted that tea and cakes disappeared at a remarkable rate, eaten mainly by agile competitors and perhaps some of those not so agile. The prizes, which were laid out on a table, remained unmolested despite the fact that they received many covetous glances, suggesting that they might be removed by a 'Tip and Run' raid at any moment.

For the next few days, Manston's units took part in a variety of different exercises involving night flying rests, practice interceptions, and fighter affiliations. Some of these were carried out with the Americans, and on the 13th, 313 Squadron's Spitfires flew to Boxted to carry out fighter affiliation with the USAF's P-47 Thunderbolts. On the same day, the Mosquitos of 406 (Canadian) Squadron, which had been based at Manston since November 1944, left for their new home at Predannack near Mullion in Cornwall. For the remainder of June, there was very little else to report in the ORB and it was just a succession of night flying tests, fighter affiliations, and other exercises.

On 1 July, the weather was fair in the morning but later there were thundery showers and there was no flying on account of it being a Sunday. RAF Manston played a game of cricket in Canterbury against Betteshanger Colliery and the game was a draw. Betteshanger was one of three Kent coal mines situated near Deal, the other two being Tilmanstone and Snowdown Colliery. On Wednesday 4 July, during sports afternoon, RAF Manston played another cricket match against RAF Hawkinge and were beaten by 90 runs, with Hawkinge scoring 143 for 5 wickets declared.

There was a lecture in the station's cinema on the 4th by a Mr E. A. Vaughan about 'The Historical Politics of the Political Parties'. There is no doubt that this was to inform and prepare the station's personnel for the General Election, which was to take place the next day. Politics is an issue rarely discussed on military bases, but given the circumstances, after five years of war, it was probably considered an appropriate measure. During the evening, there was an ENSA variety show at the Grand Hotel in Cliftonville, which was attended by a large number of airmen from Manston.

No. 310 Squadron carried our twenty-one non-operational sorties on 9 July that amounted to twenty-six hours and three minutes of flying time. They were not active at all on the 10th, but on the 11th, a party was held in the Westgate Pavilion to celebrate the squadron's fifth anniversary. No. 310 Squadron had been formed at Duxford on 10 July 1940 with mainly Czech personnel and had been equipped with the Hurricane Mk I. It had been pronounced operational on 18 August and taken part in the Battle of Britain. It had been equipped with the Spitfire IIA in October 1941, and by the time it arrived at Manston in February 1945, it had been re-equipped with the Spitfire IX.

On 13 July, there were seven non-operational visitors at Manston including one that was described in the ORB as a 'Super Fortress'. The aircraft had arrived from Bovingdon and presumably was an American Boeing B-29 Superfortress. The RAF was also later equipped with this type, which was a descendant from the B-17 Flying Fortress and known as the 'Washington'. It did not enter service with the RAF until 1950.

Exercise 'Ramrod' No. 6 was held on the 13th, which involved Spitfires from 313 Squadron that were assigned to escort twenty Lancasters that were to 'bomb' a communications centre at Southend. Some 20 miles east of North Foreland, the formation was intercepted by a dozen Mustangs, which resulted in a mock dogfight, during which four Mustangs were 'destroyed' for the loss of a single Spitfire. This exercise was part of the training for 'Tiger Force', an operation involving long-range British heavy bombers that were to have worked with American escorts to bomb Japanese forces in the Far East. Fortunately, the war came to an end before the force was deployed.

On the 15th, 29 Squadron's Sqn Ldr Bradwell and Flt Lt Schroder were flown to Tangmere to take part in a seven-week-long 'Night Fighter Leader Course'. The following day, there were two emergency landings, including one by a 65 Squadron Mustang, YT-B, from Bentwaters, flown by Fg Off. Romain, who landed on Runway 11 after experiencing hydraulic problems.

There were a couple of other emergencies over the next few days, and on the 16th, a 464 Squadron Mosquito flown by Lt Clark landed downwind when his aircraft had been damaged after he had flown into some wires over the continent. The following day, a 608 Squadron Mosquito from Downham Market made an emergency landing after its starboard engine had failed.

There were twenty-eight non-operational visitors on 21 July, including thirteen Typhoons of 181 Squadron that flew in from Denmark. Later that same day, yet another Mosquito, call sign *Playfare 40*, flown by Flt Lt Collier, made a wheels-up landing. On the same day, Sqn Ldr D. G. Benson arrived from East Kirby to take up the duties of station chaplain. That night, 29 Squadron personnel held a dance at the Oddfellows Hall in Ramsgate, which was quite a successful occasion.

There was another show on the 23rd held at Wellington House, Westgate, called Snap Happy, performed by a group called Stars in Battledress. Two days later, there was a WAAF invitation dance at the Convent, which was being used as a mess in Westgate and another good time was had by all.

On the 26th, 29 Squadron was preparing its Mosquitos for standby duties to escort the prime minister on his flight from the Potsdam Conference. Eight of its aircraft were fitted with drop tanks and were flight tested during the afternoon. There was political comment in the ORB that there was 'eager anticipation' that Churchill should have won the General Election but a mention that there had been a great Labour victory.

No. 29 Squadron was not called upon to escort Churchill's aircraft on its return flight to England, but it did provide an escort for the new prime minister's aircraft. Mr Atlee's Skymaster (DC-4) flew from Northolt to Gatow, Berlin, on the 28th when he took over the talks at Potsdam from Churchill. Eight aircraft of 29 Squadron took-off at 6 a.m. to provide the escort, with another six from 85 Squadron, and it was an honour for both units. Before their return flights, the aircraft refuelled at Calais and each crew completed seven hours' flying, having to battle their way through a severe thunderstorm to reach Manston at 8.30 p.m. Later that night, 29 Squadron held a party at Doone House, Westgate, which began at 10 p.m. and went on until the early hours.

The last day of July 1945 was a busy one and 310 Squadron flew eight sorties that lasted six hours and forty-five minutes, mainly practising formation flying. No. 29 Squadron flight tested its aircraft all afternoon, and at the end of the day, twelve Mosquitos were noted as being fully serviceable.

On the same day, Sqn Ldr Arthur V. Clowes, DFC, DFM, a Battle of Britain pilot and former CO of 145 and 94 Squadrons, was posted out to the staff college at Bracknell. Clowes had been credited with eleven enemy aircraft destroyed, but his flying career had ended unexpectedly in November 1943 when he lost any eye during a boisterous session in the mess at Uxbridge, which got out of control. Having been transferred to the secretarial branch with a permanent commission, he had become the senior administrative officer at Manston.

There were twenty-five non-operational visitors to Manston on the first day of August, and 29 Squadron personnel were busy carrying out taxi runs and air tests. Three pilots from 312 Squadron flew to Colerne in Wiltshire, two of them in Austers that were being used as 'Hacks' and another in a 29 Squadron Mosquito. Later in the day, they returned to Manston, each in a brand-new Spitfire Mk IXE. The following day, a number of pilots were flown to Colerne and Lyneham to collect another five brand-new Spitfires while the ground crews at Manston were busy painting the aircraft in Czech Air Force markings.

At 3 p.m. on 3 August, the Czech Wing was paraded in front of flying control and inspected by the Air Member for Personnel AM Sir John Slessor and AM Janoušek. The wing then marched past with the two air marshals taking the salute before work resumed in painting the Spitfires in Czech colours and preparing to fly them to Czechoslovakia. The next day, the first consignment of the Czech Wing departed from Manston in five Liberators of 311 (Czech) Squadron to fly to Prague, four of which later returned to the station.

Sqn Ldr Hrbáček of 312 Squadron addressed all the RAF ground crews on the morning of the 6th and spoke to them in English, before thanking them and their Czech colleagues. He then formally said 'Goodbye' on behalf of all the Czech airmen.

At 7 a.m. on 7 August, there was a final briefing for the squadron commander, and at 7.40 a.m. the Spitfires started their engines and slowly began to taxi from the dispersals towards the runway.

At 8 a.m. in clear weather, the first section of six aircraft, led by Wg Cdr Hlado, was airborne, and after forming up, they flew across the airfield. They were followed by 310 Squadron, led by Sqn Ldr Hartman, and 313 Squadron, led by Sqn Ldr Kučera. The final twelve Spitfires made up of three sections were led by Flt Lt Kaaal.

At 10.30 a.m., news came through that the fifteen Liberators of 311 Squadron that were to accompany the Spitfires would not be able to go because of bad weather and they were to remain at Manston. The pilots of the Spitfires that had already departed were ordered to land at Hildesheim and remain there for at least twenty-four hours. A small number 312 Squadron's Spitfires remained at Manston and were to follow on later.

On the 12th, a 44 Squadron Lancaster, flown by Fg Off. Smith arrived from Italy with twenty passengers on board. The aircraft had lost some of its hydraulics, and although its brakes failed, it made a safe landing, and nobody was injured.

The following day, it was noted in the ORB that 312 Squadron's Spitfires had flown the last leg of their journey from Hildesheim to Prague where they had all landed safely at 5 p.m. Back at Manston, twelve Spitfires put on a display for members of the Royal Observer Corps.

The 15th was VJ-Day, which was only briefly mentioned in the ORB. It was noted that 'All concentration should be applied to suitable celebrations'; however, there is no mention of what form the celebrations took, but it did state that all flying was excluded. There must have been a huge sense of relief among all those serving at Manston that the chances of them of them being posted out to the Far East had been very much reduced.

Three Austers of 312 Squadron took-off for the long flight to Prague at 6.30 a.m. on 18 August, with FS Machek in charge of the trio. He had been ordered to make five refuelling stops along the way, and the following day, three more Spitfires arrived for the unit and were painted in Czech Air Force colours.

At 7.30 a.m. on the 21st, some of the final elements of the Czech Air Force were due to depart for Prague and under the command of Wg Cdr Bibral. They taxied out to the main runway, but that was as far as they got. Because of heavy rain at Manston and the bad weather forecast along the route, it was decided to abandon the mission. The Spitfires, four from 312 Squadron, three from 310 Squadron, and four from 313, returned to dispersal.

Also on the 21st, Wg Cdr Rupert Francis Henry Clerke, DFC, arrived from Swanton Morley to take over the post of CO at RAF Manston from Wg Cdr A.

D. Murray. Clerke had been granted a permanent commission in 1937 and was a pilot who had flown in the Battle of Britain with 79 Squadron, which had been based at Acklington. Clerke was posted in from 125 Squadron, based at Church Fenton, and he had been credited with four enemy aircraft destroyed. Clerke was a highly talented pilot and had been chosen to demonstrate the Mosquito to the king and queen at Watton in 1941 and he had also broken a number of records while flying the type, of which he was best associated.

No. 567 Squadron arrived at Manston on 21 August, having been posted in from Hawkinge. The unit that had been formed at Detling on 1 December 1943 was equipped with the Spitfire Mk VB and Mk XVI, but it had already begun to re-equip with the Vultee Vengeance Mk IV.

It was the 24th before the weather improved sufficiently for the Czech Air Force Spitfires to depart, and at 8.30 a.m., they finally took off. They were ordered to route via Eindhoven and Achmer, in Lower Saxony, where they were to refuel, then proceed to Gräfendorf in Bavaria and from there to Prague.

There were ten non-operational visitors on the 27th, including an air ambulance that conveyed the wife of the Governor-General of Guernsey back to the island. On the last day of August, there were fourteen non-operational visitors, including a VIP, the details of which are not listed. No. 29 Squadron carried out a lot of local flying, including five night-flying tests and a lot of testing on the ground.

## 2

# 567 Squadron

It is unfortunate that the Operational Records for the month of September 1945 are missing from the National Archives at Kew. Nothing else of any significance is thought to have happened during the month, but it is sad that a whole month's history is missing from the records. It was in September, however, that the Transport Command Examination Unit arrived at Manston. It would be responsible for checking out aircrew and supporting those existing Transport Command crews that passed through the station.

The ORBs for those other units based at Manston, such as 567 Squadron, still exist, and on 9 September, Wg Cdr Bond met the SASO of 11 Group, Air Cdre Russell, to discuss the possibility of 567 Squadron acquiring a Meteor for fast low-level work in co-operation with the army. The air commodore authorised Bond to make his own enquiries as to where he might get a Meteor but could not help him any further. Next day, Bond had a meeting with the CO of 1335 Conversion Unit, Wg Cdr Bird Wilson. Wilson stated that he had at least one Meteor to spare, but when 11 Group was notified, it refused to authorise the loan of the aircraft.

Bad news was received by 567 Squadron on 19 September when the police notified the unit that the wreckage of a Spitfire had been found on Great Arden Moor in Yorkshire. It was almost immediately discovered that it was Flt Lt Catterns's aircraft, SM278, which had been reported as overdue while returning from Acklington three days earlier.

Flt Lt Catterns had flown the aircraft to Acklington on the 16th to take part in the Battle of Britain Anniversary weekend and had taken off from there at 2.35 p.m. to return to Manston. There had been a suggestion that he may have landed at Dishforth to refuel and that he might have become disorientated after taking off from there, but that has never been confirmed. Twenty-two-year-old John Burleigh Catterns from Westminster in London was buried in Harrogate Cemetery on 26 September.

On 1 October, Flt Lt George Eric Ball was posted in as 'B' Flight Commander on 567 Squadron. Ball had joined the RAF in 1937 and had been posted to

19 Squadron in February 1938, but he was later transferred to 242 Squadron during the height of the Battle of Britain.

The following day was very busy, with thirty non-operational landings and nine HF and two VHF homings beings made. Among the visitors was a 626 Squadron Lancaster from Glatton that landed with engine trouble, and among the passengers that arrived was the commander of the Home Fleet, Adml Reginald Maurice James Hutton.

During the first couple of weeks in October, the runway was being repaired by spraying tar on to its surface, but that did not stop a very rare visitor from landing at Manston on the 8th. The aircraft that touched down at 2.38 p.m. flown by a German pilot was a former Luftwaffe twin-engined jet, an Arado 234 (Blitz), which had entered service in late 1944 with KG 76. The type, which was the world's first operational jet bomber, had mainly been used for reconnaissance, but in its other role as a bomber, it had operated over the Normandy beaches shortly after D-Day.

Trouble was brewing the next day, and Sqn Ldr Bond, the CO of 567 Squadron, was sent for by the station commander and interviewed about a number of the unit's Spitfires that had 'Beaten Up' one of its own dispersal. The following day, Sqn Ldr Bond was ordered to report to HQ 11 Group, which suggests that his interview with Wg Cdr Clerke had not gone well.

A 29 Squadron Mosquito attempted to break the air speed record on the 13th, but there is no mention of whether it succeeded. Another of its Mosquitos flew to Bentwaters for an 'At Home' day but crashed on landing, causing Cat. 'B' damage. On the same day, an Auster made a forced landing near Deal but was repaired and flown into Manston the following day.

Manston was seemingly being used as a base for a shuttle service between England and Italy, and on the 17th, a Lancaster was airborne for Italy at dawn, while another landed from Italy at dusk. The following day, a 5 Group Lancaster took-off at 7 a.m., destined for Italy with twenty passengers.

Sqn Ldr Bond was posted out on the 18th and Flt Lt Ball assumed command of 567 Squadron. Two days later, he addressed members of the squadron and spoke to them about discipline and efficiency, which suggests that this was in connection with the 'Beat Up' of the airfield on the 8th and possible the reason why Sqn Ldr Bond had been replaced as the CO. Wg Cdr Evans also arrived from 11 Group HQ and promised to provide two more Vengeance aircraft very soon.

A model of RAF Manston that had been built by the intelligence section was taken to Ramsgate on the 19th and exhibited for 'Savings Week'. Tar spraying continued on the runway, though by this time work had progressed to the centre section. No. 29 Squadron was active on night-flying and flew sorties to Drem and Gatwick, while four Mosquitos were engaged on 'Bull's Eye' exercises and 'destroyed' a large number of enemy bombers during the exercise.

No. 567 Squadron had a detachment at Eastchurch, and on 23 October, Flt Lt Ball flew there to inspect it. He also visited Maj. Fisher, CO of a Royal Marine's unit based in Sandwich, and discussed how they could co-operate in the future. Flt Lt Ball was promoted to acting squadron leader on the 26th and posted to 222 Squadron. Unfortunately, on 1 February 1946, he was killed when the Meteor that he was flying crashed while practising aerobatics at Fairmile in Devon. The evening that Ball was posted out, what was described a 'terrific party' was held in Doone House, Westgate, to celebrate the imminent departure of 29 Squadron and its move to West Malling.

The new CO of 567 Squadron, who would not arrive until the beginning of November, was Sqn Ldr John Minchin Hewson, DFC, a veteran of both the Battle of France and the Battle of Britain. He had joined the RAF on a short service commission in 1937, and after being posted to 142 Squadron, he had flown the Fairey Battle. He had then requested a posting to Fighter Command and joined 616 Squadron but was later selected as a flying instructor.

During the morning of the 27th, the station commander held a conference with all section commanders regarding personnel that were to carry out general station duties. At the top of the list was guard duty, but help was also needed in the cookhouse for menial work such as peeling potatoes. The Ashford district of the Royal Observer Corps visited the station during the afternoon and was shown around flying control and the station intelligence offices.

No. 29 Squadron moved out on 29 October, and Sqn Ldr Baldwin, who had served as the intelligence officer since September 1943, was also posted out. He was posted to 100 PDC, and from there, he was to be discharged from the RAF. At 3 p.m., he gave a final lecture in the intelligence office and talked about the war in the Far East. Although the war with Japan was over, airmen and officers were still being posted there as part of the occupation force.

3

# High-Speed Flight

On 30 October 1945, Grp Capt. Hugh Joseph Wilson, AFC, Commandant of the Empire Test Pilot's School, and Mr Eric Stanley Greenwood, Chief Test Pilot of Gloster Aircraft Company, arrived at Manston to prepare for an attempt to break the world air speed record. They flew in two specially adapted Gloster Meteor F.4s that had been stripped down of all unnecessary equipment. One of them represented the RAF, EE454 (*Britannia*), and the other Gloster Aviation, EE455 (*Yellow Peril*). The event was to be covered by the world's press, and later in the day, a converted Lancaster arrived with a party of accredited journalists on board.

The press was a source of discontent for those involved in the project, and when the Air Ministry stopped some journalists from getting access to Manston, two of them decided on a devious way to get around the security and chartered an aircraft to fly in. They got as far as the doors of the hangar where the Meteors were being kept, but, unfortunately, they were soon recognised and dealt with by being put under 'arrest'. After being taken to the guardroom, the men were charged with gaining entry to secret premises and were kept there until further notice.

The course for the attempt on the record had been especially prepared and ran to the east for 3 kilometres from Herne Bay Pier towards the ruined remains of Reculver Tower; several observation platforms were situated at both ends, equipped with cameras and timers. The sensitive equipment was connected by landline to the National Physical Laboratory at Teddington. One other stipulation was that the course was to be flown at exactly 200 feet. At that height, there was no room for mistakes.

The two Meteors were kept under guard in a hangar at Manston, along with another Meteor that was being used to check the weather and the course for any problems with the time and testing equipment. The third Meteor was normally flown by Flt Lt Clarke.

As an addendum to the ORB on the last day of October 1945, there were a couple of paragraphs titled 'Padre's Notes'. In them, it was noted that the

Red Cross 'Penny a Week' fund had been closed but had raised £221 14*s* and, in addition to that, another £45 had been raised by the efforts of the mayor of Margate.

The model of RAF Manston that had been loaned to the town of Ramsgate to help it to promote 'Savings Week' was returned to the station on 1 November. The next day, it was noted that tar spraying was still being carried out on the runway and the circle and lead-in lights were now fully functional and being used by flying control. A Dakota, which, for some reason, was unable to land anywhere else in Britain or the continent, landed at Manston, but the ORB does not explain where it came from.

Nos 130 and 165 Squadrons, both equipped with the Spitfire IX, arrived at Manston on 4 November, having flown from Norway where they had been supporting the Norwegian Air Force. Immediately upon their arrival, all personnel were sent on disembarkation leave.

Also on the 4th, a Halifax from 38 Group made an emergency landing at Manston after it had lost the power from one of its engines. The aircraft had taken off from Earls Colne and was flying to Malta carrying the diplomatic mail. The mail was offloaded and taken to the control tower for safekeeping and a guard was maintained on the Halifax throughout the night.

Sqn Ldr Day visited Manston on the 7th in connection with a Canadian Flying Fortress that had passed through three days earlier and later crashed on the

A line up of 130 Squadron Spitfire Mk IXs at Manston in early 1946, prior to its move to Acklington. The aircraft second in the line appears to be a Harvard, which was probably used as a squadron hack.

continent. The flight had originated in Ottawa, Canada, and it was carrying medical aid in the form of thirty-nine cases of penicillin that was destined for Poland. The aircraft, serial number 9202, which belonged to 168 Heavy Transport Squadron (RCAF), had landed at Manston on the 3rd, having flown in from Prestwick after crossing the Atlantic. The aircraft, which had been the first B-17 (formerly 43-3160) to be transferred from the USAAF to the RCAF, was being used for VIP and mail flights. It had crashed near Halle in Germany while flying low and after hitting some trees in bad weather, with the impact killing all five crew.

It was on Wednesday 7 November 1945 that Grp Capt. Wilson and Eric Greenwood attempted to break the air speed record over the course agreed upon by international law. The previous record had been set by a German pilot, Fritz Wendel, on 26 April 1939 when he had achieved a speed of 469.22 mph while flying in a Messerschmitt 209. There was a lot of work to be carried out before the first attempt on the record could take place, as the 'sound barrier' was still something of a mystery. Speed over the course was only increased gradually so that the pilots could gain confidence as they approached unknown territory.

Later that day, members of both teams sat around waiting for the experts to evaluate the results, but the initial figures indicated that the Gloster company pilot, Eric Greenwood, had flown at just over 600 mph, while Wilson's RAF Meteor was at least 10 mph slower. Needless to say, the Gloster contingent began to celebrate and immediately started to organise a party. Unfortunately, the celebrations were a little premature.

When the figures were checked again and all the data had been analysed by the laboratory at Teddington, it was found that Wilson had flown faster than Greenwood. Wilson's Meteor had achieved an average speed of 606 mph, while Greenwood's trailed by just 3 mph at 603 mph. It had been a close-run thing, but the RAF had beaten the Gloster Aircraft Company. RAF Manston had played its part in the high-speed record attempt and it was another first for the station.

No. 438 Air Training Corps Squadron visited Manston the following day and was taken flying by 567 Squadron in the unit's Airspeed Oxford. No. 567 Squadron also carried out several flights for 71 Brigade, demonstrating radar equipment to the Swiss authorities.

It was a busy day on the 11th, with forty-six aircraft diverted to Manston. The Air Training Corps was on the station again, studying aircraft recognition before being shown an air combat film. Over the next two days, several Austers passed through Manston—nine on the 12th and another two on the 13th—on their way from the continent to RAF Andover.

The Poles were back at Manston on 13 November in the form of 303 and 316 Squadrons, which flew in from Andrews Field in Essex to take part in exercise 'Johnny'. Both units had converted and re-equipped with the Mustang in April. The first patrol the following morning had to be cancelled, but at 1.32 p.m., they took-off and rendezvoused over Beachy Head at 1.55 p.m., flying at 5,000 feet where they came under the control of HMS *Boxer* (F121), a former tank landing ship that had been converted to a fighter direction vessel in 1944.

The exercise continued the next day with the Mustangs patrolling an area between Selsey Bill and Beachy Head, again under the control of HMS *Boxer*. Maj. Mallinson of the 4th Regiment Royal Artillery was taken into the air by Flt Lt Lenton of 567 Squadron, to observe the gun emplacements that were under his control around Dover. He was later entertained in the officers' mess. Exercise 'Johnny' was completed on the 16th, and 303 and 316 Squadrons returned to Andrews Field the following day.

It was a memorable day on 20 November when a Mosquito made the first ever landing at Manston aided by the ground control approach radar. The station was one of the first to have the equipment, along with Lyneham in Wiltshire and Prestwick in Scotland.

Also known as precision approach radar, it enabled a controller on the ground to pass information to the pilot about his aircraft's height (elevation) and position (azimuth) in relation to the runway threshold. This covered the aircraft's descent and approach on a 3-degree glide path right down to a quarter of a mile from touch down. The controller informed the pilot of his exact position in relation to the ground, runway threshold, and centre line, and effectively 'talked him down'.

There were thirty-three types aircraft from Transport Command diverted to Manston on 23 November, the day that the station was visited the AOC of 46 Group, the former AOC of Fighter Command, Air Chief Marshal Sholto Douglas. He was accompanied by AVM William Elliot, Assistant Chief at the Ministry of Aircraft Production. No. 567 Squadron lost an aircraft when Fg Off. De Harn experienced engine failure while flying a Vultee Vengeance and had to make a forced landing near Graveley.

Several aircraft were talked down by GCA controllers on the 25th and there was what was described in the ORB as 'another large-scale diversion of passenger carrying aircraft from the continent'. One potential visitor, had it arrived, would have been another former Luftwaffe Ju 52, but it was diverted from Croydon. Unfortunately, the aircraft had to make a forced landing near Maidstone, but there were no casualties among those on board.

The Meteors of 245 Squadron arrived at Manston during the morning of the 27th to take part in exercise 'Tweakem One', along with the Spitfire IXs of short-term resident unit 130 Squadron, which had moved from Acklington, and 165 Squadron, which was based at Duxford. Nos 130 and 165 were scrambled at 1.50 p.m. and, having intercepted a mixed force of Mustangs and Mosquitos south of North Foreland, they gave a good account of themselves in action. No. 245 Squadron was scrambled at 2.15 p.m. and later claimed to have 'destroyed' no less than seven Mustangs and two Mosquitos for the loss of two of its own Meteors. There were twenty-five diversions on the 27th, including a Lancaster that arrived from Italy and landed on just two engines.

The following day, the exercise controller sent his congratulations to Manston on how its staff had handled the previous day's exercise. It was another busy day with twenty-five diversions, including three Ju 52s that were on their way to Brize Norton in Wiltshire. Another German type, a Siebel, on its way to Farnborough, made a forced-landing in the sea off the coast of Dover and the two-man crew were picked up by the men on duty in a light vessel. This was probably a Siebel Fh 104, a twin-engined, medium-sized aircraft that had regularly been used by senior German staff officers.

There were sixteen non-operational visitors on 1 December, including a Dakota that had been diverted from Prestwick in Scotland. That night, another Dakota landed after being diverted from Prestwick, along with a B-17 Flying Fortress from Thurleigh. On the 3rd, the CO Wg Cdr Clerke held a conference in the briefing room at the station intelligence offices. The next day, advance ground parties of both 130 and 165 Squadrons left Manston for Charter Hall, an airfield 15 miles from Berwick, where the units were to spend six weeks on an air firing course. The pilots flew the aircraft out to Charter Hall the following day.

There had been some problems with the airfield lighting system, but by 9 December, it had been modified so that the lighting on the loop, on the south-west of the airfield, could be turned on whatever runway was in use. Four Meteors arrived at Manston to practise using the ground-controlled approach system, but there is no mention which unit they were from.

There were a number of incidents between the 10th and 13th, starting with a Mosquito of 162 Squadron that made an emergency landing at 5.28 a.m. on 10 December because its starboard engine had failed. An Airspeed Oxford of 567 Squadron was on an air test on the 12th when one of its engines failed and the pilot, Flt Lt Turnbull, had to make a wheels-up landing close to No. 4 crash bay. Work began laying concrete on parts of runway at No. 2 point of runway 29.

Two Dakotas were diverted to Manston from Hurn, Bournemouth, on the 27th, one of them, which was in the service of the state airline BOAC, landed at 8.46 p.m., and between them, they were carrying forty-six passengers. Over the next few days, the weather interfered with operations, and on the 30th, strong winds meant that aircraft were diverted from Manston to other airfields. The grass runway 06/24 was waterlogged and remained closed.

4

# A New Role for Manston

During the month of December, a conference had been held by Fighter Command and the Air Ministry to decide what the peacetime establishment of RAF Manston should be. On the last day of 1945, it was recorded in the ORB that, in the future, two day-fighter squadrons should be based at Manston and a single anti-aircraft unit. Also, it was decided that Transport Command should set up a staging post to deal with the increasing number of aircraft that were being diverted there. It would be classified as 'Lodger Unit' but be responsible to the station commander at Manston.

The first few days of 1946 at Manston were quiet, and on 1 January, there were just two visiting aircraft, Dakotas, one from Croydon and the other from Blackbush. The next day, Flt Lt Valentine paid a staff visit to the equipment section but otherwise there was very little to report in the ORB. Four representatives from Transport Command arrived on the 4th to investigate the situation as regarding the setting up of the recently proposed staging post.

The most serious incident into the new year happened on 7 January at 2.15 p.m. when twenty-six-year-old Sqn Ldr Davidson was killed after his Spitfire, TZ106, had crashed and burnt out in a wood between Ashford and Maidstone. Davidson, who belonged to 450 Squadron, was flying from Dunsdorf (B116) to Gatwick, accompanied by Fg Off. Adams who had been flying in a Typhoon.

Shortly before the Spitfire crashed, Adams had called over the R/T to say that he did not like the look of the weather and thought that they should divert to Manston; Davidson was heard to agree with him. Adams's Typhoon was homed to Manston and landed safely, but there was no further contact with Davidson. Eyewitnesses claimed that Davidson's Spitfire had entered low cloud at no more than a few hundred feet before re-emerging and crashing into the ground.

Wg Cdr Clerke attended a station commander's conference at 11 Group HQ on the 8th, but operations at Manston were badly affected by the weather and a number of gale warnings. The gale warnings were only cancelled at midnight on the 12th, and on the 13th, Flt Lt Mason from 'P' Staff Fighter Command arrived to further discuss and review the manning situation at Manston.

During the morning of the 14th, Flt Lt Linton, the 'B' Flight commander, gave a lecture to 567 Squadron personnel in the briefing room. Later in the day, Wg Cdr Stopley arrived from 84 Group to chair the court of inquiry into the accident involving the death of Sqn Ldr Davidson. He was accompanied by Flt Lt Spier and Flt Lt Bateman, who made up the other members of the board.

The 16th was the final day of the air firing course for 130 Squadron at Charter Hall, and the next day, pilots helped the ground crews prepare the aircraft for the return to Manston. The next morning, twelve Spitfires from 130 Squadron took-off from Charter Hall but they all had to turn back when the pilots encountered a huge bank of snow near Middleborough. Some pilots and all of the ground crew travelled back to Thanet in a special train that departed during the early evening. It was the 28th before the twelve Spitfires managed to get back to Manston, but three of the unit's aircraft had been left behind at Charter Hall, unserviceable.

Not everyone was happy with the service that they received at Manston, and on the 28th, Wg Cdr Spencer complained about the refuelling facilities. He was a passenger in an Avro Anson engaged on communication duties that had landed from the continent at 11.35 a.m. The aircraft had taken-off at 1.21 p.m. and had been on the ground for less than two hours, on what was a busy day for the station with twenty-seven visiting aircraft, including six Mosquitos of former resident unit 29 Squadron.

On the 29th, airfield serviceability was reported as being in good condition, but there was 'Jointing' taking place on the main runway and 'Harrowing' on the grass runway. The Spitfires of Australian units 451 and 453 Squadrons, which had landed at Manston on the 27th, departed for High Ercall in Shropshire. Technically, both units had already been disbanded in Germany on the 21st and their return to the UK was just a formality.

On 30 January, it was claimed that Manston was the only airfield in the country not to have been affected by bad weather and remained open for business with four Dakotas among the many aircraft that were diverted there. During the last day of January 1946, 130 Squadron flew a number of cine-gun exercises and its CO, Sqn Ldr Woolley, later gave a talk in the intelligence section to his pilots on general flying.

There were thirty-two visiting aircraft on 1 February, including a Dakota that was diverted from Croydon with hydraulic problems affecting its undercarriage. The pilot managed to get the wheels down and managed to make a successful emergency landing. A batch of Proctors passed through Manston the next day *en route* for France, although one of them made a forced landing at Brooklands on the way. Sqn Ldr Thompson and Sqn Ldr Simpson arrived at the station in connection with another court of inquiry.

Sqn Ldr Eve from Fighter Command visited the station on the 6th, and for a two-day period, 130 Squadron carried out air-to-ground firing practice on the range at Leysdown using cannon. A district court martial was held at Manston on the 8th, with Wg Cdr Murray presiding, but there is no mention in the ORB of the serviceman who was involved. Bad weather prevented normal flying operation on the 9th when a Miles Aerovan was one of the few visiting aircraft.

There was another incident involving a 'beat up' on the 11th when Sqn Ldr Plages, flying a Spitfire VB, thundered very low over the 567 Squadron dispersals. His actions were observed by a number of officers who were not impressed by the display and he was subsequently reported to his base station at Bentwaters.

Tracking Exercise No. 1 took place on 19 February with the pilots of 130 and 567 Squadrons checking the accuracy of the Inland Stations Chain Reporting Systems. During the afternoon, there was a lecture given by Capt. Hebblethwaite from Biggin Hill about the organisation and co-operation with the Army. The following day, the AOC of Fighter Command visited the station and, along with Grp Capt. Robinson, visited Flying Control.

Wg Cdr Holmes arrived at Manston on the 21st in connection with a Dakota that had crashed at Warlingham, south of Croydon, on the 13th and the death of eight of the eighteen passengers on board. The aircraft, serial number KG397 from 435 (RCAF) Squadron, had been operated by a Canadian crew and flown from Buckenburg in Germany but had landed at Manston because its destination airfield, Croydon, was affected by bad weather.

Having landed at Manston, the pilot, Sqn Ldr R. G. Joyce, had been given an updated weather report, suggesting that the weather at Croydon had improved; he took off again at 10.55 a.m., and the Dakota was overhead just before 11.30 a.m. The aircraft flew over Croydon and then began to let down but crashed into an 800-foot ridge near Chelsham, Surrey, at 11.35 a.m. in an area already known to some airmen as the 'Valley of Death'. The aircraft was carrying four crew and twenty passengers, and among them, the only civilian on board, was thirty-six-year-old Dr John Brittain.

Dr Brittain was an explosives and rocket projectiles expert who was returning from Germany after observing a number of test launches of the V-2 rocket. Having been educated at King Edward VII School in Lytham, he had gained a BSc at the University of Manchester and worked in the chemist and explosives department at Woolwich. He was one of the foremost and leading scientists in his field, and on returning to London, he was due to sail to the USA where he would have taken up a post as a rocket expert to the 'Scientific Investigation Explosives Project'. Dr Brittain, who left behind a widow and a young son, was buried in Sevenoaks Cemetery.

A conference was held in Wg Cdr Clerke's office on the 25th about the closure of the road across the airfield. Wg Cdr Mallinson and Sqn Ldr Seymour attended the conference on behalf of Fighter Command, while Sqn Ldr Higginson came from 16 Group and Mr Haines from the Ministry of War Supply. On the same day, another district court martial was held in the intelligence offices with Grp Capt. Robinson presiding.

On 1 March, there were twenty-two visiting aircraft, including a batch of Tiger Moths that were destined for France. It was noted that the two resident units were more co-operative with Flying Control than was usual, which allowed a greater number of practice GCA approaches to be made. The next day, a Dakota that was *en route* from Berlin to Croydon made an emergency landing with a damaged propeller blade and an Anson flying to Down Ampney carrying stretcher cases also made an emergency landing having lost its hydraulics. There were very few movements on the 3rd because of bad weather and the weather's state remained at 'Red' all day.

Sqn Ldr Pike, the C of E chaplain, flew to Detmold in Germany on the 8th on board an Airspeed Oxford of 567 Squadron. There were thirteen practice flying sorties carried out by 130 Squadron and a single Spitfire was flown to Eastleigh, Hampshire, for a much-needed overhaul.

Field Marshal Montgomery's aircraft, a Dakota, arrived from RAF Blackbushe on the 10th, but the ORB does not state whether he was he was on board. After the war, Montgomery had been appointed as the chief of the Imperial General Staff and was awarded the title Viscount Montgomery of El Alamein. Montgomery's aircraft was scheduled to depart from Manston the following day, but the flight was cancelled.

Another batch of fifteen Tiger Moths, which were destined for the Belgian Air Force, passed through Manston on the 13th on their way to Diest, north-west of Brussels. The final two aircraft transited through on the 18th and were given radio and navigational assistance across the Channel.

On Thursday 21 March, six aircraft from 130 Squadron carried out a search from Orford Ness to the Naze from 9.05 a.m. until 3.40 p.m., looking for a launch that was missing from Broadstairs, but nothing was found. A number of newspaper reporters from the *Daily Mail* and the *Daily Express* visited the station in connection with this incident, which involved a stolen 20-foot half-decked motor cruiser.

The boat, called *The Babs*, had been found to be missing from Broadstairs on Sunday 17 March, and the theft had immediately been connected with the fact that four local men had also gone missing after lunch on Sunday. The four youths were known to be interested in the sea and one of them had recently studied charts of the Channel.

The *Isle of Thanet Gazette* named the men as nineteen-year-old Bert Stubbings, seventeen-year-old Peter Perry, eighteen-year-old Arthur Shiel, and eighteen-year-old John Skinner, all from Ramsgate. The men had stolen petrol from other boats in Broadstairs to allow them to get further out to sea and the launch had last been seen off Walton-on-the Naze. It was heading towards Harwich, but it did not enter any other port and was never seen again.

Sqn Ldr Shaw, DFC, the senior admin officer, was posted out to Nether Wallop on the 28th and he was replaced by a veteran of the Battle of France, former 73 Squadron pilot Sqn Ldr Peter Vigne Ayerst. The squadron leader was no stranger to Manston and had previously been stationed there while he was serving with 124 Squadron in late 1944 and early 1945. As a pilot on 73 Squadron, Sqn Ldr Peter Ayerst had been involved in some of the earliest aerial activity of the Second World War, having flown with pilots such as Dickie Martin and Edgar 'Cobber' Kain.

On one occasion in France, he had inadvertently flown into a swarm of Bf 109 fighters of the Luftwaffe, thinking that they were friendly aircraft. He got quite a surprise when he recognised them and found himself being chased by no less than twenty-seven enemy fighters. He was eventually credited with nine enemy aircraft destroyed and a third share of a He 111, which he shot down when acting as an instructor at 7 OTU Hawarden, Chester.

In his book *Spirit of the Blue*, Peter wrote that he took the post at Manston because it was in the area that he intended to settle down when he left the RAF, close to his 'spiritual' home of Canterbury. He said that the position was effectively that of the CO because Wg Cdr Clerke was often away. It is noted in the ORB that on 1 April, Sqn Ldr Ayerst assumed command of the station while Wg Cdr Clerke went on leave. Peter was a very generous man and when the author (Joe Bamford) contacted him in 2003, he wrote back and sent a number of photographs.

No. 91 Staging Post was formed at Manston on 1 April 1946 for the purpose of handling Transport Command aircraft that might be diverted there. The unit was commanded by Sqn Ldr W. Deaves who was transferred from Transport Command. The airfield was now classed as a RAF and Civil Customs Airfield and a new chapter opened in the history of RAF Manston as the airfield could regularly be used by civilian aircraft.

An unusual event that occurred on the 1st was when thirty German POWs were transferred to Manston from No. 1 German POW Camp at King's Cliff Camp, Peterborough. King's Cliff POW camp had opened in March 1946 and it was basically a holding unit where Germans would be processed before passing on to other camps. The site near Peterborough was part of RAF King's Cliff, an airfield that had opened in 1943 and it was known to the Americans as Station 367. An interesting note is that Glenn Miller had played his last concert at RAF King's Cliff in a hangar there on 3 October 1944.

On 3 April, 91 Staging Post handled twenty-five aircraft, and the following day, another sixteen, including five Ju 52s of the Luftwaffe. A number of Avro Yorks arrived from Stradishall on the 5th and carried out night flying. The aircraft belonged to a newly formed company called Skyways, and they would soon carry out the first regular commercial flights from Manston.

The airline had been set up by former BOAC director Brig.-Gen. Alfred Cecil Critchley; its deputy chairman was Alan Cobham, who had learnt to fly at Manston during the First World War. The airline was based at Langley and it would soon become the largest operator of non-scheduled flights in Britain and Europe.

A Spitfire *en route* from airfield B78 (Eindhoven) to Manston crashed in East Flanders on the 6th, and another one, also flying from B78 to Manston, was reported as overdue. Visibility, though, was reported as being excellent and four Spitfires of 130 Squadron flew service trials up to 30,000 feet.

Aerodrome discipline, which had recently been improved, broke down on the 10th when two Meteors from 245 Squadron took-off on the wrong runway without making contact with air traffic control. Their actions could have caused a serious accident and both pilots were reported to their destination airfield at Colerne. No. 91 Staging Post was visited by the Establishment Committee on a day when it handled twenty-six visiting aircraft, including one carrying a VIP, AVM Percy Eric Maitland, the AOC of 84 Group.

Twenty-four pupils from the School of Flying Control at Watchfield visited Manston on the 13th, and later that afternoon, they were given a demonstration of FIDO. The school had opened at Watchfield in 1941, and after being moved to Bridgenorth, it returned there and remained open until 1950 when it moved to Shawbury.

Another convoy of Tiger Moths arrived at Manston on the 14th, *en route* from Gatwick to Coxyde, and over the next few days, listening watches were maintained for aircraft crossing the Channel. Air Cdre Barnabas Henry Cross Russell, AOC of 11 Group, arrived in an Anson on the 16th and carried out an inspection of the station. He was just one of a number of senior officers who visited Manston during this period and AVM William Forster Dickson also arrived flying in a Proctor on the 18th.

The next week or so was relatively quiet, and on the 21st, 91 Staging Post stood down as many personnel as was possible but kept on a staff of four officers, four senior NCOs, and six airmen. On the 22nd, Easter Sunday, there were no movements at all recorded in the ORB, and on the 23rd, 91 Staging Post handled seven aircraft, including another former Luftwaffe Ju 52. Air Cdre John Gosset Hawtrey, Director of RAF Intelligence Operations, departed for Spittlegate after spending two days at Manston. No. 91 Staging Post personnel were paid by their own adjutant on the 26th to relieve the pressure on the station's pay accounts section.

No. 567 Squadron departed Manston on 26 April and flew out with its Vultee Vengeance IV to West Malling. The unit had been at Manston since 21 August 1945, but by June, it would be disbanded.

On the last day of April, there were just three visiting aircraft, including a Mosquito that landed after making a GCA approach with the cloud base down to less than 300 feet. A staff party visited 91 Staging Post and made some suggestions for improvements on handling aircraft and confirmed that the policy of the post was that it was there only to provide support for Transport Command aircraft that were diverted to Manston. No. 130 Squadron flew fourteen sorties, raising its total for April to 247, having flown 208 hours minutes by day and twelve hours at night.

There were twenty-eight visiting aircraft on May Day and fourteen movements by those from the Manston flights, one of the visitors being wartime ace Grp Capt. Johnny Johnson. Tar spraying was in progress for most of the day on the main runway, 29/11.

5

# The First Civil Traffic

Notice was received on 12 May 1946 that Skyways would be operating a regular air service between Manston, the Middle East, and Switzerland on the 14th, and on that day, the first aircraft, an Avro York, duly arrived from the Middle East with twenty-five passengers. These flights were carried out on behalf of the Anglo-Iranian Oil Company that had chartered the aircraft to carry troops and oil industry related material between the UK and Basra, Iraq, via Manston, Malta, Cairo, and Lydda. These were the first regular civil flights to operate from RAF Manston.

Over the next few days, Sqn Ldr Wooley of 130 Squadron continued to lead his unit, practicing for the Victory Parade Fly Past, Operation Big Bull, which was to take place on 8 June. On the 14th, he and Flt Lt Ponsford led a formation of aircraft over Romford for further low-level training.

Another Avro York of Skyways arrived at Manston from the Middle East at 7.50 p.m. on the 16th with thirty passengers who were cleared through customs by 10 p.m. and taken to London by coach. The following day, another Skyways York was among twenty visiting aircraft that arrived from Egypt, and after refuelling, it took-off for the company's base at Langley.

A USAAF Dakota from Bremen diverted to Manston because of bad weather on the 20th and two air maintenance assistants were posted to 91 Staging Post to relieve the shortage of staff. No. 130 Squadron's Spitfires flew a total of twenty sorties, practicing GCA approaches, formation flying, and navigation.

The Belgian Minister of Labour arrived at 1.20 p.m. on 22 May and departed later that night at 11.40 p.m. The CO, Wg Cdr Clerke, inspected the whole of 91 Staging Post, and the following day, it received some more personnel, who were led by Sqn Ldr Walker.

On the 24th, there were twenty-three visitors, most of whom were attending Wg Cdr Clerk's 'Flypast Conference'; No. 130 Squadron flew a dozen sorties, carrying out formation flying and cine-gun camera exercises. The following day, Wg Cdr Deaves, CO of 91 Staging Post, held a conference to discuss the best way to deal with the extra traffic over the 'Victory Parade' period.

Personnel from the British Air Force of Occupation, known as BAFO, were expected from Gütersloh on the 27th, but bad weather delayed their arrival and the three Dakotas that were carrying a large number of ground staff did not land until the next day. Tar spraying of the runway was completed on 30 May on the day when there were fifteen visiting aircraft, including six Dakotas from Gütersloh that carried 607 lb of freight. No. 130 Squadron flew ten sorties to raise the monthly total to 300 flying hours, with Flt Lt Beeby flying the route of the 'Victory Flypast' to check the timing.

On the last day of May, Sqn Ldr Deaves visited 46 (Transport) Group HQ for a conference led by AOC Air Cdre William Ernest Staton. No. 130 Squadron flew only four sorties but were given a lecture by the CO, Sqn Ldr Woolley, on the use of radar. During the evening, the unit held what was described as a very successful mess party.

On the first day of June, thirty-two Mosquitos and forty-five Tempest from the British Air Force of Occupation (BAFO) arrived at Manston in connection with the 'Victory Parade Flypast'. On the same day, five Vampires passed through *en route* to being delivered to the Swedish Air Force and this was the first time the type had been seen at Manston.

The SASO of 84 Group arrived on the 6th to observe a full dress-rehearsal for the Victory Parade Flypast in London, but the weather was threatening to interfere with the arrangements. The following day, Friday 7 June, a large number of personnel were issued with leave passes for the Whitsun weekend, although many of those involved with the flypast, scheduled for the following day, had to stay behind.

The weather on the 8th was appalling but the flypast went ahead even though visibility was described as being 'Nil', with aircraft passing the saluting base on Pall Mall at 400 feet. No. 130 Squadron returned to Manston via the coastal towns, while other units had to be homed back. Wg Cdr Corkby, wing leader of the Mosquitos, suffered an engine failure and had to return on a single power plant. The Tempest squadrons returned to the continent on the 12th, along with five Dakotas packed with personnel from BAFO, while 130 Squadron prepared to leave Manston and move to Acklington on a permanent basis. The 14th was the day that the main party of the unit departed.

The mayors of Dunkirk, Calais, and Boulogne visited Manston on the 19th and were met by the mayor of Ramsgate, Alderman S. E. Austin. The purpose of the visit was, as reported in the *East Kent Times*, to cement the friendship of the towns on both sides of the Channel. The French party arrived at Manston by air, in two silver-painted Dakotas that had flown in from Merville aerodrome in Northern France. The weather was so bad when they landed that the conditions were described as being like the Artic.

The main French party consisted of *Monsieur* Henneguelle, Mayor of Boulogne; *Monsieur* Defachelle, Mayor of Calais, and *Monsieur* Robelet, Mayor of Dunkirk. They were met at Manston by the acting CO Sqn Ldr Peter Ayerst, the vicar of Ramsgate, and many other senior members of Ramsgate Council before being invited to inspect a guard of honour. Several interpreters were present, and much credit went to the mayor of Ramsgate's secretary, Mr Vincent, for his organisation. The main translator credited for bringing the French and English parties together in their understanding was Dr E. A. Woolf.

During the reception speeches, the mayor of Boulogne said that the cross-Channel ferries should be resumed as soon as possible, with a weekly service like that in place before the war. There were also calls for a regular air service between London and Paris to be resumed, and it was claimed by Mr Ivor Thomas MP, Secretary for the Ministry of Civil Aviation, that very soon flights would leave every fifteen minutes.

Three Dakotas and a York were diverted to Manston on the 25th and one of the Dakotas was so short of fuel that it had to land on the downwind leg of its approach. A Ju 52 and twenty-five Spitfires were among the visitors on the 28th and the aircraft that were from 129 and 19 Squadrons were dispatched to the continent the next day.

The last entry for June 1946 merely states that there were ten visiting aircraft. For some inexplicable reason, there are no further records available for RAF Manston until April 1947. This may be because they have been removed and lost during the subsequent years in question. There were also no references to RAF Manston in the local newspapers.

However, there were a number of incidents and events that were well reported during the intervening period, including one that happened on 14 September 1946 during a practice formation flight for the Battle of Britain Flypast involving a Hawker Tempest from 3 Squadron. From 1–12 June 1946, the unit had been based at Manston but had then moved out to Dedelstorf in Germany. A Tempest that was being flown by WO Cruse, SN334, was number two in a formation of three aircraft when it struck the leader's aircraft, SN171, before dropping back and colliding with SN221.

The accident happened in what was described as turbulent conditions. Cruse tried to make a forced landing but was killed when the Tempest crashed a short distance from the airfield in Hogben's Orchard on Stirling Way, Ramsgate. Thirty-year-old WO Edward Charles Cruse was killed by the impact, while Plt Off. Campbell, in SN221, survived after making a forced landing in a field near Margate Cemetery.

Also in October 1946, the command of Manston changed again and Grp Capt. Richard Grice took over from Wg Cdr R. F. H. Clerke who had been the station's CO since September 1945. Grice was a veteran of the First World War who had been commissioned as a second lieutenant in June 1917. He arrived at Manston from Biggin Hill, a station that he had commanded in 1938 and he had seen it through the period of the Battle of Britain.

Another new unit arrived at Manston from Stoney Cross on 11 October—46 Squadron, which was equipped with Dakota Mk IIIs and IVs. The unit that had previously been equipped with the Short Stirling V was commanded by Wg Cdr George Burges who had taken over in July. The unit remained at Manston for just over two months and moved out to Abingdon on 16 December 1946.

From July 1947, the ORB gives very little detail about operations or events at Manston and merely records 'outward' and 'inward' movements. There were few movements of any interest during the first week of July except for a number of Avro Ansons that were flying to Valkenburg in Holland and a Dakota that arrived on the 4th with four Dutch civilian passengers. In the ORB, aircraft were only identified by the last three digits of their serial number, such as Dakota 665 (KN665), which arrived from Geneva on the 6th; Avro York 267, which arrived from Fassberg in Germany; and Vampires 287, 297,307, 308, and 309 from Lincolnshire.

A Ju 86 passed though Manston on the 9th, along with two passengers who were noted as being of Swedish nationality. On the same day, there was a rare mention of things other than aircraft movements when it was noted that there were two casualties among the passengers. They were A. C. Chandler, who had a lacerated hand, and J. Moston, Esq., who worked for the NAAFI and had been diagnosed with obstructive jaundice. There was also a Pte Parsons who had arrived from the 94th British Military Hospital in Hamburg and who was pronounced fit enough to proceed to Farnborough.

Captured Ju 52s became regular visitors to Manston, and on the 24th, one of them departed for Le Bourget with 2,690 lb of French freight on board. Another three of them flew in and out of Manston on the same day to Vélizy-Villacoublay, with one carrying eighteen French passengers inbound and another nineteen outbound. On the final day of July, there was another Ju 52 inbound from Vélizy-Villacoublay with two French passengers.

A Lincoln, Oxford, Proctor, and five Spitfires were among the aircraft handled on 1 August, but there were few movements over the next few days with 'Nil Return' being noted on the 5th. A rare visitor on the 6th was a Ju 86 that belonged to the Swedish Air Force. The twin-engined aircraft had been designed as a transport aircraft in 1934 but was later converted to a bomber for the Luftwaffe. There was also a high-altitude reconnaissance version of the aircraft, the Ju 86 P-1 and P-2, but the version the Swedes had was the Ju 86K bomber.

An Avro Lancaster, noted as number 881, was a regular visitor to Manston during this period, flying backwards and forwards to Fuhlsbüttel Airport, Hamburg, with as many as fourteen passengers. There was also an Avro York (244) transiting from Bückeburg that arrived on the 10th with eighteen senior officers destined for the RAF Staff College.

A summer camp was held for members of the Air Training Corps in August, although the ORB does not mention what squadrons were involved. A band competition was held between the participating units in Northdown Park, Margate, on the 24th, and 61st (Eastern Reserve) Group later received a message thanking its staff for co-operation with the ATC.

There was an unfortunate incident on Thursday 28 August when a Dakota (KJ984) crashed into a ploughed field near Westgate while flying in the circuit around the airfield. Both occupants of the aircraft, Flt Lt Cooke (the pilot) and Flt Lt Roberts (the navigator), were killed on impact. The Dakota was on a training flight from the Transport Command Examination Unit, which was based at Manston. It was later claimed that the aircraft crashed after reducing power on one engine and it had entered a spin from which the pilot was unable to recover.

KJ984 had taken-off at 2.22 p.m. and was in contact with the control tower until 3 p.m. when the crash occurred. Flt Lt Cooke was an experienced pilot who had flown forty-two operations with 49 Squadron, but the investigator subsequently blamed him for turning the Dakota into the direction of the dead engine after cutting power on the other one. That effectively caused the aircraft to enter the spin.

It was a disappointing end to August 1947 for another reason: there was a serious outbreak of diarrhoea that involved forty-five members of the ATC and a number of airmen on the station. The source of the infection was found to be contaminated meat pies, which had been consumed the previous day, and a medical report had to be quickly written up and sent off to HQ 46 Group HQ. Some forty members of Ramsgate ATC who were due to join the summer camp were forced to be examined before proceeding to Manston, but all were pronounced fit enough to join the camp.

6

# Transport Command

The Transport Command Examining Unit was still working out of Manston in September 1947 and there were a large number of arrivals and departures with staff being posted in and out to airfields like Fairford, Hullavington, and Bassingbourn for what was termed categorisation duties.

This meant that aircrew, mainly pilots but also navigators, were assessed and rated on such aspects as instruments flying, navigation, and conversion to type. They were also 'route checked' by another more experienced pilot on every aspect of their ability to operate such aircraft as the Avro York and Douglas Dakota. Flt Lt Cook, the navigator on the ill-fated KJ984, was on the last stages of his training and was due to be sent to Hullavington for his final check.

Among the movements noted in the ORB on 1 September was Dakota 513 flying out to Vienna with four passengers, including Maj.-Gen. Oxley. There were also two Lancasters, noted as numbers 303 and 910, outbound to Gatow. The Fire School gets its first mention on the 2nd when the medical officer gave a lecture on first aid to the existing course, on a day when the station was visited by Wg Cdr Barnes from Transport Command HQ.

Air Cdre David Francis Atcherley, Director of Air Support and Transport Operations, flew out of Manston on 3 September in a Percival Proctor, serial number 298. Along with his twin brother, Air Cdre Richard Llewelyn Atcherley, he was a legend in the RAF who had flown during the Battle of Britain and had later commanded a number of fighter squadrons. Many years later, in August 1952, after he had been appointed as the AOC of 205 Group, the Meteor FR 10 that he was flying from Egypt to Cyprus mysteriously disappeared and neither the aircraft nor his body were ever found.

Another Ju 86 arrived at Manston on the 9th, carrying five officers from the Swedish Air Force that were destined for the Radio School at Debden. The aircraft departed the next day for Malmo. A ceremonial Battle of Britain parade was held on the 12th and the RAF Central Band provided the music. The parade was also attended by a flight of ex-servicemen.

In September, preparations were being made for Operation Longstop, a Transport Command exercise that involved a large number of Dakotas from 77 Squadron and Horsa Gliders. There is not an exact date that the unit arrived at Manston, but it had previously been based at Broadwell in Oxfordshire, where it had been since December 1946.

The aim of the operation was to test the transport system and train the crews to carry troops and equipment on air drops, such as those carried out over Salisbury Plain. It was claimed that it was the biggest deployment of airborne troops since the Arnhem operation in September 1944. Over two dozen Dakotas were parked up on the 'loop' on the extreme western side of the airfield, from where many of the troops involved in the Arnhem raid had departed. That is the part of the airfield that has not been used for many years and is now as a business park.

On 21 September, AVM Charles Basil Slater Packman, AOC of 19 Group (GR Coastal Command), was one of five senior officers who arrived at Manston from Bückeburg to observe the exercise. On the same day, the medical officer gave a lecture on first aid to a group of glider pilots who were about to take part in the exercise and who might possibly need their recently acquired medical knowledge.

Two days later, on the 23rd, a Ju 52 arrived from Le Bourget with eighteen French officers who had been invited to observe Operation Longstop. On the same day, the station's medical officer carried out a 'freedom from infection' (FFI) inspection on half of the staff at SHQ. Whether this was just routine check or whether there were substantial grounds for such a thing to take place is not mentioned in the ORB.

There are few details of Operation Longstop in the ORB or of the date that it took place at Manston, but according to *Flight* magazine, it was on 23 September. AVM Packman departed and returned to Bückeburg in an Avro Anson on the 24th. Rocky Stockman provided some details of the operation in his book *The History of RAF Manston* (third edition, 1986), but what is clear is that Manston was not the only airfield involved with the exercise and others, such as RAF Brize Norton and RAF Netheravon, played their part. Altogether, there were a total of twelve Dakotas from 4 Group; six Dakotas and nine Hamilcar gliders from 38 Group; and fifty Dakotas and twelve Horsa Gliders from 46 Group taking part. Manston's 77 Squadron was part of 46 Group.

As part of the operation at Manston, there were typically twenty-six parachutist in each stick loaded on to a Dakota, which towed a Horsa glider into the air, which was also packed with troops and equipment. The glider would become airborne first when it was approximately halfway down the runway, then the Dakota would become airborne. Once in the air, the pilots of the Dakotas and gliders would practice various manoeuvres while flying above Thanet at no more than 2,000–3,000 feet. For those who witnessed it, the formation of so many aircraft and gliders was a sight never to be forgotten.

The landing procedure was also a sight to behold as the Dakotas and their tugs flew over Birchington on the approach to runway 11. The glider pilots had to decide when to cut the link to the Dakotas, and while the aircraft flew straight down the runway, the Horsa glider pilots had to break left and aim to land on the ground between the main runway and the northern grass. Then the Dakotas would form up and enter the circuit to land on runway 11. A total of 2,400 parachutist were involved in the exercise and 170 tons of supplies and equipment were dropped.

A station commander's parade was held on 24 September, and that evening, Pathé Pictures visited the station to film aircraft that were making night landings. They also visited flying control and recorded conversations between pilots and air traffic control over the R/T. Wg Cdr Miller from 46 Group HQ visited the station on the 26th for a meeting with the equipment officer. Wg Cdr Peters took over command of Manston on the same day, when it was noted in the ORB that Grp Capt. Grice was 'absent on duty'.

On the last day of September 1947, a 24 Squadron Lancaster (VM727) departed Manston on a training flight to the North African town of El Adam. The aircraft had had its nose turret removed and replaced by a large nacelle and had effectively been converted to a Lancastrian, although some documents still referred to it as a Lancaster PR1. Two de Havilland Hornets and a Lincoln were among a small number of other aircraft that passed through the airfield, while the Transport Command WAAF medical officer inspected her girls (FFI).

Another station commander's parade was held on 1 October, and the WAAF contingent was under the spotlight again when Sqn Ldr M. E. Sherwell supervised an FFI inspection. Manston was becoming a truly international airfield, and the following day, a 24 Squadron York (MW228) departed on a training flight to New Zealand, routing via Luqa in Malta. It was carrying just six passengers and 400 lb of freight. Two 77 Squadron Dakotas, KN393 and KN131, which had recently taken part in Operation Longstop, departed for Istres. Both aircraft returned the following day carrying three passengers. Wg Cdr Peters was noted as having taken over command of the station after Grp Capt. Grice was again noted as being 'absent on duty'.

A civilian aircraft, an Airspeed Consul, G-AIDY, was diverted to Manston from London on the 5th, along with Dakota KN607, which was carrying four passengers. The Consul was actually a former RAF Oxford (LX263) that had been converted and sold after the war. Meanwhile, the medical officer was keeping up the pressure and another FFI inspection was held for all RAF personnel.

There were no inbound or outbound aircraft on the 9th and no outbound on the 10th either, on a day when there were just three visiting aircraft, which included an American Beechcraft from Paris Orly. There was a RAF 'P3' scheduled arrival from Bückeburg in the form of RAF Dakota KN552 on the 13th that was carrying fourteen passengers. Another civilian aircraft, Dakota

OO-AUX, which belonged to the Belgian airline Sabena, diverted to Manston from Northolt because of the weather.

AVM Phillip Herbert Mackworth, Air Officer Administration (AOA) for Transport Command, passed through on the 16th along with Grp Capt. Hobbs and Grp Capt. Watts. Mackworth, who had been awarded the Royal Aero Club Certificate number 3540 in August 1919, was a specialist navigation officer who had taken part in a number of long-range flights to India and South Africa. They were accompanied on the short flight from West Malling in an Avro Anson by Wg Cdr McInley of 46 Group.

The following day, VM727—this time noted as a Lancastrian belonging to BOAC—arrived at Manston from Luqa, having been on a 24 Squadron training flight to Cape Town. There was another BOAC Lancastrian at Manston this day, G-AGLS (previously RAF serial VD238), which arrived from Castel Benito, having diverted from London Heathrow Airport.

The AOC of Transport Command, AM Brian Edmund Bake, DSO, MC, arrived from Hendon on the 20th in an Avro Anson. The AOC was another veteran of the First World War, who had twelve confirmed victories. He was one of three senior officers to arrive on this day, along with Air Cdre Frederick Edward Vernon, SASO of Technical Training Command, who also flew himself to Manston in an Anson. The AOC of 46 Group flew in another separate Anson from Hendon, hence there being three senior officers in three separate aircraft.

They were at Manston for a high-level meeting, and two days later, on the 22nd, delegations from the Ministry of Civil Aviation and British European Airways arrived. The purpose of their visit was to evaluate the airfield and its facilities in case there was an urgent need to divert aircraft from London Heathrow Airport. Mr Ruddock and Mr Monroe from the ministry met with Mr MacGregor and Mr Mackeson from BEA to discuss the proposal. Afterwards, the delegation met Grp Capt. Grice and he talked to both parties and expressed his views on the subject.

Whatever the outcome, it did not take long for the first BEA aircraft to arrive, and on the 24th, Vickers Viking G-AHPL diverted from London with nine passengers. It was one of several civil aircraft diverted to Manston that day, and a DC-4 that belonged to Skyways, G-AJPL, was also diverted from London with nine passengers. The Viking had arrived from Lisbon while the Skyways DC-4 had flown from Castel Benito in Libya. There were also a couple of RAF Dakotas, one diverted from Northolt and another from Abingdon, carrying a total of fourteen passengers.

The most interesting entry in the ORB concerned a lady, noted as being the wife of 2Lt Zacharewice of No. 3 Polish Holding Unit, British Army of the Rhine. She had been accompanied during a flight in an Anson from Gütersloh by a nursing sister and her husband and had extensive burns to her trunk, limbs, and face. She was examined at Manston by Medical Officers and was pronounced fit enough to proceed to RAF Lyenham, but there is no mention of what caused her condition

A Dakota from the Transport Command Examining Unit left Manston for Japan, and on the 28th, it was noted that all the crew had been vaccinated against cholera. Within a few days (3 November), the Transport Command Examination Unit would leave Manston when it was posted to RAF Brize Norton, but this failed to get a mention in the Manston ORB.

Three Avro Lincolns arrived on the 30th from the Suez Canal region, and all water and food that they were carrying had to be immediately discarded because the threat of disease from imported goods was being taken very seriously. The crew's medical form 1427s were examined and two of them were given vaccinations against cholera. It was not the only threat to health, and on the same day, the MO gave a lecture to fifty airmen at RAF Hawkinge about venereal disease.

A civilian aircraft, a Fairchild UC-61 Argus, G-AJSW, made an emergency landing on 1 November, after having taken off from Croydon. The aircraft could not have been seriously damaged because the next day it departed for Le Touquet with two passengers. The same day (2 November), an Avro Anson, TX222, arrived from what was described as a 'secret airfield' and its passengers were noted as being a number of Polish VIPs, but no names were mentioned.

There were several diversions on the 5th, including a BEA Dakota, G-ACIP, that arrived from Vienna with twenty-eight passengers, along with an Avro York, MW197, from Castel Benito with thirteen passengers. Among the outbound aircraft was a de Havilland Dove that flew to Karup with a Swedish Air Force officer, Col. Jacabbson. A number of Thunderbolts of the French Air Force also passed through on their way to Paris.

A Remembrance Day Service was held in the station's church on Sunday 9 November 1947. At some point on the same day, Lancaster TW909 arrived from Malta with five passengers. American Ambassador Mr Murphy was one of two passengers on board an American DC-4 Skymaster, 9052, that arrived on the 11th. The aircraft remained at Manston overnight and departed for Rhine-Maine the next day. Station commander's parades were a regular event and they took place on both 11 and 17 November. General dress regulations appeared in station routine orders stating that disciplinary action would be taken against any of those who infringed them.

Lancaster VM725 took-off for a long flight to Habbaniya in Iraq on the 20th, a distant airfield, where in May 1941, a little-known battle had taken place that could have affected the outcome of the Second World War. A rebel leader, Rashid Ali, assisted by the Germans, attacked Habbaniya and threatened Iraq and the whole of the Middle East. The situation was so desperate that it was one of the few occasions in the Second World War that volunteer untrained aircrew of 4 FTS were called upon to fly on operations.

7

# A Mixed Bag

There was an unfortunate incident on the 20th when controllers at Manston were informed that RP500—a Vickers Wellington Mk X from No. 1 School of Air Navigation based at RAF Topcliffe in Yorkshire—had ditched into the sea 4 miles off the coast of Margate. The aircraft had landed at Manston during a training sortie, and after taking-off, its starboard engine had failed, and the pilot decided to return to Manston. At 800 feet, the aircraft had entered a bank of cloud and stalled, with the pilot unable to recover and prevent it diving towards the sea.

It was later discovered that the aircraft had actually ditched on a sandbank off the coast of Ramsgate and that four of the crew of five had survived and been picked up by the Royal Navy survey vessel HMS *Franklin*. They were then taken to Sheerness Docks before being driven to Manston.

The missing crewmember was the pilot and captain, WO Zdzisław Stępień. The four survivors were cadet navigators: 3002984 P. Markham; 2265103 I. A. Lambert; 3040372 P. J. Ellis; and Fg Off. A.B. Landells, the co-pilot. It was the early hours of morning on the 21st by the time they arrived at Manston, where they were checked over by the MOs, Flt Lt Clayton and Fg Off. Nicholson. They were treated for minor injuries and it was found that they each suffered from various degrees of bruising but otherwise were in excellent spirits. The four airmen were then given temporary accommodation in the transit mess.

RAF Sandwich, a radar station and a satellite of RAF Manston, got a mention on the 21st when Flt Lt Clayton medically inspected over 100 personnel and found them all free from infection (FFI). The unit had opened in April 1942, and after operating as a mobile unit with ground control interception (GCI) radar, it had become a permanent static site. Clayton also inspected their billets and the cookhouse and, without exception, found them to be clean and free from infection of skin disease.

Mr Bull, an employee of the Air Ministry who worked at RAF Manston, died suddenly on the 29th. Fg Off. Nicholson inspected the body and then referred the matter to the coroner as a case of 'sudden death'. Flt Lt Clayton visited RAF Sandwich again where he medically inspected another forty-five personnel.

On the final day of November, Lancastrian TW909 passed through Manston again on its way to Castel Benito with seventeen passengers. There were two aircraft diverted to Manston, Lancasters SW290 and TW900, which should have landed at Stradishall.

There were a number of interesting types of aircraft on the airfield in the first few days of December, the first one being what was described as a 'Lancashire Airways' Halifax (Lancashire Aircraft Corporation), registered G-AIHU, which had arrived from Geneva on the 1st with seventeen passengers. It was the last time the aircraft would appear at Manston, and on 5 December, the Halifax crashed in the Welsh mountains, killing all of its four-man crew.

On the 3rd, an Aer Lingus Constellation arrived, EI-ADA, and this was the first mention of both the type of aircraft and the airline at Manston. The aircraft flew out to Dublin and returned the same day with twenty-seven passengers. There was also a USAF B-29, 44-62303, that arrived from Wiesbaden in Germany.

An all ranks' dance was held in the Westcliffe Ballroom, Ramsgate, in honour of 77 Squadron, which was being posted out to Waterbeach. Grp Capt. Grice, the CO, made a speech and handed out a number of prizes. There was another 'farewell' dance held in the officers' mess on the 5th, which was also attended by Grp Capt. Grice and Wg Cdr Peters, the CO of 77 Squadron.

Two Dakotas were amongst a number of aircraft diverted to Manston on the 11th, with KJ810 having flown from Luqa in Malta and KN832 from Bückeburg in Germany. Both aircraft were carrying eighteen passengers and KN832 had 3 lb of diplomatic mail on board. An Anson arrived on the 13th that was ferrying three stretcher cases to RAF Broughton. Flt Lt Girard was suffering from a cerebral haemorrhage, while FS Parr had had his leg amputated above the knee.

A civilian aircraft, an Auster, crashed after taking-off on the 20th, ironically coming down at Coffin House in Margate. Fortunately, Mr Duncan (the pilot) sustained only a fractured right femur and other minor injuries, while his passenger, a Dutch man, Mr Schuller, sustained only light injuries. Both men were taken to Margate Hospital.

Another two medical evacuations arrived at Manston on the 30th, aboard Anson PH765, which had flown in from Bückeburg with one stretcher case and one sitting wounded. Pte O'Donnel and AC Savage were suffering a number of different fractures and were to be transferred to the Queen Victoria Cottage Hospital at East Grinstead, where the surgeon Archie McIndoe was working on his 'guinea pigs'.

The Technical Training Section was formed on 1 January 1948 from the Station Servicing Section and all available warrant officers and senior NCOs were attached for instructional duties. RAF Manston had a long history of technical training, with the original Technical Training School having been formed there in 1920. Over the next few days, pre-course training was given to airmen described as 'recruits'; the use of that term suggest they had only recently joined the RAF.

A number of airmen were being trained as air movement assistants and given up to four hours' instruction a day up to the end of January.

A civil aircraft, a Percival Proctor (G-AHWP), was diverted to Manston on the 6th but was unable to land because the cloud base was down to 600 feet and visibility was less than 200 yards. The pilot, Sqn Ldr George Coleman (ret'd), DFC, and his passenger, George Dawson, were flying from Zurich to Stanstead. Coleman was a veteran who had served with 256 and 600 Squadrons, and he had been credited with seven enemy aircraft destroyed. Dawson, whose profession was given as an engineer, was also a pilot and held Royal Aero Club Certificate Number 22993.

The former squadron leader had made R/T contact with Manston at 5.50 p.m. and requested a bearing, but it was not until 7.55 p.m. that he declared his remaining fuel endurance was only twenty-five minutes and that landing at Manston was his only option. At one point, he claimed that he could see the searchlights on the airfield but radio contact with the pilot was lost at 8.36 p.m., although it was later reported that it was still circling Ramsgate at 8.42 p.m. RAF Uxbridge was made aware of the situation and had alerted the Margate lifeboat at 8.34 p.m.

It was subsequently presumed that the aircraft had crashed into the sea and the Margate lifeboat was launched at 9 p.m. Flt Lt Robinson, Duty MO, proceeded to Margate Harbour where it was thought the men may have been brought ashore. A Lockheed Constellation that was flying from Brussels to London was diverted to search the area where it was thought the aircraft might have come down. It circled the sea for some time but—despite that and the fact that both the Ramsgate and Margate lifeboats continued to search until 3.30 a.m.—nothing was found. The Margate lifeboat was launched again at 6.30 a.m. and continued to search in conjunction with aircraft from Manston until 11.30 a.m., when it was called off. Nothing was ever found of the aircraft or the two men.

Grp Capt. Maynard Crichton-Biggie, DFC, assumed command of RAF Manston from Grp Capt. Grice on 14 January. Grice was later posted to RAF Tengah and retired on 23 January 1950, retaining the rank of air commodore. Crichton-Biggie had been promoted to the substantive rank of group captain in October 1947, and from 1942, he had been the long-standing CO of 83 Squadron. In May 1943, he had been awarded the DFC for flying a number of bombing sorties over Italy and Germany during the summer of 1942.

The WAAFs came under a lot of scrutiny in January, and on 16–17 January, WAAF Advisory Staff Officer Transport Command Wg Off. Pitter inspected their accommodation. On the 20th, Squadron Officer Downs, the WAAF Advisory Officer for 46 Group, paid them a visit and inspected the WAAF Section. On the final day of the month, the senior air traffic control officer reported that there had been 286 movements during the month and that thirty-nine aircraft had diverted to Manston.

On 1 February, the only movement recorded was that of a Dakota (KN665) from the RCAF that had departed for Stockholm. The following day, there was another incident involving a Proctor (G-AIIK), which made an emergency landing while returning from Brussels. There was another emergency landing on the 6th involving an Airspeed Oxford of the FAA that arrived from Ford. There are no other details of either incident. There was another emergency landing on the 14th by a Spitfire of the RAAF.

On the 16th, the AOC of 46 Group, AVM John William Frederick Merer flew in from Hendon in Anson TX227, returning with four passengers later the same day. Vickers Viking VL248 was a regular visitor in February, ferrying between Benson and Manston and never carrying more than six passengers.

There were also a small number of USAAF B-29s arriving from and returning to Fürstenfeldbruck, a former Luftwaffe airfield in Bavaria, which had been one of its main training bases. B-29s 44-84122 and 45-21782 must have been a spectacular sight as they flew low over Ramsgate at 2.30 p.m. before landing at 2.40 p.m. There was a third B-29 noted as being number '7299' that arrived from Wiesbaden, but it is not known if it was connected with the other two aircraft. Although the ORB notes the B-29s as belonging to the 'USAAF', technically, they were now part of the USAF that had only recently been formed in September 1947.

Royal Netherlands Air Force (RNLAF) B-25 Mitchell 181 was another regular visitor flying between Manston, Valkenburg, and Hucknall on the 26–27th. The American presence was made up by a USAF Dakota, 50806, that had arrived from Rhine-Maine with eight passengers and 340 lb of freight.

The 29th, the last day of the month, was a very busy one, with eight Lincolns arriving from Shallufa in Egypt on what was called Operation Sunray. Lincolns RF358, RF405, RF471, RF482, RF510, and RF513 carried four passengers each, while RF409 and RF478 flew in with just three passengers. Senior Canadian Liaison Officer AVM Ralph Edward McBurney passed through Manston, arriving in RCAF Dakota KN665 from Le Bourget.

Wg Cdr Miller, the 46 Group equipment officer, visited the station on 2 March. By this time, the Air Movements Section was writing up its own ORB, which gave a more detailed account of aircraft visiting the station. Vickers Vikings, especially those of BEA, were by this time regular visitors and G-AIVE arrived from Northolt on the 4th with fourteen passengers, 820 lb of freight, and 18 lb of mail. Its 'sister ship' G-AIVF also flew in from Northolt on the same day, along with a Lancaster from Upwood and an American DC-4 from Berlin.

On 5 March, a station commanders' conference was held when a proposal to move a number of other units of Transport Command to Manston was discussed. It was agreed that the AOC of 38 Group, AVM Alfred Sharp, should visit the station and inspect both the quality and quantity of accommodation available.

A prestigious ceremony took place at Ramsgate railway station on 9 March when a Battle of Britain-class locomotive (34070) was named after the RAF station, *Manston*. The unveiling ceremony was carried out by Lord Balfour and a photo was taken of the occasion that was later presented to the station commander. The engine had been designed by Chief Mechanical Engineer of the Southern Region Oliver Vaughan Snell Bulleid and built in Brighton in 1947. Also known as *Light Pacifics*, each of the 100 or so engines built were named after towns in the West Country, RAF stations, types of aircraft, or those officers who were best associated with the Battle of Britain. *Manston* was the last engine built for Southern Railways before nationalisation of the railway system.

Sport was always an active part of service life and, at Manston, personnel participated in various aspects of what was available. ACW Walters took part in .22-calibre trial shoot at Digby, and on the 17th, it was subsequently noted that she had been selected for the WAAF shooting team. Fencing classes were held twice a week and AC Lawrence was selected to join the Junior Master of Arms competition at RAF Cosford. AC Humberstone was selected to play in the Transport Command football final that was to be held at RAF Hendon.

On 18 March, another American B-29 passed through Manston, serial number 44-86430, and the aircraft was one of those that had participated in the Bikini Atoll atomic bomb trials on the Marshall Islands in 1946. It belonged to the 509th Bomb Group, the very same group that had dropped the atomic bombs on Japan in August 1945. According to the ORB, the aircraft arrived from Washington, but some sources state that the departure airfield was Roswell in New Mexico, the scene of the incident in 1947, where it was alleged that a 'flying saucer' had crash-landed there.

There was a station stand down from 12 p.m. on the 25th to 12 p.m. hours the 30th, and all non-essential personnel were allowed leave for the Easter break. The airfield remained busy despite that, and on the 27th, B-29 44-86430 *Bikini Atoll* departed for Washington with two passengers and 1,300 lb of freight. RCAF Dakota KN665 was also kept busy ferrying passengers between Bassingbourn and Le Bourget, with various numbers of passengers. On the final day of March, the only movement logged was that of a B-25 Mitchell of the RNLAF that arrived from and departed to Valkenburg.

The movements for April noted in the ORB are few, but on the 5th, it was noted that Wg Cdr Gaines, Signals Officer for Transport Command, visited the station. The following day, a party of airmen from 90 Group monitored the moving and repositioning of the outer marker of the Standard Beam Approach system. It was later tested, and everything was found to be working satisfactorily. On the 13th, there was a visit by personnel from the Admiralty and a refitting party from 90 Group regarding of the radio beacon, known as 'Yanky Golf'.

It was a big day on the 15th when the International Civil Aviation Organisation (ICAO) system of signalling was brought into use at Manston in air traffic control. Some difficulty was experienced on the first day while staff became familiar with the new way of working, and the Air Traffic Control Centre at Uxbridge had to be contacted on several occasions. The concept of ICAO had been proposed in December 1944, but it was not founded until April 1947 as an agency of the UN. Its aims were to promote flight safety and standardise and maintain codes within the aviation industry. Each airport and airfield was allocated a four-letter code to identify it on flight plans and other signals; Manston was allocated the letters EGMN.

Practice shoots by the station's miniature rifle team were carried out at the Lydden Spout ranges on the 12th, 14th, 26th, and 28th. The standard of shooting was classed as above average and good scores were obtained by all those who took part.

It was noted in the ORB that there had been an interest in sporting activities by all ranks in April, especially in football—the station team had lost only one match during the month. Badminton had become particularly popular and games were played most evenings. There had also been a lot of interest by the station's WAAF community in the game of cricket and, being well ahead of their time, there were plans that the women should form their own team.

The station commander was keen on recreational and physical exercise and insisted that all personnel should take part in it for at least fifteen minutes every day. There was exercise of a different form and two station dances were held in April that proved to be very popular and well attended. A station concert party was being formed with an enigmatic note in the ORB, promising that fresh talent would soon be arriving from RAF Pershore.

For two weeks in April, the Air Training Corps spent its Easter Camp at Manston and Flt Lt Knight, Training Liaison Officer, had ensured that the cadets were kept busy with lectures pertaining to air force life, being held every day. The Air Training Corps' cadets had also taken part in sporting activities and the station fencing team had played and beaten them in a fencing competition by seven points to two.

On 30 April, the senior ATC reported on the number aircraft movements during April. There had been 426 RAF movements, 118 foreign movements, twenty-three civil, and nine diversions.

The so-called 'fresh talent' arrived from Pershore on 1 May in the form of a detachment of personnel under the command of Flt Lt Barnes. He had arrived to commence work on the formation of the Technical Wing under the command of a 3 Wing organisation that was to be formed within the next week.

There were a couple of minor incidents at the beginning of the month, and on the 5th, a 14 Squadron Mosquito (TV594) burst a tyre as it prepared to take-off, but the aircraft was not damaged. The following day, a Proctor (LZ681) made an emergency descent after its engine had failed, but it also landed safely, and it was later found that the problem was faulty plugs.

Wg Cdr Millar, OBE, arrived from Pershore on the 9th to take command of the Technical Wing. The following day, the 3 Wing organisation came into effect and sections at RAF Manston were divided into the Administration, Flying, and Technical Wings. Sqn Ldr J. S. Tucker was put in command of the Admin Wing; Wg Cdr W. C. M. Booth, the Flying Wing; and Wg Cdr Millar, the Technical Wing.

An all ranks' station dance was held in the NAAFI on the 12th, and two days later, all those airmen and airwomen who could be spared were allowed a stand down again for the Whitsun holiday.

# 8

# Czech Mates

There was a bit of a 'flap on' during 18 May 1948, when a twin-engined Siebel aircraft landed with eight former airmen of Czech Air Force on board, five of them being former RAF officers and three NCOs. The aircraft had made no radio contact and its arrival caused the authorities immediate concern. During interrogation by Flt Lt Andrews, the station's intelligence officer, the men said that they had 'borrowed' the aircraft to fly to England to join their wives, who had been sent back to England by their government.

They informed him that they had been persecuted by their government and dismissed from the Czech Air Force for marrying British women. The three NCOs, who were mechanics, were single men. After they had been interrogated, complied with immigration procedures, and interviewed by the BBC, the men were supplied with British currency and eventually allowed to leave the station to join their wives.

At the time, the identity of the men was closely guarded, and no photographs were allowed to be taken of their faces for security reasons. One photo was taken of the men's backs, walking away from the aircraft with the nose of the machine in the foreground. We now know that the five former RAF officers were former Sqn Ldr Vladimír Kopeček, Flt Lt Josef Doubrava, Flt Lt Jiří Mikulecký; Flt Lt Vaclav Ruprecht, and Plt Off. Vladimír Soukup. Like many other airmen who had served in the RAF during the war, and especially those who had married British women, they had come in for 'special' treatment from the communist government that had taken over Czechoslovakia in February 1948.

All five former officers were pilots who had served on 311 and 312 Squadrons, and to reach Manston, they had taken-off from České Budějovice, their base in Czechoslovakia, and then flown to an American base in Germany. There they got a cool reception from the Americans who told them that they should return to Czechoslovakia, but the Czech airmen pleaded with the USAF authorities, pointing out that just a few years before, they had flown in support of American aircraft on bombing raids in Europe. They also told them that if they returned home, they would certainly be imprisoned, but it was more likely that they would be executed.

Despite their pleas, the men were taken into custody and detained for several days before being released and measured up for civilian suits. A senior US officer told them that they were free to go and that their aircraft had been refuelled. He informed them that he was under strict orders from his superior officer to ensure that they returned to Czechoslovakia; however, he pointed out that after they took-off, it was up to them to decide whether they flew east or west.

After the communist coup in January, even former AM Karel Janoušek, the most senior officer in the Czech Air Force, had been arrested and put on trial. On 3 August 1945, he had taken the salute at Manston as the Czech Air Force had prepared to leave and he had returned home to become the deputy chief of staff. At a trial that was held in secret, he was sentenced to eighteen years in prison, which was increased on appeal to nineteen years. He was eventually released in 1960 but was stripped of his military rank and pension. Many of those airmen who fled Czechoslovakia after the communist coup could have expected the same treatment, or worse.

A few days later, the new Czech Government announced that it had arrested a number of people in connection with the theft of an aircraft and the defection of the eight men. It also announced that it was negotiating with the west about the return of the aircraft. At the back of the Spitfire & Hurricane Memorial Building (Museum) at former RAF Manston, a plaque on the wall of the main memorial commemorates this incident and the fact that the Czech airmen escaped persecution by the brutal communist government.

Another unit moved into Manston on 17 May, but its arrival was not noted in the ORB, most probably because of the Czechoslovakian incident. This was No. 1 Ferry Unit, which was immediately retitled No. 1 Overseas Ferry Unit. It had originally been formed in March 1944 from the merger of 301 Ferry Training Unit and 1 Ferry Crew Pool, as part of 44 Group and then based at Pershore. It had mainly been involved in ferrying Beaufighters, Mosquitos, and Dakotas, but at Manston, the Overseas Ferry Unit would be moving a much wider range of aircraft.

On 22 May, 140 officers and sixty-five other ranks of 504 Squadron arrived at Manston for the unit's summer camp. The unit that was based at Hucknall was equipped with the Mosquito NF.30, but it was about to be re-equipped with the Spitfire F.22. Three days later, the station commander, Grp Capt. Crichton-Biggie, along with the three commanders of the recently formed wings, proceeded to 46 Group HQ to discuss changes being made to the wing organisation.

The Standard Beam Approach was checked on 28 May and found to be working correctly after reports of interference with the Gee chain. On the same day, Mr Shaw, from the Ministry of Aviation, visited the station and fitted a new coding unit to the MF radio beacon.

It was a busy day on 1 June, and there were a number of high-profile visitors to Manston, including Grp Capt. Noel Christie Singer, Director of Accident Prevention at the Air Ministry, along with Sqn Ldr J. R. Hawkins, also from the ministry. Along with several other senior officers, they were at Manston to witness the deliberate crashing of a Mosquito that was filmed by the Air Ministry Film Unit. Fourteen aircraft had crashed during the ensuing months and the film was being made for reasons of flight safety. In light of events that were to occur on the airfield within the next few months, it was quite ironic that the film was made at Manston.

An inspector from Ramsgate police visited the station on the 6th in connection with reports that a civilian glider had been seen landing in the local area. A police search had found nothing, and it was thought that the reports were a case of mistaken identity and the 'glider' was actually a Bristol Freighter, registration G-AGJD. That was also a case of mistaken identity, and if that registration was correct, it would have been an Avro York. Maybe it was a glider after all.

Sqn Ldr Popham, Flt Lt G. Goodacre, and a Mr L. J. Austin from 46 Group HQ visited the station on the 11th. On the same day, Fg Off. Lucas, FS Butler, and LAC Turner visited Bisley to be presented with their shooting medals by ACM Sir Alfred Guy Roland Garrod, who had just returned from the USA where he had been the head of the RAF delegation in Washington.

There was also a visit from a party from 90 Group (Signals) that were calibrating the VHF homing system. A member of the team that was from RAF Watton, FS Brooks, was injured when he fell from the top of the Eureka aerial mast.

At 3.30 a.m. on 14 June, a former USAF DC-3 in Czech Air Force colours, serial number 43-48406, landed at Manston with another twenty-one political refugees on board. The aircraft had been stolen from Prague's Kbely air base and flown by pilots Josef Bernat and Hugo Hrbáček. Those on board included seventeen men, two women, and two boys. For security reasons, no details of their names or backgrounds were published.

Between the 21st and the 24th, there were a number of visits by senior officers from Transport Command, including a party that made up a Board of Survey to decide on the location of a number of new sites for the beam approach beacon system (BABS). The WAAF medical staff officer paid a visit on the 25th and inspected all of its personnel. Sqn Ldr Sherwell from Transport Command HQ visited the station on the 26th and there were several other visits from officers of 46 Group. It would appear RAF Manston was becoming increasingly important to both 46 Group and Transport Command.

During the month of June, the ferry unit had despatched twenty-five aircraft overseas and flown a total of 1,110 flying hours, of which 185 were for crew training. The senior ATC also gave a series of talks with the hope that they would improve the R/T procedures of those pilots flying in and around Manston.

On 24 June, the Berlin Airlift had begun, with RAF and USAF aircraft flying supplies into West Berlin, but its operations had no immediate effect upon operations at RAF Manston.

The ORB was signed off in June by Battle of Britain ace Grp Capt. James Rankin, DSO*, DFC* (* denoting awarded twice), who had been credited with seventeen enemy aircraft destroyed and five shared. It is not known where Grp Capt. Crichton-Biggie went, and he had last been mentioned in the ORB at the end of May. As he signed as the 'CO RAF Manston', we can only assume that Grp Capt. Rankin had taken over command of Manston from Grp Capt. Crichton-Biggie. That, however, is not confirmed in the ORB.

Rankin had joined the RAF and been commissioned in 1935, and after a brief attachment to the FAA in 1939, he had been posted to 5 OTU as an instructor. By June 1940, he had been promoted to the rank of flight lieutenant, and by February 1941, he was serving with 64 Squadron as a supernumerary squadron leader; he later commanded 92 Squadron. He had completed his first tour of operational duty at the end of 1941, and having been promoted to wing commander, he had been posted as a wing leader to Biggin Hill. He commanded 125 Wing over Normandy and was promoted to acting air commodore in 1945 but was reverted to the rank of group captain after the war.

There was a station athletic meeting on 1 July, but the month was plagued by a series of flying accidents and minor incidents, with the first one occurring on the 5th when a Spitfire IX damaged its port mainplane while landing in a crosswind. The aircraft (MJ409) that was being flown by a Norwegian pilot suffered Category 'A' damage to its airframe.

On the 7th, Halifax RT832 made an emergency landing without brakes, but there was no damage to the aircraft. Two days later, Spitfire SL721 from Hendon made a wheels-up landing, but the pilot escaped serious injury and the damage to the aircraft was assessed as Category 'AC'.

It was discovered that there was a 5 per cent error in the high-frequency direction finding equipment on the 14th, and a Mr Wiggins was called in from the Signals Development Unit at Henlow to investigate. The problems with the signals' equipment had nothing to do with the next incident, though, when a Vampire (VV191) lost its port overload tank and had to make an emergency landing. This aircraft was also assessed as sustaining Category 'AC' damage.

On 22 July, a Mosquito (PF659) had a window blow out while in flight and had to make an emergency landing, while a 612 Squadron Spitfire (RB169) caught fire while being started, because fuel vapour had collected in the engine compartment. It was quickly extinguished but the fire caused serious damage to the aircraft. The following day, there were two more minor incidents when an Anson (NK716) and a 609 Squadron Spitfire (TB625) collided on the runway while taxiing. Spitfire TB181 hit and damaged a monitoring aerial but was not badly damaged.

At the end of the month, the VHF specifically used by Transport Command aircraft on the approach to Manston, 120.96, was discontinued. The final incident of the month occurred on the 29th when a Vampire Mk III (VV192) was damaged in a heavy landing.

If anyone thought that August would put an end to the series of accidents, they would have been very disappointed, and on the 5th, a glider stalled while taking off. Although it was badly damaged, the pilot, Flt Lt Harris, survived without serious injury.

A delay unit fitted to the BABS system was tested by aircraft from RAF Shepherds Grove in Suffolk on the 6th. A W/T air-to-ground channel was opened up on the 10th to receive meteorological reports from aircraft flying over Germany. This was in connection with Operation Hardiness.

On the 11th, another glider came to grief when it collided with a fuel bowser, but the pilot, Cadet Cpl Wilkins, was not injured. Two days later, Dakota KN664, flying in from Turnhouse, made a hard landing and broke both undercarriage legs.

It was a busy day on the 15th when fifty-three Lockheed P-80 Shooting Stars passed through Manston to be refuelled and serviced. There is no mention of their intended destination. The P-80, which had first flown in January 1944, was the first jet fighter to enter service with the USAAF. The next day, a Spitfire (LA313) flown by Plt Off. Judge struck and demolished the BABS beacon when it swerved off the runway while landing.

A working party from de Havilland Aircraft Company arrived at Manston on the 17th to effect modifications to two Mosquitos, HJ993 and TW106. There were further changes to the frequencies used by ATC and 102.42 was brought into effect for local control. There was yet another incident involving a Spitfire on the 19th, when the undercarriage of a 615 Squadron aircraft collapsed on landing. The pilot, Sqn Ldr Killet, of the RAAF escaped serious injury.

Mr Kaye, a representative from Rolls-Royce, visited the station on the 24th, his second visit during the month, having previously been on the station during the 3rd. The mobile VHF Homer was sited and calibrated for Operation Dagger. Also, in connection with Operation Dagger, an additional teleprinter circuit was provided along with three additional VHF channels in ATC. A mobile radar unit was also provided for the duration of the exercise for homing. Operation Dagger was a major air defence exercise between 'Southern Command' forces commanded by AM A. B. Ellwood and the 'Northern Forces' commanded by AM Sir William Elliot.

A number of officers from Transport Command HQ and 90 Group (Signals) visited the station on the 27th in connection with the installation of FGRI 5417 equipment. This was a console in ATC—where the duty air traffic controller sat—that was fitted with four VHF radio channels. There were more visitors on the final day of August when Sqn Ldr Miles from the Air Ministry visited the station in connection with Motor Transport (MT) matters.

On 1 September, 54, 72, and 247 Squadrons arrived on the station from Odiham to take part in Operation Dagger, and all three units were equipped with Vampires. A pilot flying a Vampire from one of the units inadvertently dropped its fuel overload tank during a fuel consumption test, but the aircraft was not damaged.

The following day, Sqn Ldr King of the Technical Wing carried out a pre-air officer commanding's (AOC) inspection and two additional channels were installed in the control tower in connection with Operation Dagger.

It appeared that there were more chiefs than 'Indians' at Manston on the 7th, when Sqn Ldr Pearce, Sqn Ldr Knight, and Sqn Ldr Penman from 46 Group HQ visited the station, along with Flt Lt Gordon, Flt Lt Burke, and Flt Lt Rowe, for another pre-AOC's inspection. Nos 54, 72, and 247 Squadrons returned to Odiham after taking part in Operation Dagger. On the 9th, the Tempest F.2s of 16 Squadron arrived in Transit from RAF Gütersloh.

9

# Disaster at Manston

On 18 September 1948, RAF Manston was open to the public for Battle of Britain Day and there were several exhibits on display, including a model of a VHF and HF radio system and a DF homing loop. The domestic display opened up to the public the airmen's quarters, the messes, station church, and rifle range. The RAF fire service put its equipment on display and there was a continuous film being shown in the station cinema about life in the RAF. Despite all that, the main thing the public wanted to see were aircraft in the air and the flying programme promised not to disappoint.

The flying display was scheduled to begin at 2 p.m. and featured a flypast by a number of Avro Lincoln bombers and later by Meteors, Tempests, and American T-33 Shooting Stars. There was also a display by 54 Squadron's Vampires, which had recently returned from a historical flight over the Atlantic. There was jumping from static balloons that featured men from the 6th Airborne Division, some of whom had taken part in the Invasion of Normandy. The flying displays were scheduled to continue until 6 p.m., and the event was advertised as being the first time that the public had been allowed full access to the famous Battle of Britain airfield.

At approximately 3.30 p.m., however, one of the displays went tragically wrong and the station experienced the worst disaster ever to occur on the airfield. Flt Lt Geoffrey Alan Hanson, twenty-nine years old, was flying Mosquito TE808 when it crashed into the ground and killed ten members of the public who were watching the display. Among the crowd of 15,000 people was the pilot's wife.

The accident at Manston was the third incident involving a Mosquito in two weeks, and on 4 September, a Mosquito (RL192) from 29 Squadron had crashed at West Malling while returning from an air defence exercise. On the 13th, a second Mosquito had crashed at West Malling after colliding with another aircraft when its pilot, thirty-five-year-old Flt Lt Hart, failed to keep position while flying in formation during severe turbulent conditions.

Like all aircraft accidents, the eyewitnesses gave slightly different versions of the events that led up the accident at Manston, but it is claimed that the

Mosquito flew across the airfield at approximately 200 feet before climbing up to 400 feet .The pilot then completed what was described as a faultless slow roll, but then instead of steadying the aircraft, it went into a second roll from which the pilot failed to recover.

The Mosquito had crashed into the ground inverted, throwing up a huge ball of black smoke, with wreckage striking members of the public who were watching the display and others in a line of cars who were waiting for admission on the Margate Road (B2190). Ten civilians were killed instantly, along with the pilot and the aircraft's navigator, Flt Lt Martin.

Some of those who witnessed the tragedy had also seen the rehearsals in the week leading up to the Battle of Britain display and claimed that the pilot had deviated from what he had done in practice. It was later claimed that the heavy casualties were caused by the pilot's failure to adhere to the display briefing and his harsh handling of the controls.

The names of those who were killed: Miss Marjorie Grace Dorlanda Astell, aged forty-four; Miss Francis Claire Lewis, aged thirteen; Master Stuart Graham Chiesman, aged thirteen; Mr Peter Charles Scott, aged nineteen; Mr Charles Edward Taylor, aged thirty-five; Mrs Muriel Lawrence, aged forty-eight; Mrs Gertrude May Andrews, aged thirty-eight; Master Brent Andrews, aged three; Mr Frederick Austin, aged sixty-seven; Mr Edward Ruston, aged sixty-six; and Miss Marie Helen Allen, aged twenty-one.

Another fifty-five people who were passengers on a double-decker bus that was taking them to the air display had a very lucky escape when the driver, Mr Alfred Cope of Margate, stopped at a junction to allow other traffic to proceed. Seconds later, the Mosquito crashed immediately in front of the bus, which was hit by flying debris. Mr Cope reversed the bus away from a wall of flame that threatened to engulf the vehicle, despite the fact that one of its front tyres was on fire.

Among those who were seriously injured was twenty-five-year-old John Charles Higgins from Bermondsey, who was the fiancé of Miss Allen, who had died in hospital the day after the disaster. His fifty-four-year-old mother, Mrs Ivy Higgins, was also among those seriously injured, along with fifty-eight-year-old Frederick Yarrow of London.

There are claims that the air show and flying display was cancelled after the Mosquito crashed, but author John Williams recalls that, after a short interval, it carried on. He was only five years old at the time, and when the incident occurred, he was looking around a Wellington aircraft that was on static display with his father. Like many others, despite being so young at the time, he still has vivid memories of what happened that day.

During the remainder of September, there were no further entries in the ORB relating to the incident and only a small number concerning staff visits by officers from Transport Command and 46 Group.

New VHF homing equipment was accepted on 1 October after the installation had been calibrated by technicians from 90 Group. There was nothing of great interest mentioned in the ORB until the 14th, when there was a breakdown in the control tower. From 7 p.m. until 11 p.m., all VHF speech channels were rendered unserviceable.

There were further visits from a Mr Trayner of de Havilland and a Mr Kaye of Rolls-Royce on the 22nd and 27th respectively. It is possible that these two men, from the companies that built that Mosquito and its engines, were involved in the inquiry.

Compared to the previous months, there were far fewer incidents, but on 29 October, a Wellington X (RP558) from Middleton St George made an emergency landing in the dark after losing an engine. The aircraft had been airborne for three and a half hours on a long cross-country flight when number twelve cylinder on the port-side engine blew out. Apart from engine failure, the aircraft also suffered a complete R/T failure and the pilot, Plt Off. Clifford, decided to make a complete wheels-up landing There were no reported injuries among the crew and little damage caused to the aircraft. Clifford was later rewarded with a 'Green' endorsement in his logbook.

Sites for the location of SCS51 (instrument approach localiser) were surveyed by the Air Ministry Works Department on 1 November, and over the next week, the radio navigation aids on the station were checked out by representatives from IRIS. There were further problems with navigational aids when, on the 19th, it was discovered that a section of cable from the outer marker beacon at Ramsgate had been cut. On the 23rd, an error of 3 degrees was found on the station's HF/DF beacon and it was placed unserviceable. It remained unserviceable for two days.

# 10

# The Station is Honoured

November 1948 was a momentous month for RAF Manston because the station received its coat of arms from the Royal College of Heraldry. A badge became a major part of a RAF unit's identity, appearing on everything from its standard to its stationary. The criteria for a station or a unit to be awarded a badge (sometimes referred to as a crest) is that the established unit should have existed for at least two years and was likely to remain permanent. It was also stipulated that its role should be one that merited a badge being awarded.

RAF Manston had clearly fulfilled that criteria because it had existed as a RAF station since April 1918 and for another two years before that as a Royal Naval Air Station. Since 1918, it had been occupied by every single command and was currently a key station in the service of Transport Command. The original copy of Manston's badge was signed in the top right-hand corner by the king and in the bottom left Chester Herald, Inspector of RAF Badges. The post of inspector, which is always held by an officer from the College of Arms, provides advice to the RAF on all heraldic matters.

Nothing of any significance occurred during the early part of December, and the only things recorded are a number of staff visits. Flt Lt Wake of the Accounts Department, Transport Command, arrived on the 3rd, and Wg Cdr Trippett of Transport Command HQ arrived a few days later. The new installation of FGRI 5417 (four channel remote VHF equipment) was accepted on the 16th, and Flt Lt Grever, the electrical engineering officer of Transport Command, made a technical inspection of the station.

There was yet another staff visit on the 21st when Wg Cdr Barthold from 46 Group HQ arrived. On the same day, service trials for the voice rotating beacon began. Avro Anson PH838 picked up a spoke in its wheels while taxiing on the airfield on the 30th and was categorised as receiving Class 'A' damage. On the final day of December 1948, the RAF Manston ORB was again signed off by Grp Capt. James Rankin.

The ORB details for the whole of January 1949 are missing, but those for February are available and the month began with a visit from Grp Capt. G. D. Alexander from Transport Command on engineering matters. On the 2nd, an Avro Anson (PH667) that was *en route* from 23 Maintenance Unit to BAFO in Germany made an emergency landing after its emergency hatch had been lost while it was in flight.

There was damage to an aircraft on the airfield during the night of the 8th when the elevators of Lancaster RF313 were badly damaged during a gale. Having served in the Far East, the aircraft belonged to 279 Squadron, but it had later been transferred to Flight Refuelling Ltd. The following day, there were further changes to the new installation of FGRI 5417 VHF radio when a new frequency of 118.1 was brought into use for civil traffic.

There were a few further incidents in the middle of February, and on the 14th, a Meteor (VT193) from Thorney Island ran out of fuel while flying in the vicinity of Canterbury. The pilot, Flt Lt Lewis, baled out and landed by parachute but was only slightly injured. It was later discovered that Lewis had taken-off without being aware that the aircraft had R/T problems and it should have been air tested before being flown. During a cine-gun camera sortie, he had become lost and flown the aircraft until the fuel ran out.

The following day, an Avro Lincoln (RF443) from Lindholme made a wheels-up landing in the dark. Few details are available, but it is known that none of the crew were injured.

Technical developments on the airfield continued, and on the 25th, modifications were made to the Standard Beam Approach, which was tested and categorised as 'A1'. This was the Lorenz blind landing system that had first been installed at airports in Europe as early as 1932. The frequency of 6440 Kcs for civil air traffic on the HF band was discontinued and replaced by 3255 Kcs.

There is very little information in the ORB for the month of March 1949 except for details of the many staff visits to the station by officers from 46 Group and Transport Command. It was noted on the 26th that seventy-six HF/DF bearings and 735 VHF bearings had been passed to aircraft during the month.

April began with more staff visits, and on the 5th, Wg Cdr P. Wicks, the technical officer of 47 Group (Transport), arrived, along with Wg Cdr Hodgson, an engineering officer from 46 Group. The catering section was also inspected by Wg Cdr Roach, the catering officer from Transport Command HQ.

No. 3617 Fighter Control Unit arrived at Manston on the 9th for its annual training, and on the same day, there were further technical problems when the HF/DF system became unserviceable. Former Vice-Chief of the Air Staff, ACM Douglas Evill, who had recently retired, had been appointed as the honorary air commodore of the unit, which covered the air defence of Hampshire and the Isle of Wight. He was an Australian who had joined the forces in 1910 when he had served as a midshipman on HMS *Vincent*. No. 3617 FCU remained at Manston until the 23rd.

An established review of the station was carried out on the 20th by Wg Cdr Gough and Wg Cdr Mitchell and Sqn Ldr Walker and Sqn Ldr Langlois, all of them from the Air Ministry.

On 1 May, RAF Manston was transferred from 46 Group to 47 Group (Transport Command), although within a short while, 47 Group was absorbed into 46 Group. On the 4th, the station was visited by Sqn Ldr Hades from Fighter Command to discuss the requirements for exercise Foil. Extra VHF channels were provided on 106.56 Mcs and 107.28 Mcs, and a direct line to 11 Group HQ was installed. The outer marker for the Standard Beam Approach on runway 29 was repositioned in Ramsgate on the 17th to the yard of the borough's police station.

There was another change of command at the end of May when Grp Capt. T. W. G. Eady took over from Grp Capt. Rankin. A lot of what we know about Eady comes from an article that he wrote for the *Motor Sport* magazine in May 1982. He had joined the London Aeroplane Club in 1925 when he was working as an apprentice in an engineering works in Basingstoke. He had begun flying lessons at Stag Lane, to where he had travelled on an old motor bike and paid £1 an hour for dual instruction.

After carrying out his first spin, he had felt ill and decided that flying was not for him, but after a chance encounter with comedian and actor Will Hay at Stag Lane, he changed his mind. Hay also happened to be a member of the club and told the young Eady that the same thing had happened to him and he persuaded him to have another go.

Eady went solo for the first time on 17 February 1927, flying the prototype DH.60 Moth G-EBKT, which Alan Cobham had flown in the King's Cup Air Race. He was only allowed to go solo because Eady's flying instructor had made an error and mistaken him for a pupil who was more advanced. The instructor had realised his mistake just before Eady took-off and shouted for him to stop, but his cries went unheard over the noise of the engine.

After getting into the air, Eady became lost but found his way back after identifying the church at Harrow on the Hill. He made a mess of the landing, as he later did when taking his test for the 'A' license, after the observer had fallen asleep and failed to notice that Eady had made a complete mess of his approach and landing. It was only after trying to make a life as a tea planter in Assam that Eady had returned to the UK and applied for a short service commission in the RAF.

It was announced on 1 June that one of the station's officers, Sqn Ldr J. H. Holloway, had been awarded the MBE for services during Operation Plainfare, the UK's contribution to the Berlin Airlift. On the same day, Sqn Ldr Pawson from 47 Group made a staff visit to the station.

On 10 June, the *Isle of Thanet Gazette* reported that Margate and Broadstairs Council, along with Ramsgate, had agreed to adopt RAF Manston as part of a municipal liaison scheme. The object was to promote good feeling between the public and the RAF and to stimulate recruiting. It was suggested that the station should have an 'At Home' every September and regular official visits should be arranged. Personal contact between the RAF and the public would be encouraged by organised games, events, and entertainment.

Throughout the rest of the month, there were further preparations for the forthcoming Operation Foil, and on the 17th, Sqn Ldr Bennett and Flt Lt Holdings from Transport Command arrived to discuss arrangements to set up a signals section. An 'A'-type summer camp was set up on the 19th for the Air Training Corps units from 65 Group.

Exercise Foil began on the 23rd when 1 and 43 Squadrons arrived from Tangmere, with both units being equipped with Meteor F.4s. The next day, 500 Squadron, which was equipped with the Gloster Meteor F.3, flew in from West Malling to take part in the exercise. The unit had been originally formed at Manston in March 1931 as a Special Reserve Unit, and when the Auxiliary Air Force had been reformed in May 1946, 500 Squadron had resumed recruiting in that capacity in Kent. Exercise Foil was a very important full-scale test and air defence exercise that involved a large number of auxiliary squadrons.

There was an incident involving a Spitfire from 604 Squadron on 26 June when TE467 crashed on take-off after its engine had failed. It was another auxiliary unit that was based at North Weald, and although the aircraft was written-off, the pilot escaped injury. There was another accident on the 28th when a RNLAF Firefly from Holland crashed on landing, but few other details are available.

On 4 July, exercise Foil was completed, and so 1 and 43 Squadrons returned to Tangmere and 500 Squadron to West Malling, The next day, there was another tragic accident when a Tiger Moth (N6644) from No. 15 Reserve Flying School at Redhill crashed in a small field adjacent to Manston village. It was claimed that the pilot, Plt Off. Michael Forster, had lost control after entering a steep turn at 200 feet, allowing the Tiger Moth to dive towards the ground. In some documentation, including the ORB, Forster's rank is given as 'PII', which was a senior NCO rank equal to that of sergeant.

The aircraft caught fire after the impact, and despite the brave efforts of several locals, including Fred Davis and Percy and Ronald Pickett of Jubilee Cottages, they were unable to save the young passenger. Air Cadet Cpl Raymond Webster, of Lillington Street, London, who was a member of 291 (Chelsea) Air Training Corps Squadron, died on the scene. He was buried in Margate cemetery. There was another much more minor incident on the same day when an Avro Anson (FH592) made an emergency landing after suffering an engine failure.

A working party from Vickers-Armstrongs arrived at Manston on the 23rd to make modifications to the RAF's fleet of Valetta aircraft. The type, which had entered service in 1948 as a replacement for the Dakota, was a 'tail dragger', powered by two Bristol Hercules engines, and it was widely used by Transport Command in both the Middle and Far East.

In July 1949, a Short Sunderland flying boat from RAF Coastal Command paid a courtesy visit to Margate and anchored in the harbour only a few yards from the jetty extension. It arrived just after 10 a.m. and had only recently been involved in a search for a missing aircraft, a Handley Page Halifax, which had been on a meteorological flight over the Atlantic Ocean. The Sunderland was accompanied by HM Air Force vessel, HMS *Bridport*, and officers from the ship and the aircraft were entertained to lunch by the mayor, Alderman W. J. Perkins. Councillors were later allowed to look around the Sunderland.

August was a bleak month as far as information in the ORB was concerned, it mainly being about the large number of staff visits to the station. On the 3rd, the HF/VHF DF system was inspected by a party from RAF Henlow, and on the 19th, a number of representatives from Avro arrived to check work to be done on Avro Anson PH645. Several officers visited Manston on the 26th to discuss arrangements to be made for the implementation for a flight information service.

The Type 'A' Cadet Training Camp, which had been operating since 19 June, was closed down on 4 September. It had been staffed by 61 (Eastern Reserve) Group personnel and a total of 2,227 cadets had received training.

11

# Battle of Britain Day

On 14 September 1949, a representative from an American oil company visited the station in connection with refuelling arrangements that were being made for aircraft from the USAF that were to take part in the forthcoming Battle of Britain Day celebrations, then in its ninth year. The event took place on Saturday 17 September at 2 p.m., nearly a year after the incident involving the Mosquito that had killed so many people. That tragedy must have been fresh in the minds of local people, but they still turned out in large numbers to see a flying display and static aircraft from a number of foreign air forces. A special bus service was set up from the towns of Thanet to Manston to help keep the roads clear of traffic. There were the usual displays of fighters such as the Spitfire and a demonstration by a Dakota of 'snatching' a Hadrian glider from the ground by means of a hook and a nylon rope.

Of the sixteen items scheduled in the display, the main attractions were to have been the de Havilland Comet, the first ever passenger jet that had flown for the first time in July. The innovative giant eight-engined (four contour rotating propellers) Bristol Brabazon was another very special aircraft on the flying programme. The event was widely covered in the local media and security was quite tight, one of the conditions of entry being that no cameras were allowed.

As it happened, neither the Comet nor the Brabazon appeared because the former developed hydraulic problems and failed an air test just an hour before departing for Manston, while the latter was grounded at Filton in Bristol. Early in the afternoon, a Harvard flew over the airfield performing aerobatics and that was followed by a Tiger Moth carrying out a number of stunts.

The crowd was bitterly disappointed with the event, and although a flight of Meteors flew across the airfield, along with formation displays by Spitfires and Mosquitos, there were gaps of half an hour or more when there was nothing in the air at all. Many of those present thought that the RAF should have concentrated more on putting planes into the air rather than just organising them for static displays. One of the highlights of the afternoon was the casting off and landing of a Horsa glider and the dropping of a stick of paratroopers.

It was claimed by the local press that model aircraft actually stole the show from the real planes and the Thanet Aero Model Club gave what was said to have been the first demonstration of radio-controlled aircraft on a RAF airfield. A Mr Taplin from Birchington, well-known among model makers, put his so-called 'Model Queen' through nine minutes of stunting before landing it just yards from the appreciative crowd.

On Sunday the 18th, there was a service held at the bomb-shattered ruins of Holy Trinity Church, Margate, and there was also with a short service at the war memorial. Before the service began, the RAF standard was placed at the altar of the church and lessons were read by Mr Girling and Flt Lt J. Rootes, DFC. Members of the RAF, WAAF, and ATC stood to attention as Mr J. W. Girling, the president of the local branch of RAFA laid a wreath that was in the shape of a pilot's wings.

In his sermon, Reverend F. R. St John, who was also a flight lieutenant in the RAF, talked about the Battle of Britain. He likened it to the 'Battle of Good Against Evil' and said that the service was being held for three reasons: to thank God, to honour those who had paid the supreme sacrifice, and to rededicate oneself to the service of God.

Almost as soon as the Battle of Britain celebrations were over, preparations began for another exercise called Bulldog and Sqn Ldr Eades, the Metropolitan Signals Staff Officer, arrived to make arrangements for the operation on 20 September. The following day, Wg Cdr J. H. Irwin from 90 Group arrived to inspect ground radio facilities on behalf of the Inspectorate of Radio Services.

Exercise Bulldog was primarily designed mainly to give experience to Bomber Command crews for attacks on defended targets by both day and night. Fighter Command was also involved, and three squadrons were detached to Manston for the period of the exercise that began at 7 p.m. on the 23rd.

The USAF took part in the exercise along with the RNLAF, and for the first time since the end of the war, there was participation by the French and Belgian Air Forces. They contributed aircraft to the defending force, control, and reporting facilities, also providing personnel to help man the radar stations. Also, for the first time, 300 volunteers from the RAuxAF manned a complete fighter sector in the south-west. They were flown in from airfields near their hometowns all over the country just to do a period of duty lasting just twenty-four hours.

The exercise, under the command of AM Sir Aubrey Elwood, the AOC-in-C of Bomber Command, continued until the 27th. The main attacking force consisted of Lincolns, Lancasters, and Mosquitos, with another additional force from the USAF's Third Air Division, made up of a number of B-29 Superfortresses and B-50s, a modified version of the B-29. The main defending force, under the command of AM Sir Basil Edward Embrey, was comprised of Meteor jet fighters and de Havilland Hornets.

On the day that exercise Bulldog finished, the Air Ministry Constabulary Training School moved into Manston from Harrogate in Yorkshire. The unit was established with a policy of training up to 250 constables a year. The Air Ministry Constabulary, which had been formed in 1942 to police all major airfields, was later given the responsibility for the control and policing of just military airfields. In 1946, the establishment of the constabulary had undergone a change of policy and had been broken up, when policing of civil airports had been handed over to the newly formed Civil Aviation Constabulary.

There were several changes to the communication services on the station at the beginning of October when the teleprinter services for ATC and other sections was centralised in the control tower. On the 13th, the transmitter and receiver for the flight information service became operable.

It seems that were some problems with the fuel system on a number of de Havilland Vampires, although the exact nature of the issue or the unit to which the aircraft belonged is not known. On the 20th, a Mr Oakley from 5 MU at Kemble visited Manston in connection with faulty fuel pipes and assembly joints on the type.

On the last day of October, Manston was issued with station callsigns, both for radio and wireless transmissions. There were two call signs for R/T messages, 'Kiwi' and 'Eggstar', while the letters 'MMCI' were used for W/T transmissions.

With the station having been transferred from the control of 46 Group to 47 Group in May, on 1 November, it was transferred back to 46 Group. It was stated in the ORB that this was just a numerical change in the group HQ. Flt Lt Nixon from the Air Ministry visited the station on the 2nd in connection with technical facilities that were to be given to the Air Ministry's Film Unit. On the 9th, a representative from the Gloster Aircraft Company arrived to make arrangements for Meteors that were to be ferried through Manston to Denmark. A total of forty Meteor F.4 and F.8 aircraft were delivered to the Danish Air Force in 1949.

On 14 November, RAF Manston joined the French Air Transport point to point W/T network that was operating on 6,990 Kcs and direct communication with Paris, Dijon, and Istres was established. The exact purpose of this link is not known, but it is understood to have been established to help co-ordinate the ferrying of aircraft through French airspace. Vital information concerning such factors as the weather in France and beyond would have also been relayed to Manston.

The RAF Regiment School, the establishment of which is another element missing from the ORB, was inspected by AVM Harold Edward Lydford on the 17th. Lydford, who was a veteran of the First World War, had received a permanent commission in 1919 and had been appointed as commandant of the RAF regiment in June 1948.

Towards the end of the November, a beacon specifically operating for the use of the Royal Navy was set up with the code letters 'YG'. Another connection with the Navy and FAA was when a representative from Hawker Aircraft Company arrived to deal with a number of issues relating to the Hawker Fury. On the 29th, Manston won the 46 Group Rugby Cup by beating a team from 46 Group HQ, 6–0.

Some 1,178 VHF DF and fifty-six HF bearings were passed to aircraft during November and there were three successful approaches made using the BABS.

On 1 December, Flt Lt Harper visited the station in relation to resettlement issues and most of the entries in the ORB in for the month concern routine visits to the station by staff officers from 46 Group HQ. On the 15th, Sqn Ldr Halford from Transport Command HQ arrived, dealing with business concerning the RAF Regiment School, and the following day, another two officers arrived from Transport Command HQ in connection with the training of teleprinter operators. During the month of December, ATC dealt with request for 1,150 VHF bearings and ninety-seven HF/DF bearings.

The flight information service went live on 1 January 1950 on the VHF frequencies 106.02 and 116.1. A few days later, a second teleprinter was installed in the control tower to facilitate air traffic communications for signals such as flight plans and arrival/departure messages. On the same day, two Spitfires from Brize Norton made emergency landings, and it was later discovered that both aircraft had badly damaged propeller blades.

Sqn Ldr Beattie from 46 Group HQ visited Manston on the 9th in connection with a programme to ferry Meteors through the station. There is no mention of to which air force the aircraft were to be delivered, but they scheduled to transit through Istres, Dijon, and El Aouina. Wg Cdr Carpenter was also involved in the programme and his role was to solve several problems concerning refuelling.

Tragedy struck the south-east during the evening of 12 January when a Royal Navy submarine, HMS *Truculent* (*P315*) sank after colliding with a Swedish oil tanker, the *Divina*, in the Thames Estuary. The submarine had been launched at Barrow in 1942, and it was heading for Sheerness during sea trials after undergoing a refit in Chatham Dockyard. During the early hours of the 13th, a Sea Otter (RD871) arrived at Manston to refuel and co-ordinate the search for the submarine.

Despite an extensive search and rescue operation carried out over a few days, the weather and other factors prevented the submarine and most of its crew from being saved. Eighteen of the seventy-nine-man crew were dockyard workers, but in the end, only a total of fifteen of those on board were rescued and fifty-seven were swept away and drowned. More bodies were found inside the vessel when it was salvaged, and the final death toll was sixty-four.

To add to the death toll, a Lancaster (SW363) from Coastal Command crashed while taking-off from Kinloss on its way to Leuchars to pick a team of navy divers and fly them to Manston to take part in the rescue operation. Flt Lt George Harris, the pilot, was the only member of the five-man crew to survive the initial impact but had suffered multiple injuries and shock, and he died in the ambulance on the way to hospital. The other members of the crew who were killed were second pilot, Flt Lt Gwynn Williams; navigator, Sgt John Cunningham; flight engineer, Flt Lt Alfred Stephens; and wireless operator, Sgt Ernest Geal.

There was another incident on Friday the 20th of a more personal and local nature when forty-three-year-old FS William George James Bradbury was knocked off his bicycle and killed when he came into contact with a taxi near Vincent Farm on the Margate Road. The flight sergeant was returning to his living out quarters after the completion of his duty on the station.

One of the witnesses to the accident was fellow RAF Cpl Maurice Sharpe who was a passenger in the taxi, and he saw Bradbury just a few yards from the junction. He said he did not expect the cyclist to come out, but to stop when he saw the car approaching him, and he did not see any lights on the bicycle. Another RAF serviceman, AC Dennis Mahoney, who was in the front seat of the taxi, confirmed that the cyclist was riding in the middle of the road. He said that although the taxi driver braked hard and dipped his lights, he could not avoid the cyclist, although the vehicle was only travelling at 30 mph.

At the subsequent inquest held in Margate town hall, the coroner returned a verdict of 'death by misadventure' and recommended that a 'halt' sign should be installed at the junction. FS Bradbury, who was married to Gladys Louisa Bradbury, had been stationed at Manston since 1949. He was buried with full military honours just a short distance from where he had been killed, in Margate's St John's Cemetery on the 25th.

The mayor of Hastings visited the station on the 24th to present a plaque from the borough to 47 Squadron, Transport Command, in connection with the naming of the type of aircraft the Handley Page Hastings. The Hastings was a transport aircraft powered by four Bristol Hercules engines that had first flown in May 1946. It had entered service with 47 Squadron at Dishforth in September 1948 but soon moved to West Germany where it had played an important part in the Berlin Airlift. The station presented a guard of honour, and it was also reported in the local press that the councils of Broadstairs and Margate had agreed to adopt RAF Manston under the terms of the municipal liaison scheme. Ramsgate Council had already agreed to the adoption, and the aim of the connection was to promote good feeling between the public and the RAF and to stimulate recruitment. AM Sir Brian Baker was present to meet the mayor, along with the AOC of 46 Group who had arrived by air.

There is a rather confusing note in the ORB on 6 February 1950 stating that Grp Capt. Eady had taken over command of the station from Grp Capt. Crichton-Biggie, who had not been mentioned for nearly two years. According to the records, Crichton-Biggie had handed over command of the station to Grp Capt. Rankin in May 1948 and, in turn, Rankin had passed on the command to Grp Capt. Eady in February 1950. It is a confusing picture, but it is possible that Eady had been ill or sent on a detachment.

On the 13th, the Central Signals Unit from RAF Watton tested the Standard Beam Approach and Eureka Beacon. The 'YG' naval beacon that had been established the previous November was also tested and found to be fully serviceable.

A Wellington (PG347) from RAF Swinderby in Lincoln made a forced landing on the 16th after the pilot had noticed a loss of oil pressure in the starboard engine. It was the second Wellington from Swinderby to make an emergency landing in less than a week; on the 10th, NB118 had diverted to Manston for exactly the same reason.

Wg Cdr Denneby, representing the high commissioner's air traffic advisory service for India, passed through Manston on 20 February. The purpose of his visit was to discuss arrangements for a monthly Dakota flight to India. The flights had previously been organised and flown from RAF Oakington. At about the same time, a number of high-ranking officers arrived to discuss another air defence exercise, which had been named Stardust.

Vampires from 54, 72, and 247 Squadrons arrived at Manston on 6 March to provide an escort for the visit of the president of France to England. The aircraft remained at Manston until the 10th, when they returned to Odiham.

No. 3617 FCU returned to Manston on 1 April for its summer camp, having previously visited the station in March 1949. The unit also received a few visits from senior officers during this time, including Grp Capt. Newbigging from Reserve Command on the 5th.

The following day, 120 air cadets arrived on the station for their Easter camp, along with the twelve officers and three warrant officers who were to supervise them. The camp had been organised by 65 (London Reserve) Group, and it lasted until the 11th. There was a lot of activity and staff visits during this period, and on the 12th, the station hosted ACM Douglas Claude Strathern Evill, the former vice-chief of air staff, accompanied by Wg Cdr C. A. Stevens of 62 (Southern Reserve) Group, the air chief marshal was visiting the summer camp held by 3617 FCU.

Two representatives from BEA visited the station on the 13th. There is no mention of what business Mr Millward and Mr Scott-Fell were on, but judging from what had occurred during previous visits by officers from BEA, it would have been to discuss the airline's access and use of the station for its fleet of aircraft.

The build up to the air defence exercise Stardust was not without its problems, and on the 16th, there had been a collision between a Vampire (VV565) from 246 Squadron and an Avro Lincoln from 100 Squadron. At 1.45 p.m., the Vampire, while making a mock head-on attack, hit the port wing of the Lincoln, of which the pilot managed to maintain control and make a safe landing, despite losing 3 feet of its wing and aileron. The pilot of the Vampire, Plt Off. Trench, baled out over the sea 12 miles off the coast of Swanage, but despite successfully ejecting from the Vampire, he died of exposure in the water. Such were the perils of air defence exercises.

Nos 1 and 43 Squadrons arrived at Manston on 21 April to take part in exercise Stardust. Both units were equipped with the Meteor F.4 and based at Tangmere. A number of vehicles from nearby RAF Sandwich also arrived on the station to help out with the technical side of things such as providing additional signals and radar. The RVT vehicles that were carrying the portable radar equipment had to be correctly sited and then calibrated.

Other equipment, such as a Magneto Type 10 line switchboard, was fitted in the control tower along with a Mobile Pack Radio set type TR1430. Unfortunately, the BABS that had experienced interference from 26 April had to be downgraded to Category 'D'.

On the last day of April, Manston was visited by the AOC of Fighter Command, AM Sir Basil Edward Embry, DSO*, DFC. Embry was probably was one of the most distinguished RAF officers who had been closely associated with 2 Group. He had personally led attacks on enemy positions during the war, including three on German Gestapo HQ at Aarhus, Copenhagen, and Odense. Even after being appointed as the AOC of 2 Group, Embry had continued to fly on operations using the name of 'Wg Cdr Smith'. The air marshal was inspecting and evaluating exercise Stardust and how the units taking part were performing during the period that it ran, from 30 April to 1 May.

On 1 May, Manston was visited by another high-ranking officer, the AOC of 11 Group, AVM Thomas Geoffrey Pike, DFC*, who flew in from Tangmere. He was visiting the station in connection with another air defence exercise called Bulldog, but the main reason he was there was to inspect the radar equipment at RAF Sandwich, 3 miles down the road from Manston. The station at Sandwich had become fully operational again as an SOC/GCI unit on 1 April, and it took part in the air defence exercises as part of its 'warming up' period. Both 1 and 43 Squadrons returned to Tangmere on 2 May after participating in both exercise Stardust and Bulldog.

The BABS was rendered unserviceable on the 6th because of continual interference from the Royal Navy's beacon 'Yankee Golf'. A Mr Stanley from the Admiralty was called in to sort the problem out.

Not directly connected to Manston, but another incident that involved a local airman and officer who was a member of the Overseas Ferry Flight occurred on 17 May when thirty-year-old Flt Lt William Makepeace Strathern, DFC*, a New Zealander, was killed at Istres in France. Strathern had taken-off from Manston at 10.30 a.m. to ferry a Vampire F.3 (VG699) to Istres, where he had carried out a test flight on the aircraft.

The aircraft crashed and exploded close to the airfield at Istres after being overstressed, and Strathern was killed instantly. Strathern was a veteran of the Second World War, during which he had served with 138 Squadron, ferrying agents out to France and the Netherlands in a variety of aircraft, including the Lysander and Halifax. His address at the time of his death was 19 Canterbury Road, Westgate.

There were a number of staff visits from officers from Transport Command HQ on the 23rd and the 24th involving Wg Cdr Maycock and Sqn Ldr Hook from accounts and Sqn Ldr Neal from engineering. During the month of May, a total of seventy-seven HF/DF and 538 VHF/DF Bearings had been given to pilots. In addition, two BABS approaches had been successfully carried out.

On 1 June, the VHF 'distress' frequency was changed from 116.1 to 121.5 MHz, and the same frequency is still in use today by civil aircraft. The UHF frequency used by military aircraft is 243.0 MHz, exactly twice that of the civil frequency. The reason for that is because it is possible that any transmission broadcast on 121.5 might break through to 243.0.

On 3 June, No. 3620 FCU (Norwich) arrived at Manston for its summer camp training. Wg Cdr Pawson from Transport Command HQ visited the station on the 7th to present a trophy to the Technical Wing. It had taken part in and won the Inter Wing Cup that had been held as part of RAF Manston's annual sports meeting. The following day, the whole station turned out on parade to celebrate the king's birthday.

Over the next few days, there were further staff visits, including one on the 12th by AVM Lawrence Darvall, the AOC of 23 Group (Flying Training Command). Darvall had joined the service in 1916 and had joined the Green Howards before remustering to the RFC the following year. During Operation Overlord, he had flown on D-Day on one of the lead aircraft as second pilot, leading from the front.

Darvall was visiting 3620 FCU, which received another staff visit the following day by Wg Cdr Roach from the catering office of Transport Command HQ; Sqn Ldr Cuthbert also arrived at the same time. There were further staff visits on the 13th by AM Robert Mordaunt Foster, the AOC of Reserve Command, who inspected both the FCU and 438 ATC Squadron that had also arrived for its summer camp. He was accompanied by AVM Theodore Neuman McEvoy, the AOC of 61 Group (Eastern). The final visit to the FCU was on the 15th by ace pilot and former CO of the Biggin Hill Wing, Wg Cdr Al Deere, DSO, OBE, DFC*, who was also stationed at 61 Group HQ.

No. 3620 FCU returned to Norwich on 17 June, but the following day, another group, comprising of ATC cadets from 343 and 1999 Squadrons, arrived for their summer camps. They, in turn, received a staff visit from Sqn Ldr Collinson from 65 Group (London) HQ on the 22nd—Manston was a very busy place.

On 1 July, another FCU arrived for its annual training camp, this time it was No. 3608 from Middlesbrough. The following day, 46F and 329 Air Training Squadrons arrived for their summer camps and they remained at Manston until the 9th.

# 12

# The American Years

In July 1950, RAF Manston became the first station in the country to be used as a rotational base for the Fighter Bomber Groups of SAC that were on ninety days' temporary duty. Duncan Curtis has written an excellent book about the USAF's occupation of RAF Manston and what follows here is not meant to undermine his work.

The Americans were based at Manston from 1950 to 1958, and our account merely gives an overview of that period and covers a number of major incidents that occurred in the intervening years. The 7512th Air Base Squadron was the first unit to arrive on 15 July 1950, and it was directly under the command of the 3rd Air Division based at South Ruislip. Its role was to provide administration and support for the SAC units when they arrived.

On 12 July, arrangements for the arrival and accommodation of No. 20 Group, USAF, were discussed between the staff of the station and Lt-Col. A. Bocous of the USAF, Wg Cdr M. K. Sewell (Org.1) of Fighter Command HQ, and Sqn Ldr R. D. Stephens (equipment).

RAF Manston was transferred from Transport Command to 11 Group, Fighter Command, on 14 July. What was described as the 'taking-over board' was formed under the presidency of Sqn Ldr E. G. R Downey, with the other members being Sqn Ldr Johnson and Flt Lt Jones. Those RAF units that remained began to move out to various other locations and the RAF summer camps ended on the 16th. Nos 291, 342, 409, 1481, and 2096 ATC Squadrons had completed their training and any further summer camps that were scheduled for Manston were moved to RAF Oakington.

The following day, the advance party of the USAF base component arrived on the station and the first elements of the Technical School were moved out to Chivenor by air, while the RAF Regiment Training School moved to Oakington. Sqn Ldr Morgan arrived from Fighter Command HQ to discuss a new establishment for the station. There were many staff officers visiting the station over the next few days, and on the 18th, AVM Stanley Flamank Vincent from Fighter Command HQ and Grp Capt. Earle White, the command's account officer, were among them. Vincent was a veteran of the First World War and had begun his service life with 2 Reserve Squadron in 1915 as a U/T pilot.

The main body of the RAF's Technical Wing departed on the 20th by rail, and Grp Capt. Eady handed over command of the station to Grp Capt. Rankin. Over the next few days, there were several technical changes, such as those to the frequencies used on the airfield. The airfield control channel was changed to 108.7 Mcs and the 11 Group 'Guard' frequency was brought into use. The Transport Command frequency of 117.18 Mcs was disconnected.

The first aircraft to arrive were the Republic F-84D Thunderjets of the 20th Fighter Bomber Wing that flew in on 26 July, although this historic event is not mentioned in the ORB of RAF Manston. The wing comprised of the 55th, 77th, and 79th Fighter Bomber Squadrons. Its arrival was described as being very impressive as they flew across the Thames Estuary during the late afternoon of a glorious day in tight formation. The F-84s left individual black smoke trails, and it was claimed that a solid black cloud was visible long before they were heard or seen.

On 29 July, a newly installed ground-controlled approach installation was used for the first time, and despite the American presence, the airfield continued to be used by the RAF and the British establishment. The duke and duchess of Gloucester flew in from Northolt for what was described as an official function at Dover College. The royal couple returned to Northolt during the evening.

An Avro Anson C.12 (PH611) from RAF Manston's station flight was forced to ditch into the Thames Estuary on 18 July after the aircraft had suffered engine failure. The Anson ditched into the sea 10 miles north-east of Margate after the pilot found he could not maintain height on a single engine. Exact details of this incident are not known, but it is thought that the two-man crew were later picked up and escaped without injury.

Another incident involving a RAF aircraft occurred on 20 October 1950 when a Wellington T.10 (RP320) from 2 Air Navigation School, based at Thorney Island, collided with a Mosquito (MM757 (MB-18)) from the Belgian Air Force. The Wellington, captained by twenty-six-year-old Allan Worboys, was on a night-training exercise called Emperor and was climbing out over the Thames Estuary. It crashed on marshland somewhere between Birchington and Herne Bay, but the wreckage of the aircraft was never actually found.

With the pilot were five members of the crew, which included FS Arthur Gordon (the signaller) and Sgt Ronald Geroge Stanley Stansby (the staff navigator). The other two men on board were student navigators, Officer Cadets Alan Frederick George Marshal and Peter Alister MacIntosh. The Wellington T.10 was the final version of the Second World War bomber to remain in service with the RAF, and it had a faired nose to replace the nose turret.

The Mosquito was being flown by Capt. Christian Henrahrd and navigator Sgt Joseph Tytgat who were from 10 Squadron from Belgische Luctmacht.

Because the Mosquito was mainly made of wood, some of the wreckage from it was found floating in the sea, but the two airmen's bodies were never found.

The 20th Fighter Bomber Group remained at Manston until 10 December 1950 when it returned to Shaw Field, Carolina, in the USA. On 3 January 1951, it was replaced by the 31st Fighter Escort Wing that comprised of 307th, 308th, and 309th Squadrons that were equipped with the F-84E.

Just three weeks after the 31st had arrived at Manston, on 24 January, the USAF experienced its first major incident when F-84 49-2105 crashed into Nash Gardens, Margate. The aircraft was being flown by Lt Cdr William D. Biggers who was the executive officer of the 308th Squadron. He was actually a member of the US Navy and on loan to the USAF.

The flight by four F-84s had begun with a briefing for a routine cine-gun mission that was to be carried out at 15,000 feet using the callsign 'Norman White Flight'. The individual callsigns were 'Norman White Leader' and 'Norman White 1, 2, and 3'. Biggers was given the position and callsign of 'Norman 2'. All times that are mentioned here are given in 'Zulu', which is the time used by ATC and is basically another name for GMT.

Take-off went as normal and the flight arrived in the designated area for the cine-gun exercise at 12.10 p.m. with Norman White 2 moving into attack position and proceeding to make passes on Norman White Leader. Norman White 3's take-off was delayed because of a 'wet start', but at 12.29 p.m., it was airborne, and the pilot called for a rendezvous over Manston, which was made at 15,000 feet at 12.35 p.m. While Norman White 3 commenced cine-gun passes, Norman White 2 pulled up into close formation with Norman White Leader. At that point, Biggers made his only radio transmission when he told pilots in another flight to use their correct callsigns.

At approximately 12.40 p.m., Norman White 2 began to make a slow right turn away from Norman White Leader, before making another gradual left turn. Norman White Leader followed Biggers's aircraft, keeping a position 500 to 600 feet astern and observed it pulling up sharply, before rolling over. He noticed that the aircraft seemed to falter in the air for a moment before falling rapidly in what he described as a split 'S' manoeuvre. The aircraft then fell vertically, made a fast half roll, pulled up before entering a constant roll, and then collided with the ground and exploded at 12.40 p.m.

The aircraft had crashed into the garden of 10 Nash Gardens, Margate, leaving a crater 20 feet long and 12 feet deep. Rather miraculously, nobody other than the pilot, Lt Cdr Biggers, was killed and he stood no chance of surviving the impact. The cause of the crash was later found to be contamination of Biggers's oxygen system that had caused a condition known as hypoxia.

The 12th Fighter Escort Wing arrived at Manston on 18 July 1951 and it was made up of 559th, 560th, and 561st Fighter Escort Squadrons that were equipped with the F-84E. It replaced the 31st Wing, which returned to Turner Field, Georgia, USA, on 6 August.

The remains of Lt Cdr Biggers' F-84 in Nash Gardens, Margate. The aircraft crashed on 24 January 1951 after taking-off from Manston.

The 123rd Fighter Bomber Wing (Air National Guard) arrived at Manston in December 1951, comprising of the 156th, 165th, and 1677th Fighter Bomber squadrons from the North Carolina and Kentucky Air Guards. These units took over the F-84s that had been used by the 12th Fighter Escort Wing that had returned to the USA in January 1952.

It was one of these aircraft that was involved in the second major incident that occurred on Sunday 27 April 1952 when a F-84E of the 123rd Fighter Bomber Wing crashed in St Peter's. The aircraft, serial number 49-2111A, was being flown by Capt. Clifford Vincent Foggarty from Long Island, New York. The duty ATC that day was an RAF officer, Flt Lt G. F. Lincoln, and at 11.05 a.m., he was contacted on 147.42 M/cs and gave Foggarty's flight of four aircraft taxi clearance for take-off on runway 11.

Instructions were passed over the air before take-off that after getting airborne, all aircraft should avoid flying over Ramsgate between 10 a.m. and 11.30 a.m., after a message to that effect had been received from USAF Combat Operations. 'Red Leader' acknowledged the message and the flight was cleared for take-off at 11.14 a.m. Foggarty had been assigned to fly in the number two position in a four-ship formation, which was on a high-altitude mission, but things went wrong from the start. The pilot flying number three noticed that there was fire coming from the area of number two's dive break just one minute and thirty seconds after taking-off. At 11.15 a.m., Red 3 called on 147.42 M/cs: 'You have smoke and fire coming from the back. Land as soon as possible'.

Foggarty was told over the R/T to put the aircraft down in the nearest field, but he remained with the aircraft and made no attempt to eject. According to the official account from the USAF, the F-84 turned left, lost altitude, and there was an explosion as it flew over the centre of town. At 11.16 a.m., Red Leader called Manston tower and stated: 'We have an emergency aircraft crashed. Plenty of smoke. Position 15 degrees left of the runway. Request you inform crash crews and fire tenders'. Flt Lt Lincoln carried out the appropriate crash action and informed the civilian fire services at Ramsgate and Broadstairs.

Rescue work was put into effect immediately, and when Police Constable Harris arrived on the scene, an ambulance was already in attendance. He had been on duty at the junction of Luton Road and Ramsgate Road in Broadstairs accompanied by Police Sergeant Marshal when he had seen four American jets flying in line abreast in a northerly direction. It was clear to both officers that one of them was in trouble because the machine on the left of the formation was on fire. As it turned towards St Peter's, they could clearly see that the whole of the fuselage was on fire and they realised that a crash was inevitable. Almost immediately, a black cloud of smoke had arisen from the direction of St Peter's.

Harris cycled towards the scene of the crash while Sgt Marshal proceeded towards St Peter's with Chief Inspector Hann in a car. At the scene, they found that Lloyds Bank and 44 The High Street were a blazing inferno and ammunition from the American jet was exploding all around. The aircraft had been fitted with six .50-calibre Browning machine guns. Members of the USAF's rescue team soon arrived on the scene and Harris immediately began to search for the pilot; at about 12.30 p.m., he found Capt. Fogarty's remains in an evergreen bush approximately 30 yards from the crash site. His red and white parachute was also found close by his remains.

The F-84 had been heading towards an open field and might have made it but failed to clear one row of houses and had crashed into 44 The High Street, St Peter's, killing two occupants of a house—seventy-nine-year-old Mr William Read and his wife, fifty-five-year-old Mrs Evelyn Read. Mrs Ellen Collier later died of her injuries several weeks later on 27 May at Queen Victoria Hospital, and her death was due to shock and extensive burns.

Dr J. C. McNaught examined the bodies of Mr and Mrs Read and stated that they had suffered extensive burns and lacerations and death was due to being crushed. The Reads had lived in St Peter's since 1935, and during the war, Mr Read had served with the Canadian Army. After the war, he had owned an ironmonger's shop on the High Street in St Peter's, which was also destroyed by the crash. The funeral of Mr and Mrs Read took place at Charing Crematorium on 5 May 1952. Mrs Read had two daughters, one who lived in Oxfordshire and another in Canada. The American Government paid for the air fare for her to be flown over for the funeral.

The medical report concluded that the pilot had been in a good position at about 600 feet and flying at 300 mph when he was told to put his aircraft down in the nearest field: 'Pilot apparently pilot made no attempt to eject himself and was headed for an open field if he had cleared one row of houses. Pilot was blown clear of the plane and in the direction of other pieces of the aircraft'.

After an investigation of the wreckage, it was found that there had been a failure of part of the fuel nozzle, part number 5230443 on the Allison J-35 engine and possibly part number AN832-6D. The failure had been caused by damage while handling on the ground due to the vulnerable position of the assembly; inherent weakness of union metal; and high-frequency vibration during engine operation. A subsequent report stated that qualified engineering personnel and safety sections should be sent to Fürstenfeldbruck Air Force Base in Germany to gain knowledge of such events on other aircraft.

Sometime later, Capt. Foggarty's widow, Mrs Sonia Foggarty, wrote to the mayor of Margate, responding to a letter of sympathy sent to her by Mrs B. M. Giles (councillor). Writing from her home in Brooklyn, New York, she thanked the mayor for her beautiful letter, which Mrs Foggarty said she would save for her son to read when he grew up.

In reply to a letter sent to Col. Philip Ardery, CO of the 123rd Fighter Bomber Wing, he wrote to the chairman, Councillor A. T. Tucker: 'Your letter of sympathy has reached me and I am pleased to convey your sentiments to all members of my command and particularly to Mrs Foggarty. I think the spirit of

Capt. Walker of the USAF's 156th Fighter Bomber Wing being rescued by the pilot boat *Foreness* on 14 May 1952 after his F-84 had crashed into the sea.

Capt. Walker being interviewed after his rescue from the sea off Foreness Point.

British goodwill and good sportsmanship has shone forth brightly in the time of this misfortune. We hope you all know that we too, sympathise with you in the suffering experienced by your people'.

Just a few weeks later, on 14 May, there was another incident when Capt. C. K. Walker of 156th Fighter Bomber Squadron crashed into the sea a mile off the coast of Foreness. His aircraft was an F-84E (49-2074) and he was fortunate enough to safely bale out and be picked up and taken aboard the pilot boat *Foreness*.

Soon after these events, the command of RAF Manston changed, and Grp Capt. Eric S. Finch took over as CO from Grp Capt. Rankin. Finch had held his first command in April 1937 when, then as a squadron leader, he had taken over 73 Squadron that had been equipped with the Hawker Fury. The squadron later became part of the Advanced Air Striking Force in France and Finch served with such 'aces' as Fg Off. 'Cobber' Kaine and Fg Off. 'Fanny' Orton. He had been promoted to the rank of group captain in June 1944, and shortly afterwards, he had been given the post of air *attaché* in Bolivia.

In between all the American activity at Manston, on Saturday 27 June 1953, there was what was described as a 'grand reopening' of the local Ramsgate Airport and an international flying display. The airport had been completely devastated by enemy bombing during the war and the land had been returned to agricultural purposes until it had been reclaimed for flying in the spring of 1952.

The flying display featured demonstrations by a Tiger Moth, a Hawker Hurricane, and a Gloster Meteor from 500 Squadron (County of Kent), led by Sqn Ldr De Villiers. One of the organisers of the event was Wg Cdr Hugh Kennard, who had led one of the American 'Eagle' Squadrons, 121 Squadron, made up of American volunteers, during the war. In 1953, he was a director of Air Kruise, but he was also later involved with several other airlines, including Silver City, but he was best associated with Invicta Airways.

Some years ago, I met a former RAF airman who had served at Hawkinge towards the end of the war and he told me an interesting story about Wg Cdr Kennard. Tom Smith, who was an engine fitter, had just arrived at Hawkinge when he momentarily stopped to look at a Hawker Tempest that was parked up with someone working on it. The man shouted down to Tom, 'Do you know anything about these bloody things?' Tom replied that he did and that he had worked on them before. With that, the dirty looking 'airman', who Tom presumed to be a fitter, asked him to give him a hand to get the engine started.

For over an hour, Tom and his companion, both by now covered in oil and grease, worked in shirt sleeves and struggled to get the engine started; eventually, it did burst into life. A few moments later, the other airman jumped down, rolled down his sleeves, and put on his tunic. Tom was astounded to see that there were three bars on the shoulder indicating that he was a wing commander, in fact it was the CO of RAF Hawkinge, Wg Cdr Hugh Charles Kennard.

It was after Wg Cdr Kennard had left the RAF in June 1946 that he had formed Air Kruise, which was equipped with a number of Bristol Freighters and C.47s. Some time later, he traced Tom to his home in Glasgow and offered him the job of chief engineer with the company. Unfortunately, by then, Tom had got married and had found himself a good job. He seriously considered the wing commander's offer but because of his circumstances, he had to turn him down. They kept in touch for many years and Tom never forgot the humility and friendship shown by Hugh Kennard. In May 1954, Air Kruise was taken over by Britavia, a group of companies that included Silver City Airways, and Wg Cdr Kennard became involved with its management.

There was another incident involving a RAF aircraft on 21 January 1954, when a Meteor NF.11 (WM175) crashed while attempting to land at Manston. The pilot, Fg Off. Ronald Albert Moore, had first attempted to land at RAF West Malling but overshot from a ground-controlled approach (PAR) and was diverted to Manston. To begin with, Moore was well-positioned for a landing but then failed to respond to corrective information passed to him from the control tower and he again missed his approach.

Moore then informed the controller that he had insufficient fuel for another approach and said that he was going to climb to 10,000 feet and abandon the aircraft. The aircraft was in the vicinity of Whitstable but over the sea when it disappeared off the radar screens without trace. The other member of the crew was Fg Off. David Brian Pattison, and it was presumed that both he and Moore had drowned. The Meteor and its crew belonged to 85 Squadron, which was based at West Malling.

Just three days later, on the 24th, there was another accident involving a Meteor from 257 Squadron that was being flown by Plt Off. John Cardinal Goodwin. Meteor F.8 WH298 crashed in Poulders Gardens estate in Sandwich, and it was believed that the aircraft had undergone a catastrophic failure of the oxygen system. Then it had subsequently suffered structural failure in flight. The unit was based at Wattisham in Suffolk and commanded by an officer from the USAF, Maj. H. N. Tanner.

On the night of 26–27 November 1954, there was a disaster out at sea when the *South Goodwin Lighthouse* anchor chains failed in a storm and it capsized on its starboard side with the crew trapped in the galley under water. At approximately 1.15 a.m., the vessel's sister ship on the East Goodwin's spotted the lighthouse drifting past 6 miles off its station heading towards the Goodwin Sands. There was little that could be done immediately, but at low tide, during the morning of the 27th, an S-55 helicopter of the USAF from Manston was dispatched and landed on a sand bar close to where the wreck of the lighthouse had ended up.

The helicopter from 66th Air-Sea Rescue Squadron, flown by Maj. Paul Parker, hovered as low as 30 feet above the heaving deck and its crew managed to rescue twenty-two-year-old Mr Ronald Murton who was flown to hospital. The rescue took place on its second sortie of the morning at 9 a.m., and Murton was snatched from a precarious position on the side of the vessel's hull. Ironically, Murton was not a regular member of the crew but had been employed by the Minister of Agriculture to carry out a study of bird migration.

Severe bad weather continued and prevented any further rescue attempts until the 28th, when divers and rescue equipment were dropped on the sands and the vessel searched for the rest of the crew. It was soon realised that there was nobody else on board and that the bodies of the rest of the crew had been washed out to sea. It was a very brave effort by the USAF's helicopter crew, and for their gallantry, they were presented with Vellum Scrolls. The helicopter's commander, Capt. E. Parkins, received the DFC and the Silver Medal of the Royal Lifeboat Institution. Other members of the crew were awarded the Air Medal.

During the American occupation of RAF Manston, the USAF's operations were supported by a number of aircraft and helicopters for the purpose of ASR, from both the 9th and 66th Air-Sea Rescue Squadrons. One of them was the Grumman Albatross SA-16 (originally HU-16), the USAF's version of the amphibious twin-engined aircraft widely used by the US Navy.

On Wednesday 17 August 1955, an Albatross and its crew had to itself be rescued after it had floundered during an exercise practising sea landing at Margate. After being taken in tow by the Margate lifeboat, the aircraft was taken ashore on the old naval slipway at Westgate where, during the First World War, many ancient seaplane pilots of the RNAS had found themselves in similar circumstances. The aircraft was being flown by Capt. V. Dixon and Col. Marshal Stricker, the CO of the 9th Air Rescue Operations. The Albatross was not badly damaged, and it was repaired and flown out at high tide the following day.

A Grumman Albatross of the USAF's 9th Air-Sea Rescue Squadron taking off using its auxiliary jet pack.

13

# The Manston Spitfire

No book about former RAF Manston would be complete without a mention of Spitfire Mk XVI TB752, which has over the years become better known as the 'Manston Spitfire'. The aircraft arrived at Manston in September 1955 during the American occupation of the station, although the station log records the event as being June 1956.

When it arrived at Manston, TB752 was painted a dull silver, but within a short while, it was repainted in what has been described as 'Spurious' Battle of Britain colours. Initially, the Spitfire was placed outside the officers' mess (later the sergeants' mess), but it was later moved to be on public display outside SHQ.

It is claimed that former RAF fighter pilot Sqn Ldr 'Tubby' Mayne, who lived locally in Birchington and had become a local councillor, began the campaign to acquire a Spitfire for RAF Manston. The CO at the time, Grp Capt. Oldbury, also had a stake in claiming a Spitfire for the station. Grp Capt. William George Oldbury, OBE, DFC, had taken over command of Manston in April 1955 from Grp Capt. Finch. Finch retired from the service on 28 May 1955.

Oldbury had joined the RAF in 1936 and had learnt to fly at the Artwork Reserve Flying School in Perth. He had previously served at Manston in 1938, and as a flying officer at the School of Air Navigation. During the war, he had served as a flight commander on 620 Squadron, flying Stirling bombers, before being posted to 218 Squadron (Gold Coast) as a wing commander, again flying the Stirling. He had been promoted to the rank of group captain in January 1955 and posted to Bomber Command HQ.

It was fortunate that a small number of Spitfires had been gathered together at RAF Lyneham for the production of the film *Reach for the Sky*, the story of Wg Cdr Douglas Bader. All the aircraft in the film were painted with fictional serial numbers and so it is impossible to identify TB752. After filming had been completed in August 1955, TB752 may well have been heading for the scrap heap, but the pressure from Mayne and Oldbury worked, and the Spitfire arrived at Manston on 28 September 1955.

The wartime operational history of TB752 concerned just two units: 66 and 403 (RCAF) Squadrons. It had entered service with the RAF in March 1945 with 66 Squadron, which was then based at Fairwood Common, although the exact date is not known. The aircraft had been allocated the squadron code LZ-F, and TB752 visited Manston for the first time when the unit stayed overnight on 16 March. That was almost certainly when 66 Squadron was in the process of moving from Fairwood Common in Glamorgan to Schijndel in Holland.

The first recorded operational flight of the Spitfire was on 19 March by Plt Off. Edwards who was carrying out the role of top cover for a flight of bombers from 2 Group, which were attacking the marshalling yards at Dulmen, a small town in Germany. The following day, the Spitfire was flown by another pilot, on a bomber escort mission to Bocholt. Later that same day, Fg Off. Edwards took the aircraft on its third operation on another bomber escort mission to Dorsten.

TB752 continued to operate with 66 Squadron until 25 March, when it was damaged returning from a sortie after Plt Off. Hugo found that the starboard wheel would not lower. He made a one-wheel landing that damaged the wing and propeller, but Hugo escaped unharmed and the aircraft was classed as Category 'AC' (badly damaged) and sent to 409 Repair and Salvage Unit to be repaired. It was one of thirteen such units assigned to the 2nd Tactical Air Force and each one of them dealt with a specific type of aircraft.

On 29 March, the aircraft was reissued to 403 Squadron and was given the unit code letters KH-Z. It was on 403 Squadron and while operating from Diepholz in Lower Saxony on 21 April 1945 that TB752 destroyed its first enemy aircraft. Not

Spitfire TB752 on display outside SHQ before its refurbishment in 1980.

Former Luftwaffe ace Adolf Galland sitting in the cockpit of TB752 in 1983. Apart from his wartime operations, this was not the first time he had visited Manston, and in 1974, he had met up with RAF ace Bob Stanford Tuck, and they posed for a photo in front of the Spitfire.

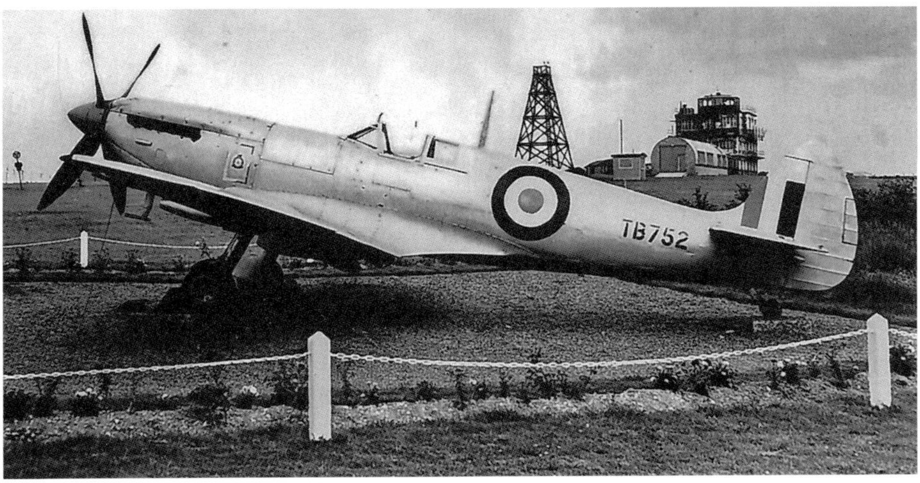


The 'Manston' Spitfire TB752 shortly after its arrival at Manston, painted in a dull silver colour scheme.

many surviving Spitfires can claim to have been in action or having destroyed a single enemy aircraft, but TB752 is one of them and it destroyed four.

The pilot who claimed TB752's first victory was the squadron's CO, Sqn Ldr Henry Paul Michael Zary, DFC, an American who had crossed the border and joined the RCAF. Before the war, Zary had been an associate professor at a university in New York. Known on 403 Squadron as 'Hank', he was already an ace, and the Bf 109 that Zary destroyed was his seventh victim. Unfortunately, Zary contracted pleurisy shortly after the war ended and he died in hospital in early 1946.

TB752's second victory went to Fg Off. David Leslie on 25 April when he destroyed an unidentified enemy aircraft while attacking a coastal airfield at Travemünde. It was later thought that the aircraft was a Focke-Wulf Fw 189, a twin-engined, twin-tail night-fighter. During the sortie, the aircraft was damaged in the starboard wing by flak, but Leslie managed to get the aircraft back safely, and after repairs on the squadron, it continued to operate with 403 Squadron. Leslie was an experienced pilot who had enlisted in the RAF as soon as he had left high school. He survived the war and later went to live in San Diego in California.

Fg Off. Bob Young claimed TB752's third victory on 1 May, a long-nosed Fw 190 that was destroyed during a raid in the Bergedt area. The Fw 190 was among twenty enemy aircraft carrying bombs and the one that Young claimed was one of two that were shot down. Bob Young was from Peterborough and he had joined the RAF in 1940. Bob survived the war and went to work for Nottingham Trent University.

Fg Off. Fred Town claimed TB752's fourth and final victory on 3 May when, after getting separated from other aircraft in the squadron, he came across a solitary He 111K. They had been carrying out a strafing raid but had insufficient machine-gun bullets and cannon shells left to fire and destroy the Heinkel. Fred Town flew a variety of aircraft during his RAF career, including the Mustang, Tempest, and Meteor. Probably the most unusual type he flew was a Fw 190 that had been was acquired by 403 Squadron at the end of the war. Fred is one of a number of TB752's former pilots who have returned to Manston to visit the museum and see his former aircraft.

The Spitfire's last recorded flight with 403 Squadron was on 19 June 1945, and after that, it was sent to No. 83 Ground Support Unit before going into storage with 29 MU at High Ercall. In September 1949, it appeared at RAF Scampton's Battle of Britain display before going back into storage at High Ercall. In 1951, TB752 was on the strength of 103 Flight Refresher School at Full Sutton in Yorkshire, but then it was moved from 49 MU at Colerne in Wiltshire to 45 MU at Kinloss before returning to 29 MU at High Ercall. In November 1953, it spent a short time at No. 5 Civilian Anti-Aircraft Co-operation Unit at Llanbedr. In December 1954, TB752 was classified as 'non-effective stock', but at an unknown date, it appeared in the film *Reach for the Sky*, before finally being sent to Manston as the Gate Guardian.

On the wall immediately behind TB752 in the Spitfire & Hurricane Memorial Building hangs the Manston 'scoreboard', which covers the confirmed claims of those units based at the station for the period 1941–45. For many years, it hung on the wall of the CO's office in Station HQ, where beneath it in a glass case sat the station's casualty record book. Together, they represented the station's wartime history and its losses during the last four years of the war.

The scoreboard is made out of wood, and at the top of it is the station's badge; below that is depicted the numbers of those squadrons that flew from Manston, specifically during the period 1941 to 1945. Beneath each squadron's number, in vertical columns that run across the board, the types of aircraft that each unit had operated are mentioned. In columns beneath those are the number of aircraft destroyed by each unit, in the air, on the ground, flying bombs destroyed; ships sunk; and ships damaged.

Those units mentioned are 605 Squadron that flew the Mosquito; 406 Squadron, Mosquito; 137 Squadron, Whirlwind, Hurricane, and Typhoon; 198 Squadron, Typhoon; 609 Squadron, Typhoon; and 3 Squadron, Hurricane and Typhoon. The total number of aircraft destroyed in the air and on the ground is given as 252, with 166 flying bombs destroyed, 113 ships sunk, and 914 damaged.

Towards the end, there is a column on the scoreboard headed 'Other Squadrons'; unfortunately, it fails to mention those units that operated out of Manston during the Battle of Britain in 1940, such as 74 and 92 Squadrons. They also destroyed significant number of enemy aircraft that are not credited on the board, but such was the chaos of the battle that exact figures would have been impossible to calculate.

Another unit not mentioned is 501 Squadron, which was equipped with the Hawker Tempest and stationed at Manston in August 1944. Its CO, Sqn Ldr Joe Berry, was credited with destroying the highest number of flying bombs, many of them while flying out of the station. Despite the omissions, the scoreboard is a wonderful piece of RAF Manston's history during the Second World War.

Shortly after the Spitfire arrived at Manston, another three aircraft landed that the Americans would not have welcomed.

They were three Russian Aeroflot Tupolev 104s, only the world's second type of passenger jet to enter service after the British de Havilland Comet. The aircraft had 150 members of the Bolshoi Ballet company on board and had been diverted from London because of fog. They were due to appear at Covent Garden's Royal Opera House to give their first performance outside Russia in 200 years.

The first aircraft landed just after 10.30 a.m., and while the Americans on the base tried to cover up or move its more interesting aircraft and equipment, the Russians were forced to remain on board the Tupolevs for over five hours until an embassy official arrived and gave permission for the passengers to disembark. It was soon clear that there was something of a language problem but that was solved by using the skills of an American airman, Polish-born Sgt Joe Olinski. He had learnt Russian while spending two years in a Soviet labour camp.

To the relief of everyone, the Russians showed no interest in the USAF's aircraft but congregated around the Spitfire TB752 and took hundreds of photos while examining the aircraft. Eventually, a fleet of East Kent coaches arrived on the station and the Russians were driven up to London. There was then a problem refuelling the aircraft when one of the flight engineers repeatedly rejected the fuel that had been offered. Eventually, Grp Capt. Oldbury convinced him that there was nothing wrong with the it and, as a final gesture, he was allowed to look around the aircraft.

The Queen Mother flew into Manston on Wednesday 23 May 1956 in a Vickers Viking of the Queen's Flight VL246. She was transported almost immediately by a Humber Pullman car to Walmer Castle near Deal, the home to the Lord Warden of the Cinque Ports, where she was a frequent visitor. The Tudor fortress had been the home to a number of distinguished people over the year, including the duke of Wellington who had died there in September 1852.

There was another tragic incident at Manston on 19 November 1956 involving an F-86 Sabre of the 514th Fighter Interceptor Squadron. It was part of the 406th Fighter Bomber Wing that had been reactivated at Manston in July 1952. The unit had then been formed out of the 123rd Fighter Bomber Wing, and in August 1953, the 406th had been re-equipped with the F-86 Sabre.

It was one of those aircraft, serial number 52-4141, that ran off the hard standing after landing on runway 11 at 5.14 p.m. on 19 November after the right main tyre had burst. The fighter hit a vehicle that was travelling along the Ramsgate–Canterbury road. Driving the car, an Austin A35, was forty-six-year-old Mr George Edward Bignell, who was travelling home from Deal where he worked at the Admiralty Depot of the Royal Marines as a foreman.

Mr Bignell, who lived in Margate Road, Herne Bay, and had three children, was killed instantly. For the pilot, Lt Edgar Lewis, it must have been a terrifying experience as it was his first night flight out of Manston, but he survived the incident. What remained of the aircraft was later dismantled and transported to the USAF base at Burtonwood in Lancashire where it was scrapped.

Wg Cdr J. A. A. Read took over command of Manston from Grp Capt. Oldbury in October 1956. Oldbury was the very last group captain to command the station. Oldbury had been posted to the Tactical Air Force in Germany. Not a lot is known about the background of Wg Cdr J. A. A. Read, the new CO, except that he was posted to Manston from RAF Horesham St Faith in Norfolk and that he was married and liked playing golf.

On 1 December 1956, RAF Manston ceased to become a self-accounting station and became a satellite of RAF Sandwich, where all the records of the station were kept and handled. In January 1957, RAF Manston was formally handed over to the USAF when it took control of the telephone exchange.

An American airman was killed on 7 March 1957 when he was sucked into the air intake of a Sabre. It was claimed that he had been working on the Sabre and was standing close its nose when the engine was suddenly started up for

The scene at a junction on the A253 at Wayhill on 14 November 1956. Motorist George Bignell was killed when his car was hit by an American F-86.

a test by another technician who was unaware of his presence. Although he was taken to the base hospital, he was dead on arrival. He was later named as twenty-year-old AC2 Joseph McMurray who was an electrician on the 514th Interception Squadron. Few details were made available to the public other than that an inquiry was to be held.

There was another first for Manston in April when three T-33s of the German Air Force landed at Manston and it was claimed that they were the first of that country's air force to arrive in the UK since the end of the war. The newly formed German Air Force, still called the Luftwaffe, had been formed in the 1956 and most of its former pilots had been retrained in the USA and had learnt to fly its new jet fleet such as the T-33 and F-104 Starfighter, with which it would soon be re-equipped. The three aircraft that landed at Manston that had been on a cross-country flight and were crewed by an instructor and a trainee pilot. On this occasion, two of the instructors were American pilots from the USAAF, 1Lt L. R. G. Lyden and Capt. R. M. Byron. All three aircraft returned to Germany the following day.

An open day was held at Manston in May 1957 and, according to reports in the local press, the airfield was turned into a 'mini Farnborough'. More than 1,000 spectators packed into the base, and among the main aircraft on view was the RAF's Vickers Valiant, the first of its 'V' bombers. Other aircraft from the USAF that were featured included the F- 86D, the H.14 Helicopter, and F-100

Super Sabre. This was one occasion when the issue of noise from jet aircraft was not an issue, at least not until the day was over.

It was in September that the first news appeared that the USAAF might be leaving Manston and that the base would be closed in an article from the *Air Force Times* (*European Section*). It stated that a spokesman for the USAAF had said that senior officers at Manston and Third Air Force HQ had disclaimed any knowledge of the move. It was also noted that the increase in the number of USAAF bases in the UK had been temporarily halted and that there were indications that the Third Air Force might be wound up because of stringent economic measures.

In December 1957, the USAAF's fire department was credited with saving a house in the local village of Minster after a fire had broken out in the early hours of the morning. The house at Dellside, Minster, was occupied by a Mr and Mrs Foley, and although the house was still severely damaged, many pieces of their lifetime collection of antiques and art were saved. The USAF team was called in by a neighbour, Sgt Klein, and the Ramsgate Fire Brigade were unable to attend because it had already been called out to a small fire in the High Street.

The RAF continued to use Manston, and on 23 January 1958, there was a tragic accident involving a Vickers Varsity from No. 2 School of Air Navigation based at Thorney Island. The aircraft was on a navigation exercise and was attempting to land at Manston when the pilot, Sgt Brading, overshot on the final turn to the approach and failed to line the aircraft up properly with the centre line of the runway. Brading did get the aircraft down on the runway, but after a

Open day at Manston during the 1950s, the crowd looking with over a F-84.

Children and members of the public examine safety equipment at the USAF's open day.

short distance, it began to turn to port and then, after moving off the runway, it hit a snowbank.

The aircraft then turned through 130 degrees and slid along the ground before catching fire and trapping three members of the crew. The pilot, twenty-eight-year-old Sgt Donald Brading, the operating navigator, Flt Lt Doulas Mallpas, and signaller, FS Frank Lomax, DFM, were all killed. Lomax had been awarded the DFM while flying Lancasters with 9 Squadron in 1944. The two student navigators escaped from the blazing aircraft unharmed.

There was another fatal incident on Wednesday 9 April, and it was very similar to that which had occurred in November 1956 and one of the last ones before the USAF left Manston. It involved a Lockheed T-33 Shooting Star (51-4474) that was being flown by forty-year-old Capt. Herman Hines from North Carolina.

The aircraft was taking-off when it veered off the runway and on to the Canterbury–Ramsgate road and struck a car, a Morris Minor, being driven by thirty-nine-year-old teacher Mr Wilfred Booth, who lived with his wife and two children in Helvellyn Avenue, Ramsgate. Unfortunately, his wife, Pauline Booth, and his two children, nine-year-old Ann and two-year-old David, were also travelling in the car and were killed alongside Mr Booth. He was a history teacher at Charles Dickens School in Broadstairs and had taught there since the school had opened in September 1955. Prior to that, he had been a master at King Ethlebert School in Birchington.

# 14

# The RAF Return

The USAF withdrew from Manston in 1958 when the final USAF unit, the 406th Fighter Wing, was deactivated, with its personnel and equipment being distributed to other stations in the UK and in Europe. On 29 March 1958, American airmen and officers carried out the last formal parade at Manston. The formalities were not completed until 5 p.m. on 15 June, when the Stars and Stripes was lowered for the last time by T/Sgt S. E. Williams and the RAF ensign was raised by Cpl K. C. Johnson of the RAF Police.

Maj. John G. Paulsick of the 406th Supply Squadron USAF took the salute alongside the RAF's CO Wg Cdr J. A. A. Read. There was a formal handover of the 'station key' from the major to the CO. The station was not formally returned to the Air Ministry until 30 June, but all flying had ceased on 13 June at 5 p.m. when it closed as an operational station. A care and maintenance party arrived at RAF Manston on 1 August, and the airfield remained closed for eight months.

There were another two RAF COs of Manston during the American period: Sqn Ldr P. A. Alt, who had taken over from Wg Cdr Read in May 1958, and Flt Lt D. R. G. Marlow, who took over from Alt as acting CO in September 1958 after the Americans had withdrawn and remained in command until April 1959.

The reason for the closure was almost certainly based on economics, but complaints about aircraft noise, especially during the American occupation, probably had an impact on the final decision. Local MP Rees-Davies had received a huge number of letters complaining about the noise levels.

The American base commander, Col. Herlick, had appeared on television with Reece Davies to discuss the problem, and even though a restriction of hours between 6 a.m. and 10 p.m. for flying had been agreed, it failed to satisfy certain elements of the local population. Despite the complaints, many local trades people and businesses were unhappy with the closure because they had relied heavily on the money spent by the airmen, officers, and their families.

By December 1958, 491 Signals Unit at RAF Sandwich had closed down and Manston took on its responsibilities. All the married quarters were vacated, and

The final parade by the USAF on 29 March 1958 as the ranks march past the saluting base on what looks like a very wet day. Note the DC-3 and other aircraft in the background. It is hard to identify where this took place, but it may have been on the 'Old Loop' on the western side.

The Stars and Stripes being lowered for the final time on 15 June 1958 and the RAF flag being raised again.

the main site was put on a care and maintenance programme, although a small part of the station remained in use for training members of the RAF Auxiliary and Fighter Control Units.

In March 1959, when the RAF had returned to Manston, the station temporarily became a satellite of RAF West Malling, which provided administration to support the acting CO, Flt Lt Marlow. In March, it was decided that the station should be reactivated and become part of 11 Group, Fighter Command. Sqn Ldr W. E. Evans took over command of the station from Flt Lt Marlow.

Shortly after Manston had reopened, an event occurred that resulted in one of the few staff working in ATC being awarded an AOC's commendation. During the early hours of 16 April 1959, SAC Parker was on duty in the control tower, monitoring the flight information frequencies, when he heard a call from the leader of a formation of four Belgian military aircraft, Hawker Hunters, whose pilots had requested a homing for an emergency landing.

Being untrained for such a situation, Parker managed to find the relevant orders for that kind of emergency and successfully talked down all four aircraft. Having worked in ATC, I can appreciate what SAC Parker did as, like him, I was only an assistant air traffic controller. Assistants are not trained to use radar or control aircraft but are mainly involved in writing up flight plans, despatching arrival and departure signals, and answering the telephone. They are also actively involved in making tea or coffee for the controllers.

Just occasionally, assistants got an opportunity to answer, send messages, and talk over the R/T, especially those working in local control, when the controller had to answer a call of nature. In the approach room, such opportunities were rare as there were normally two or three controllers on duty and the assistant's role mainly consisted of answering the telephone and updating the weather boards. It would only be only in most critical situation that an assistant might attempt to control, guide, and talk down a pilot to the very threshold of the runway. SAC E. R. Parker was presented with the AOC's commendation in August, by the then CO, Sqn Ldr Evans.

In April, civil aviation returned to Manston when Silver City, which had previously been operating out of Blackbush Airport, got permission from the Air Ministry to operate from the airfield. Its name, 'Silver City', came from the Australian mining town at Broken Hill, where one of the airline's backers, the Zinc Corporation, was based. The airline's manager at Manston, Mr Russell, operated out of the station HQ to begin with but soon moved over to the eastern side of the airfield, which soon became known as the 'Civil Side'.

The airline had been founded by Air Cdre Griffiths James Powell, who was the airline's first managing director, but Wg Cdr Hugh Kennard—who, as I have already mentioned, had connections with the local area and Ramsgate Airport—was also involved and was joint managing director. The airline operated five Handley Page Hermes from Manston, an aircraft that was powered by four

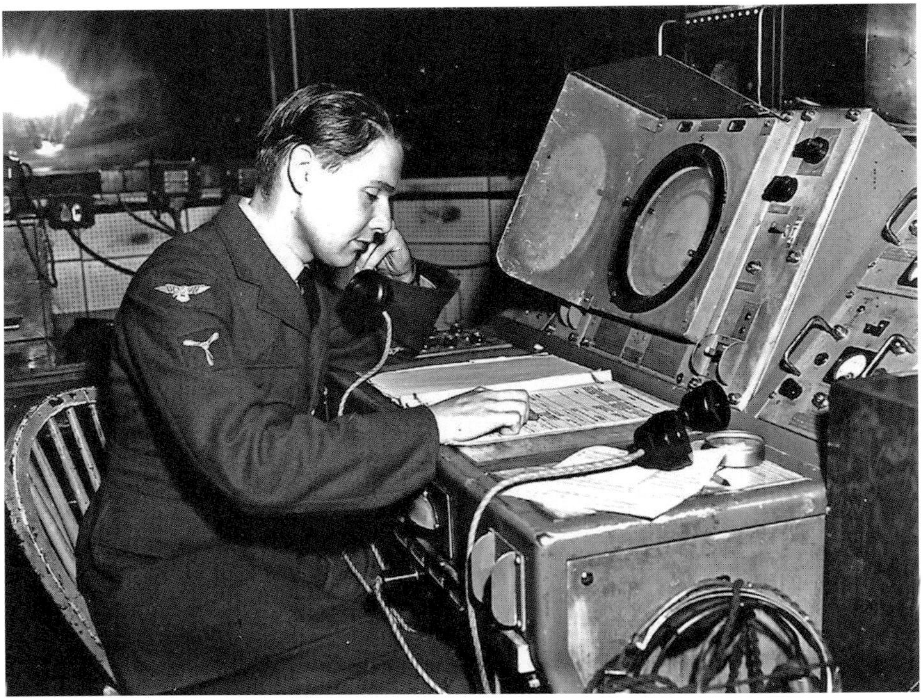

Senior Aircraftsman Parker posing at a radar console in ATC at Manston.

SAC Parker receives his AOC's commendation from Manston's CO, Sqn Ldr Evans.

Bristol Hercules engines and had been acquired from Silver City's sister airline, Britavia (British Aviation Services).

The first flight, 'CBO 3', departed in June 1959 with sixty-seven passengers destined for Le Touquet on what it called the 'Silver Arrow' service. The passengers had travelled from London to Margate by train and then the short distance to Manston by coach. Waiting to meet them was Mr John Wilkins, the managing director of the travel company that had chartered the aircraft. It was claimed that potato pickers looked up in amazement as the Hermes climbed into the air and heavy cloud of the Channel, not having seen such a sight since the Americans had left the airfield the year before.

The records for the beginning of 1960 are not very detailed and are more concerned with the weather than anything else. A medical report that covers the month of February states that the health of those working on the station was good, although there had been an outbreak of whooping cough. Twenty personnel had been taken to hospital and two admitted to the station's sick quarters. A single civilian had been injured in an accident.

Another new unit was formed at Manston in January 1960 in the form of the Air Ministry Fire Fighting School, and although it was not specifically under the control of the RAF, it did, as its name suggested, come under the control of the Air Ministry. The history of RAF firefighting goes back to 1922 when its first firefighting school had been formed at Cranwell, using instructors from the London Fire Brigade. Subsequently, the school had moved from Cranwell to Weeton in Lancashire and then to Sutton-on-Hull in 1943, where it came directly under the control of the newly formed RAF Regiment.

In 1959, the school had moved to Catterick in Yorkshire, again under the control of the RAF Regiment, and it was renamed the Fire Fighting and Special Safety Squadron. At about the same time, a decision was made to form a separate fire training school for civilian fire officers and firemen. This then became the Air Ministry Fire Training Service and the organisation that was formed at Manston in January 1960.

After it reopened, RAF Manston had been designated as a Master Diversion Airfield. That meant that it remained open twenty-four hours a day with firefighting and rescue facilities to deal with any potential emergencies involving both military and civil aircraft. The 9,000-foot runway was ideal for its new role and the control tower, along with the aircraft servicing flight, was manned seven days a week.

On 8 March, a meeting was held to discuss the final arrangements for the installation of new ATC equipment in the control tower. There were thirteen officers at the meeting, which was chaired by Sqn Ldr Preston from Fighter Command HQ. Among those present were Wg Cdr T. P. Gibson, Wg Cdr S. V. Valsey, and Wg Cdr L. F. Ralls, but there is no mention of Manston's CO, Sqn Ldr Evans. The aim of the meeting was to decide a final policy and a firm date

*Left:* Final preparations for the launch of Silver City's 'Silver Arrow' service to Le Touquet in June 1959. In the background is Handley Page Hermes G-ALDM. These two gentlemen from the travel company appear to be taking the 'Arrow' with them.

*Below:* Silver City Handley Page Hermes G-ALDM about to depart on the first 'Silver Arrow' Service in June 1959. On the bottom of the steps is the late Wg Cdr Hugh Kennard, who went on to form Invicta Airways.

for installation of the equipment. It was stressed that once a target date had been agreed upon, it must be adhered to, otherwise the installation of air traffic equipment would be out of phase with other changes taking place.

The chairman suggested a target date for the start of installation work to begin as 25 April and the resident engineer said that it could be completed in eight weeks. It was agreed that works service should be finished by 21 May and the fitting party from Signals Command HQ should arrive on 23 April. The completion date when the control tower was to be handed over to the SATCO for operations to begin was 4 July.

The chairman informed the meeting that a mobile air traffic facility was being moved from Leconfield in Yorkshire to Manston to allow the control tower to be completely vacated. A number of vehicles associated with that facility had already arrived and the last three were on their way. One vehicle contained the power and cable distribution, with another two providing facilities for local and approach ATC. Another four trucks carried transmitters and receivers: 1131JX and T1540 transmitters and type R1392 receivers.

The common frequencies to be used were 122.0 Mcs for local aerodrome control; 107.28 Fighter Command; 121.5 international distress frequency; and 139.86 for flight information. Full ultra-high-frequency channels would be provided by moving the UHF box out of the control tower to the mobile facility. The CRDF was to operate from a cable that was to be connected to the GPO frame room. While the work was being carried out the airfield was to maintain its role as a Master Diversion Airfield.

On Sunday 18 September, on the twentieth anniversary of the Battle of Britain, parades took place in Ramsgate and Margate. Former RAF fighter pilot Wg Cdr Stanford Tuck took the salute in Margate where four bands took part in the parade that marched through Cecil Square. In Ramsgate, a service was held in St George's Church, led by the vicar of Ramsgate, the Reverend J. F. C. White. One of the guest speakers in Ramsgate was the Canon Stander from Canterbury Cathedral who compared the Battle of Britain with the Spanish Armada and Nelson's efforts to prevent the French invading. Representatives of seventeen service organisations took part in the service in Ramsgate.

Throughout 1960, there were a number of changes, with RAF Manston taking on the additional role of being a customs airfield, where both civil and military aircraft cleared customs during inbound and outbound flights. Silver City extended its business when it was awarded a 'trooping' contract by the British Army. An RAF movements party was posted to the station to handle those aircraft carrying service passenger and their families, loading their baggage and military freight.

It was claimed in the local press that the use of aircraft for trooping flights rather than the more traditional shipping method would save the government over £1 million. There was to be thirty flights each month between Manston and two airfields in Germany carrying 4,500 passengers to Düsseldorf and Wildenrath. By the end of 1960, it was forecast that the numbers would rise to 7,000 passengers a month, and it was claimed that passengers flying from Manston were given VIP treatment with drinks and refreshments before boarding.

One of the first victims of the Customs Office was Mrs Lillian Rose Bentley from Highbury in London. In November, she was fined £75 for attempted evasion of duty on two handbags, a cigarette lighter, camera, a gold ring, a pair of opera glasses, and a gold bracelet. The total duty amounted to £54 14*s* 3*d*, and although she pleaded guilty, Mrs Bentley claimed that the Customs Officer had not given her the opportunity to declare the goods. There is no mention of what flight Mrs Bentley had been on, but it was almost certainly a civil flight and probably involving a Silver City aircraft.

A tragic accident occurred on 2 November when a junior technician, twenty-five-year-old Alan Rae, acting as a ground crewman, was hit on the head by a rotor blade from a Whirlwind helicopter. The aircraft was a visitor from 225 Squadron based at Andover and flown by Flt Lt Strong, it was about to lift off when the accident happened. The last communication between the pilot and technician had been the 'engaging rotors' signal that Rae had acknowledged.

The East Kent coroner, Mr W. R. Mowell, was told that the accident was the first of its type in the RAF and that a board of inquiry was being convened to investigate the incident. Flt Lt Strong told the inquest that after the rotor had been engaged, he had noticed a shock in the controls, and when he looked down, he saw Rae on the ground with his head bleeding. He immediately slowed down the rotor blades and called the control tower on the R/T. One of the factors that may have caused the accident was the wind, which was gusting at 30 to 40 mph.

The coroner admitted that he was not qualified to answer such questions as to whether a ground crewman should have been so close to the helicopter. Such decisions would have to be made by those responsible for such operations. There was no evidence to suggest that the rotor blade had malfunctioned, and the most likely cause was a drop in the wind. The coroner recorded a verdict of 'accidental death'. Junior Technician Alan Wilkie Rae (413301) was buried in Margate Cemetery.

At the beginning of January 1961, it was noted in the ORB that the position as regarding the employment of radio technicians was still difficult and that attempts had been made to recruit them locally but there had been no response. Another matter concerning signals was that several attempts to calibrate Eureka Mk VII by a party of technicians from RAF Tangmere between the 5th and the 12th had failed. Eureka was a ground-based beacon that was used to home aircraft to a particular station.

On the 13th, it was a busy day for diversions with four F-86, one T.33, and four Hunters arrived and stayed over for a night stop. An Avro Vulcan diverted to Manston on the 18th with engine trouble and, having entered operational service with 83 Squadron in July 1957, this is the first mention of the type at the station. The aircraft was repaired the following day and returned to its unit.

There was also a series of visits by officers from other groups and units, starting with Sqn Ldr W. M. McEwen from Fighter Command, whose visit was concerned with catering matters. On the same day, Flt Lt J. J. Ellams arrived to discuss business concerning education. Flt Lt D. F. Slattery paid a visit from Fighter Command, while there was a staff visit from Sqn Ldr F. W. Brown of 12 Group HQ.

Sqn Ldr Evans, the CO, and a number of civilian employees attended the funeral of former station employee Mr Would on the 19th in Broadstairs. The following day, the CO was visited by a Mr Peel and a Mr Monk from the Ministry of Civil Aviation to discuss matters concerning ATC. Sqn Ldr Evans was called upon to visits 12 Group HQ on the 25th and temporary command was assumed by Sqn Ldr E. L. Robinson. On the 28th, the station assumed full responsibilities for catering and became self-accounting, independent from RAF Hawkinge.

It was not until the 30th that the Eureka Beacon was successfully calibrated and classified as Category 'A'. The station was also visited by AVM Christopher Harold Hartley, who had until recently been the AOC of 12 Group. From 1 January, he had taken up the post of deputy chief of staff (Operational Requirements) and he later became a most influential officer, especially on matters concerning the role of the Vulcan bomber. Hartley arrived at Manston by air, made an informal inspection of the unit, and returned to Northolt later in the day.

During January, it was noted that a total of thirteen different types of aircraft had visited the station and the number of aircraft handled was forty-three, with fourteen aircraft turned around. That compared with 340 movements on the civil side and only twenty-nine piston-engine aircraft handled of the RAF. The strength of the station was sixteen officers, 118 airmen, and 148 civilians. The amount of fuel consumed by aircraft visiting the airfield was 411 gallons of AVGAS; 9,016 gallons of AVTAG; and 66 gallons of AVTUR. It was an accident-free month as far as the MT Section was concerned, with a total of 14,055 miles clocked up.

An interesting point is that during January, the Civil Service Pay Unit had arrived at RAF Manston to conduct an investigation. There is no mention of what type of investigation, but the organisation's very presence must have concerned Sqn Ldr Evans. Two courses at the Air Ministry Fire School were completed in January and another two were nearing completion.

The prospects of the station finding radio technicians were brighter in February 1961 when twelve candidates were interviewed and sat the appropriate test. On the 7th, the station received news that the AMFS was to receive six Supermarine

Swift Mk Vs, for the trainees to practise with on the fir dump. The first one flew in on the 16th.

The Swift, which was the first RAF jet to have sweptback wings and tail plane, had first flown in December 1948, and in September 1953, it had broken the world air speed record, flying at 735 mph over Libya. The Swift F.1 had entered service with 56 Squadron in February 1954 and it was the only RAF unit ever to operate the aircraft. The unit experienced a number of problems with the aircraft and restrictions were placed upon the aircraft as regarding its speed and its service ceiling.

A lot of time and administration in February was taken up with business concerning a pre-AOC's inspection and also a visit from the deputy chief constable from the Air Ministry about security on the station. Over the 2nd–3rd, the ATC examining board visited Manston, and after examining the senior ATC officer, he was appointed as the station's examining officer. Flt Lt Moore was appointed as the examining officer for ground-controlled approach radar and the airfield was classed as 'Medium Intensity'.

On the 13th, there was a liaison visit from the AMFS CTE establishment at Catterick to discuss trade testing principles and procedures. A few days later, representatives from the Air Ministry's Movements Branch visited the station to inspect available accommodation, with a view to turning it into a family hostel in the event that the trooping contract with Silver City should be extended. Sqn Ldr Evans proceeded on leave on the 20th and Sqn Ldr Robinson assumed command of the station.

On the 21st, the 69th AA Battery from Shorncliffe arrived to carry out a spotting and shooting exercise, which lasted for twenty-four hours. A visit was made by the director general of organisation of the Air Ministry on the 27th to inspect accommodation and the station's facilities as regards future policy commitments. It seems that accommodation at RAF Manston was much in demand.

The number of movements during the month of February were civil, 151; RAF jet, 149; RAF piston, thirty-six; Army, twelve; helicopter, six; RCAF, six; and German Air Force, four. There were thirty-nine diversions to Manston, thirty-two of which were practice diversions and seven actuals, with six of them caused by the weather and a single diversion because of engine trouble. There were three diversions by civil aircraft and all of them were caused by the weather.

Trade test were carried out from 7 March, and on the 9th, there was a Signals conference, which the Manston Signals Officer attended. There was a pre-AOC's inspection of the engineering and MT sections on the 14th carried out by Flt Lt Fox from 12 Group. There was another pre-AOC's inspection on the 22nd of the AMFS and CTE facilities by Flt Lt Hammond.

Representatives from the Air Ministry, Coastal Command HQ, and 22 Squadron visited the station on the 7th and inspected a number of buildings with regards to the possibility of accommodating crews from a helicopter flight of 22 Squadron. On the 16th, the CO met senior officers from the Royal Marines at

Deal to discuss the possibility of accommodating a number of Royal Marines over the coming month.

Southern television visited the disused RAF site at St Margaret's Bay on the 30th, and a film was made of the underground and domestic facilities. During the war, the station had been fitted with Type 13 and 26 radars, and in 1949, it had been transferred to 90 Group, Fighter Command. The station had closed down in 1957 when the last unit, 345 Signals Unit, had been transferred to Swingate at Dover.

March was the busiest month for aircraft movements since the airfield had reopened, with a total of 108 aircraft and twenty different types handled by the Aircraft Servicing Flight. There was what was described as the 'long-awaited arrival' of the runway control caravan, although it could still not be used because it had no radio equipment fitted. The strength of the station was sixteen officers, 114 airmen, and 143 civilians. There was a total of 252 civil movements, 220 RAF jet, and 108 RAF piston-engined aircraft. Among the visitors were ten RCAF aircraft, one USAF, twenty-six German Air Force, and two from Belgium.

A station dance was held in the airmen's mess in April, and it was attended by large number of service and station personnel. On 1 April, the Maritime HQ at Chatham and Coastal Command HQ, for which RAF Manston had parental responsibilities, was disbanded and all the personnel of 7302 Reserve Flight were relocated. Officers from Kent County Fire Brigade held a meeting with station fire officers and heads of other sections on the 7th to discuss a proposed simulated crash fire exercise that was to take place in May.

Mr Newham from Short Brothers & Harland visited the station on the 18th to discuss the servicing of one of its aircraft that were proceeding to the Paris Air Show. The aircraft was the Short SC.1, the world's first fixed-wing Vertical Take-off and Land (VTOL) aircraft in the world, and its development later contributed greatly to the construction of the P.1127 and the Harrier.

The C.1 was powered by four vertically mounted Rolls-Royce 108 engines to give it lift and a single 108 engine in the tail to provide the thrust. Although it had been built by the Short Company, it was being developed by the Royal Aircraft Establishment.

There was another pre-AOC's inspection of the AMFS and CTE by Grp Capt. Robinson from 22 Group (Training) on the same day. The actual AOC's inspection took place on 26 April when Air Cdre James Anthony Leathart, SASO of 12 Group, visited the station. Leathert's service was coming to an end, but he had distinguished himself on several occasions, especially during the 'Darkest Hour' in 1940, when after the Fall of France, he had commandeered a Miles Magister and flown to France to rescue the CO of 74 Squadron. Just a few hours after the Normandy landings, Leathart had pitched up on a beach with a small radar scanner fitted on top of a Jeep, so that he could control night-fighters on the beachhead. At Manston, a guard of honour was inspected by the air commodore, and he had a successful tour of the station that included the AMFS and Silver City Airways.

15

# New Units, New Faces

The day after the AOC's inspection, Flt Lt Hall, the CO of No. 1 Air Experience Flight based at White Waltham, arrived with a detachment of de Havilland Chipmunks that were to be used to give air experience to cadets from the Air Training Corps. The Chipmunk is a two-seater single-engined primary trainer built by de Havilland Canada that first flew in May 1946. Powered by a de Havilland 145-hp Gipsy engine, the aircraft has over the years given thousands of Air Training Corps cadets their first experience of flight.

During April, there were 329 civil movements, 166 RAF jet, and 167 RAF piston-engined movements. Other movements accounted for were two USAF jet and one USAF piston. There were forty-four military diversions with three of them being actual diversions because of customs or the weather; the rest were practice diversions. The ground-controlled approach radar was fully serviceable and available from 8.30 a.m. until 10 p.m.

At the beginning of May, it was noted that three locally recruited radio technicians had begun working at the station and their main role was to service the ground-controlled approach radar. The station went back to its roots with the Royal Navy on the 2nd when Cdr Foden and a number of other Royal Navy officers from Chatham arrived on the station. Together, with Sqn Ldr Evans, they inspected the station's empty building that might have been useful to the Naval Observer Corps.

On 3 May, instructions were received from 12 Group HQ stating that the runway controller's caravan, which had taken so long to arrive at Manston, was to be loaned to RAF Old Sarum. There was another AOC's inspection of the AMFS and CTE on 5 May when AVM Chacksfield, the AOC of Technical Training Command, held another annual inspection. That amounted to two AOC's inspections in nearly as many weeks.

On 5 May, an event described as a 'Ladies Ghost Night' took place in the officers' mess and was well patronised by local dignitaries. What exactly took place is not recorded, but over the years, there have been many reports of the paranormal in the old building that was part of Pouce's Farm. Sightings of what has been called the 'White Lady' wandering through the mess in the early hours had occurred on a regular basis over the years. It is claimed that it is the spirit of a woman who hanged herself after her betrothed left her standing at the altar. There are reports of many other ghosts being seen on the station, including that of an officer who allegedly shot himself in the mess, and Manston is reputed to have many other wandering souls.

Representatives from BEA arrived on the 10th and held meetings with Sqn Ldr Evans about the possibilities of further training flights being carried out in the coming months. An on-site review of the station's establishment took place on the 16th, with officers from Fighter Command HQ and the Air Ministry in attendance. The committee stayed overnight, and the review was concluded on the 17th.

There was further naval activity at Manston on the 19th when 200 Royal Marines arrived; they were accommodated for three nights during the period over Whitson. A BEA Vickers Vanguard arrived from London Heathrow Airport on the 21st and began local flying for the purpose of crew training. The flights continued throughout the day and finally ceased because of a heavy landing that caused a burst tyre.

The Short C.1 VTOL aircraft landed vertically on 26 May for refuelling and an overnight stop, with accommodation being provided for the pilot and ground crew. The C.1 took-off conventionally for Paris the next morning. The aircraft was accompanied to Paris by a RAF Beverly and a Meteor from the RAE, and the three aircraft departed at 7.30 a.m. the next morning.

A BEA Vanguard carried out crew training again between the 26th and the 28th, and its operations increased the total civil movements for May to 365. There were 270 RAF jet movements and 300 piston movements. There was a total of 644 military movements, including twenty-eight by the German Air Force, but just five diversions because of the weather.

June was the busiest month since the station had reopened as far as the Aircraft Servicing Flight was concerned, and on the 7th, they dealt with a variety of aircraft, including the Short C.1 that had returned from the Paris Air Show. A Vulcan diverted to Manston on the 12th because of the weather, and the following day, a party of one officer and four airmen from 6 MU at Brize Norton arrived to dismantle the five Supermarine Swifts that had arrived for fire training purposes.

Two members from General Precisions Limited visited the station on the 15th to carry out a survey of ATC in the area. Fg Off. Murphy from Fighter Command HQ arrived on the 19th to inspect the 25-yard firing range. He also inspected the FIDO facility for the purpose of giving explosive's clearance prior to servicing work being carried out. This is the first time that FIDO had been mentioned for some time, and it is not clear whether it was still in use.

Four Chipmunks that had briefly returned to White Waltham arrived back at Manston on the 28th to begin giving air experience to Air Training Corps cadets. On the same day, the inactive RAF site at St Margaret's Bay was auctioned off and bought by a contractor to use as a holiday camp. At the end of June, the establishment of RAF Manston was seventeen officers and 122 airmen. One officer had been posted in and one posted out, with twenty airmen posted in and just four posted out.

A detachment from 'D' Flight, 22 Squadron, arrived from St Mawgan on 1 July 1961 aboard helicopter XJ725 in advance of the main party. The unit was equipped with the Westland Whirlwind HAR.2, and it was based in a black hangar just off the western taxiway. It did not have to wait long before it was scrambled for the first time when a Channel swimmer was reported as missing on the 7th. It turned out the swimmer was alive and well, although the winchman was lowered on to the support vessel just to make sure that all was well.

Flt Lt Burridge, the CO of 22 Squadron, and the SAR crew standing by a Whirlwind.

A Whirlwind of 22 Squadron carrying out a SAR exercise from Manston.

The wreckage of a 22 Squadron Whirlwind that crashed in a field near Westgate on 16 December 1964. The crew consisted of pilot Flt Lt Ross, Flt Lt Stilwell, and Sgt Moore.

An interesting shot of a number of Whirlwinds from Odiham landing on the Aircraft Servicing Platform behind the control tower. A prominent feature on the right is the wartime Airfield Command Centre.

Wg Cdr W. J. Swift assumed command of RAF Manston on 17 July, taking over from Sqn Ldr Evans who had been the CO since April 1959. The arrival of the wing commander was widely reported in the press, including the fact that he had previously served at Manston during 1938 as a student on a navigation course. Before being posted to Manston, the wing commander had served in Tehran, where he had carried out the duties as the air *attaché* for three years.

During the war, Swift had served in the RAF with Coastal Command, but afterwards, he had left to join a civil airline and then he had flown his wife and daughter to Southern Rhodesia where he had set up an air taxi business. He then become a civil pilot again and chief pilot with a South African airline before returning to the UK and rejoining the RAF.

A day after his arrival, Wg Cdr Swift attended a press conference with the CO of 22 Squadron. The meeting was held to plan for publicity and arrange with local organisations as to when the 22 Squadron detachment would become operational.

Later that day, the flight commander of 22 Squadron made contact with the district coastguard officer at Deal, lifeboat crews at Ramsgate, Margate, and Walmer, and the local police and hospitals, informing them about 22 Squadron's SAR operations. Among the crew on 22 Squadron were Flt Lt P. J. Burridge, Master Pilot R. P. E. Hill, and Master Navigator H. W. Crossman.

The second helicopter of 22 Squadron (XJ727) landed on the 25th. The following day, an exercise was carried out with Ramsgate lifeboat on the Annual Lifeboat Day. Wet single, wet double, and stretcher lifts were demonstrated.

The squadron's second scramble happened on the 27th but turned out to be something of another false alarm, when a yacht, which had been reported to be overturned near the *South Goodwin Lighthouse*, was found in full sail. Night-flying was carried out on the 31st, and the squadron completed its training hours with a total of fifty-three hours and forty minutes of flying by day and night.

During the month of July, a total of 1,342 passengers were flown out of Manston on trooping flights to Wildenrath and another 1,736 to Düsseldorf. These had been carried out by twenty-one flights to Wildenrath and twenty-seven flights to Düsseldorf, all on the Handley Page Hermes of Silver City Airways.

In July, there were 434 civil movements, RAF 362 jet, and 371 pistons. Five military aircraft diverted to Manston, four of them because of the weather and a single diversion caused by an aircraft that was short of fuel.

On 1 August, seventy Marine cadets from the barracks at Deal arrived at Manston for their summer camp, which lasted until the 7th. On the 9th, Wg Cdr Swift visited the Air Ministry site at Leysdown on the Isle of Sheppey, which had previously been inspected by Sqn Ldr Evans. There is no mention of the purpose of his visit, but it probably concerned illegal occupation of the former RAF station at Eastchurch.

On the 15th, Wg Cdr Swift visited 12 Group HQ in an aircraft provided by Fighter Command Group's Communication Flight, and between the 22nd and the 23rd, he attended meetings at Fighter Command HQ. A practice rescue was carried out by 22 Squadron on the 16th, which was recorded for the radio and later broadcast on the BBC Home Service. The commentator was the well-known BBC personality Mr Bob Danvers Walker.

The CO and his wife attended the Ramsgate Carnival as guest of the mayor. On the 24th, Wg Cdr Swift went on leave and Sqn Ldr E. J. Robinson assumed command in his absence.

Mr Money, a divisional officer from Kent Fire Brigade, visited the AMFS at the end of the month to discuss the possibility of using 22 Squadron's SAR helicopters to fight fires on ships in the Channel. A deck-winching exercise was carried out on the 31st at Folkstone with the Newhaven marine craft unit launch.

On 7 September, Mr Wallace Clark from the Air Ministry's Lands Branch visited the station to discuss matters concerning Silver City Airways with Wg Cdr Swift. The airline had lost its trooping contract with the Air Ministry and the last flight was organised for the end of the month. The lease on part of the airfield by VW motors was also on the agenda.

AVM Robert Norman Batseon, AOC of 12 Group, visited the station to carry out a tour of inspection, before taking lunch in the officers' mess. The AOC's claim to fame had been that on 31 July that year, he had made the final take-off from RAF Duxford in a Meteor T.7 to mark the airfield's closure as a RAF station. A Battle of Britain Parade was held in Ramsgate on Sunday 17 September, commanded by Flt Lt Frampton. Wg Cdr Swift took the salute.

Sqn Ldr Verran, CO of 22 Squadron, visited 'D' Flight between the 26th and the 27th along with Flt Lt Cavana, the training officer. The helicopters had carried out seven scrambles in September, including its first CASEVAC from Manston.

There was a total of 411 civil movements in September, with the last trooping flight with Silver City taking place on the 29th. On the military side, there were 144 RAF jet movements, 100 RAF piston movements, and 158 helicopter movements; altogether, with a number of other movements by foreign air forces, including twenty-two RCAF and ten French Air Force, this made for a total of 474.

At the beginning of October 1961, the strength of RAF Manston was nineteen officers, 111 airmen on the station's strength, and sixty-four non-industrial civilian workers and 148 industrial workers.

On 3 October, Wg Cdr Swift met with the representative from the Air Ministry's Works Directorate, Silver City Airways, and contractors to discuss the closure of the main runway from the 17th. Although the trooping flights had ended, Silver City was still based and operating out of Manston.

There was a serious incident involving a Whirlwind of 22 Squadron's 'D' Flight on the 11th; the captain of XJ725, Master Pilot Leyden, was forced to ditch the aircraft during an exercise. The crash happened at 6 p.m., approximately one-third of a mile off West Cliff at Ramsgate, and there were four airmen on board; alongside the captain was Flt Lt Crawford, Plt Off. Raynell, and Sgt Dane.

The Whirlwind's crew had just finished the exercise after dropping the winchman, Sgt Dane, into the sea and picking him up again. Mr Arthur Verrion, the coxswain of the Ramsgate lifeboat told the *Isle of Thanet Gazette* reporter that 'One minute we were looking at her and the next she was in the sea'. It was claimed by other eyewitnesses that the tail of the helicopter suddenly dropped, and the nose was raised into the air.

One eyewitness said that he saw something fly off the helicopter just before it crashed, but Wg Cdr Swift dismissed such claims and stated that he could not say anything until an official investigation had been carried out. The crew were all wearing lifejackets and swam away from the helicopter, which quickly disappeared beneath the water. The crew were lucky that the Ramsgate lifeboat was already out at sea and returning to the harbour and so picked them all up in a matter of minutes. After the airmen had been brought ashore, a Royal Navy survey vessel arrived at the scene of the accident and dropped a market buoy in the water. Fortunately, the Whirlwind had crashed in shallow water, and it was salvaged on the 14th.

Despite the meeting about the proposed runway closure, some activity continued, and on the 18th, there was a very special flight involving a RAF Anson from Leconfield. There had been a serious outbreak of polio in Kingston upon Hull, and after an urgent call from the medical authorities, 200,000 doses of the vaccine, poliomyelitis, which was being manufactured by the Sandwich-based drug company Pfizer's, was flown to Hull.

Before the aircraft departed, the mayor of Sandwich, Alderman A. Mottershead, gave a special message to the pilot, FS F. L Buxton, to hand over to the mayor of Hull. The runway, which had been closed on the 16th, would remain closed until the 28th, but the grass runway 24/06, remained open and that is where the Anson landed and took-off from.

# 16

# Manston on the Big Screen

At the beginning of November, two local farmers, Mr Robinson and Mr Steed, visited Wg Cdr Swift and discussed the possibility of renting the disused hangar on the 'loop'. This is the area on the western side of the airfield just beyond the area where today the Bell Helicopter site is. The loop area has historic significance, and it was used as the assembly area for the gliders and their tugs during Operation Market Garden in September 1944. It had not been used for many years, and in the late 1950s, it had been cut off from the main part of the airfield.

Just before Wg Cdr Swift had been approached by the two farmers, he had a mysterious visit from two officials that arrived unannounced from the Air Ministry in London. They had asked the wing commander to take them over to the loop, where they carried out an on-site meeting and inspection of the area, which was rudely interrupted by the arrival of a large noisy aircraft. It was only at that point that the wing commander discovered that the officials were planning to build a prison on the land. They then told him that this could not now go ahead because it was too noisy.

On Sunday 12 November, a Remembrance Day parade was held in Ramsgate by a contingent from RAF Manston. Wg Cdr Swift laid a wreath on the war memorial and a service was held in St George's Church. Two days later, the CO attended a demonstration of a new Mk VIA firefighting vehicle that had the capability of dispensing foam.

In November, there were 268 civil movements, 181 RAF jet movements, and eighty-four piston movements. No. 22 Squadron's Whirlwind flew a single CASEVAC sortie from Southend to Stoke Mandeville Hospital and another scramble to a small boat that had been reported as being adrift. Between the 1st and the 3rd, and again between the 13th and the 16th, Sqn Ldr Verran, CO of 22 Squadron, and Flt Lt Cavanah carried out crew checks.

December was another busy month for Wg Cdr Swift, and on the 1st, he met Deputy Chief Constable McRae from the Air Ministry Constabulary to discuss increasing the establishment of the AMC. They also discussed the matter of the AMC taking over the duties of the RAF Police in the guardroom.

The wing commander attended the closing ceremony of RAF Hawkinge on the 8th, a station that had opened in February 1915 as RAF Folkestone. Like Manston, Hawkinge had been a key airfield during the Second World War, particularly during the Battle of Britain. After the war, it had been briefly closed before being used for training. The WAAF Cadet Officer Training unit was based there in the 1950s, with one of the commandants being Grp Off. Conan-Doyle, the daughter of author Arthur Conan-Doyle.

On the 12th, the CO attended a reception for the Military Air and Naval *Attachés* at the Iranian Embassy in London. Having served at the air *attaché* in Tehran, Wg Cdr Swift had lots of friends and connection in Iran, including the Shah who he knew on a personal level. The following day, the wing commander went on a liaison visit to Lydd Ferryfield and met representatives from Silver City Airways, before embarking on a flight to Le Touquet. On the 14th, he attended a ceremony at Cliff Hall, Ramsgate, where a member of the civic community was being awarded the Freedom of the Borough.

On the 21st, Wg Cdr Swift and a number of other officers served the traditional Christmas dinner to those of the lower ranks in the airmen's mess. Two days later, a children's party was held in the airmen's mess and it was attended by eighty-four children.

On the 28th, Mr Hall from Columbia Pictures arrived at Manston to discuss the shooting scenes for a new war film called *The War Lover*, which was based on a book by John Hersey. The story is about the pilot of a B-17 Flying Fortress named Capt. Buzz Rickson, played by Steve McQueen, and other well-known names in the film included Robert Wagner and Shirley Anne Field. It also featured a less known very young Michael Crawford, who, with a very suspect American accent, played a member of Rickson's crew. In one of the opening scenes, Rickson is accused of being a psychopath, after being given an order to abort a sortie but continues to the target at the expense of another aircraft and crew. At the end of the film, Rickson kicks another member of his crew out of the bomber and the film ends in a dramatic scene when it crashes into the White Cliffs of Dover.

During December, members of Air Training Corps from the Deal squadron visited 22 Squadron and were given flying experience in the Whirlwind on eight occasions. The unit also air lifted members of the Territorial Army on to camouflaged positions on Deal flats during an exercise and then flew above them to assess their effectiveness. Ninety-one sorties were flown during the month, which amounted to a total of seventy-six hours and five minutes of flying time. The unit carried out a single CASEVAC flight from Margate hospital to Brooke Hospital in Woolwich, London.

On the sports scene, the station played two football matches in December, winning one and losing the other. Basketball training had just begun, and several airmen and officers had taken to using the new squash and badminton courts.

In January 1962, Silver City Airways was absorbed into a newly formed company called British United Airways because its parent company, British Aviation Services, sold its shares to P&O. It then set up a new company called Air Holdings and took over Freddie Laker's company Channel Air Bridge, BAS, and British United, and Silver City's thirteen years of operations ended.

Columbia Pictures arrived at Manston on 3 January 1962 to begin shooting scenes for the film *The War Lover.* Capt. John Crewdson was one of the pilots of two B-17 Flying Fortresses used in the film. Crewdson was in charge of the flying sequences, including the filming of the final dramatic scene.

Mr Crewdson told the *Isle of Thanet Gazette* that, during the scene, he flew behind the headland, but it was still a close thing as there was not a lot of room to get the aircraft over the top. Film Aviation Services filmed several aerial shots over Thanet, and despite Manston being the company's base, Mr Crewdson told fans not to go there expecting to see any of the film's stars. Many of the scenes on the ground were filmed at RAF Bovingdon.

Two days later, after the film crew had arrived, there was a serious incident when a parachutist employed by Columbia Pictures was killed off the coast near Newhaven. This was almost certainly during the filming of the final scene when the crew are forced to abandon the aircraft. Wg Cdr Swift was not at Manston at the time because he was on leave between the 3rd and the 10th, and Sqn Ldr E. Harrison had assumed command in his absence.

*The War Lover* was not the first film to be involved with RAF Manston; in 1956, the opening scenes of another film, called *The Iron Petticoat* had been shot on the airfield. Katherine Hepburn had played the pilot of a Russian MiG fighter after she had defected from the east. The scene shows the MiG being intercepted over the coast of Thanet, where it is escorted to land at Manston and taxied up to the aircraft servicing platform. There are some excellent shots of the airfield and control tower that are the best part of the film. Bob Hope also stars in the film, which was certainly not one of his best.

On the 8th, there was a collision between two ships off the coast near the Goodwin Sands, between the SS *Sabac* and MV *Dorington Court*. A 22 Squadron Whirlwind flew two sorties to search for survivors of the *Sabac*, which had sunk, but none were found.

Superintendent Everitt from the Ramsgate Police visited the station of 12 January in connection with the police tattoo that was to take place in July. Between 15 and 19 January, Sqn Ldr Harrison assumed command of the station again when Wg Cdr Swift was sent off to a works study course.

There was regular entertainment for both the airmen and officers when a St Valentine's dance was held in the airmen's mess on the night of 1 February, and among those invited were nurses from Margate's Sea Bathing Hospital. During the evening of the 8th, there was a dining night in the officers' mess, and Sqn Ldr Robinson was 'dined out' on the occasion of his retirement from the RAF. The CO of 22 Squadron used the occasion to present a plaque to the mess.

The 22nd was a busy day when representatives from Bomber Command visited the station to assess the airfield and its facilities for potential use by the 'V' Bomber Dispersal Scheme. This involved the building of Operational Readiness Platforms (ORPs) at the end of the runway, where the aircraft would wait at immediate readiness.

Mr Bob Danvers Walker visited the station again with a Mr Haslam from the Air Ministry to make a programme for the BBC about air experience flights in the Chipmunks of No. 1 AEF. Local Air Training Corps squadrons had visited the station eight times in February and were given flying experience during five of them. Four days after the programme was recorded, the AEF returned temporarily to White Waltham. Between the 26th and 27th, Wg Cdr Swift attended the annual training conference at 12 Group HQ.

February was a quiet month, and there was just a single diversion—that of a Vulcan because of the weather. No. 22 Squadron was called out on the 6th to search for an Italian merchant vessel, *Talora*, after it had collided with a Russian tanker in the Channel. The *Talora* was found with some damage beneath the waterline, but it continued on its voyage. On the 25th, 22 Squadron was called out to search for a seaman who had been lost when a sand barge, SS *Deloe*, had sunk off Foulness Point after a collision with SS *Purbeck*. One survivor was picked up from the *Purbeck* and taken to Southend Hospital but was found dead on arrival.

During February, ASF handled seventy-six aircraft of nineteen different types. It delivered 7,700 gallons of AVTAG fuel; 1,303 gallons of AVTUR; and 5,333 of AVGAS. The strength of the station at the end of the month was twenty-three officers and 105 airmen.

Mr T. C. Cochrane from the Command Civil Administrative Officer from Command HQ visited the station and carried out a pre-AOC's inspection of the civil administration on 5 March. The same day, Sqn Ldr Trent carried out a pre-AOC's inspection of the RAF's equipment section. An Air Ministry sub-committee under the chairmanship of Wg Cdr J. C. Hutton carried out a review of the establishment on site.

On the 8th, a meeting was held at SHQ between the Air Ministry, the Ministry of Civil Aviation, Kent County Council, and Ramsgate, Margate, Borough Council about rights of way across the airfield. The issue was quite a contentious one among local farmers, since it had been proposed that a 300-yard strip of land that crossed the runway to access the main Ramsgate–Canterbury road be closed. The closure meant that they would have had to make a 3-mile detour to get to the local village of Minster; Minster Parish Council was among those who opposed the measure.

The trouble had begun when Wg Cdr Swift had written to Mr Alex Robertson who farmed land around Alland Grange, stating that in future civilians would not be allowed to use the runway and the gate leading to the main road. He also asked Mr Robertson to hand back the key that he held to the lock on the gate. Mr Robertson told the local press that there had been trouble over access before, but that this was the first time the issues had been completely out of control.

He said that the RAF had even let them use the gate during the Battle of Britain when Spitfires were regularly using the airfield.

When Mr Robertson wrote to the Air Ministry, it had referred him back to the CO, Wg Cdr Swift, and he felt that he was going 'around in circles'. His only hope was that Minster Parish Council would be able to get things sorted out. When asked to give his side of the story, Wg Cdr Swift had claimed that the issue was not of general public interest and he saw no reason to discuss it.

Over the two days of 28–29 March, two senior officers from the Air Ministry arrived along with officials from the Ministry of Aviation, the War Department, and Chemical Defence Experimental Establishment (CDEE), Porton Down, and the Research Federation. At the AMFS CTE, they carried out and witnessed tests of breathing apparatus and respirators that were to be used for nuclear firefighting. They also carried out tests on aluminium-based firefighting clothing that could be used in the tropics.

During March, the 22 Squadron helicopters carried out eighty-two hours and thirty-five minutes of flying that involved 105 sorties. Besides having visiting Air Training Corps squadrons look around the flight, lectures were given by members of the crews at Margate, Ramsgate, and Sittingbourne. All flying members of the flight visited HMS *Osprey* during March and carried out ditching drill.

April 1962 began with a successful curry lunch in the officers' mess, and on the 5th, the CTE's Social Club was formally opened by the chief fire officer from the Air Ministry, Mr. E. J. C. Collins. Social events seemed to dominate what was an accident free and uneventful month, and on the 12th, a ball was held in the airmen's mess. On the same day, trials were carried on the airfield with an Instrument Landing System (ILS), which had first been approved by ICAO in 1947 and replaced the Standard Beam Approach System that had been based on the German Lorenz blind-landing system.

On the 19th, the AOC of 19 Group, AVM Sidney Weetman Rochford Hughes, visited the station and was given a formal lunch in the officers' mess as a guest of Wg Cdr Swift. AVM Bernard Albert Chackfield, AOC of 22 Group, was another VIP visitor on the 27th when he carried out the annual inspection of the AMFS and CTE.

At the end of April 1962, six officers and eighty Air Training Corps cadets spent the whole weekend at Manston practising their routine in preparation for a ceremony in Canterbury Cathedral on 6 May. The march past and parade were to celebrate the twenty-first anniversary of the formation of the Air Training Corps. It had been founded on 5 February 1941.

On the 30th, a Mr Ives and Mr Philips from the Air Ministry visited to station in connection with an equipment audit from the closure of RAF Hawkinge. Sqn Ldr Harrison assumed command of the station again when Wg Cdr Swift went on leave until 8 May. Both Rank Films and Southern Television visited the station during the month, mainly in connection with the activities of 22 Squadron's 'D' Flight. There were 179 civil movements in April, 107 RAF jet movements, 102 RAF piston movements, and 234 helicopter sorties.

# 17

# Helicopters Galore

May 1962 was another busy month for the helicopter SAR flight, and on the 9th, there were two scrambles with one being to an overturned catamaran off the coast of Whitstable. The other one was to Southend Airport to cover an emergency landing after a Dakota flying in from overseas had suffered an engine failure.

Several airmen from the Swedish Air Force landed at Manston on the 16th in five Dakotas to clear customs while they were on their way to London. They were met by the Swedish air *attaché* and remained at the station of two days. No. 1 AEF returned from White Waltham on the 17th with five Chipmunks to provide air experience for Air Training Corps cadets. At this point, the unit was still only attached to Manston.

There was another twist in the tale of access to the airfield in May, and after three months of arguments and with questions having been asked in the Houses of Parliament, Mr Robertson won back his right to take his vehicles across the airfield to another farm at Minster. He was delighted when he was given the news but not so happy when he was told about the terms of access, the main one being that he would not be given back the key to the gate; instead, he had to inform the control tower about his intended movements and be accompanied across the airfield by a RAF vehicle, Rover 1, from ATC. Both Wg Cdr Swift and the Air Ministry thought that that was the ideal solution to the problem without prejudicing the safety of aircraft.

The records for the month of June 1962 are not available; however, from the press and other local sources, we know that in June Manston was visited by five Nord Atlas transport aircraft of the French Air Force. The aircraft that landed at 5.30 p.m. one evening were carrying 100 French cadet paratroopers from the Military Academy at Saint-Cyr. They were on their way to take part in an air drop, which was part of a large military exercise in East Anglia.

The aircraft flew into Manston to clear customs, but the crews and paratroopers were shown hospitality in the form of tea, coffee, and a meal.

Capt. A. Whitehorn of the Royal Engineers, who was based at Sandhurst, had flown with the paratroopers and he made the introductions to Sqn Ldr D. J. Green, the RAF representative at Sandhurst. After a very welcome rest, the five aircraft took off again at 8 p.m. and left to drop the parachutist on their 'DZ' in East Anglia.

July was a very bust time for 22 Squadron's 'D' Flight, and the busy month began on the 2nd when, at the request of the local police, a helicopter was sent to Colchester to search for a missing child. On the 7th, there was a scramble to a boat that was in trouble near Herne Bay and two survivors swam ashore. Not all of those on board the boat escaped, and a young girl was found was discovered under the surface of the water, having drowned. The following day, there was another scramble to a cabin cruiser off the North Foreland, and the helicopter hovered near by while it was taken in tow by a lifeboat.

On 12 July, a Whirlwind of the Queen's Flight landed for refuelling on the Queen Mother's visit to Canterbury Cathedral, though it is not clear whether the Queen Mother was on board the aircraft. A film unit from Associated-Rediffusion visited the station on the 27th to make a film that would be shown on television at a later date, but there is no mention what the subject of the programme was. There were more royal visitors on the 28th when the duke and duchess of Gloucester arrived in a helicopter and later departed in a Heron of the Queen's Flight.

On 24 July, members of the sergeants' mess had a day trip to Boulogne, and it was noted that despite the lunch of steak and chips costing £2 10*s*, a good day was had by all. In July, there was a total of 220 civil movements, 212 RAF jet movements, and seventy-eight piston movements. No. 22 Squadron flew a total of twenty-two hours and ten minutes on SAR duties and CASEVAC sorties.

Sqn Ldr C. W. P. Lishman, former CO of West Malling, and Sqn Ldr W. J. Merrick, who had succeeded him in the post, paid a staff visit to the station on 14 August. Manston was acting as the parent unit for West Malling. Two days later, Wg Cdr Swift visited Leysdown on the Isle of Sheppey (RAF Eastchurch, closed 1946), another former station of which Manston was the parent unit.

On Tuesday 21 August, what may have been the quickest rescue carried out by 22 Squadron took place, after an eight-year-old girl, Barbara Ann Cook, had drifted out to sea on a lilo half a mile off the coast of Pegwell Bay. The call was received at Manston at 1.36 p.m. from the Deal coastguard, and just four minutes later, Sgt Hill, the winchman, was lowered into the water to pull her to safety. Apart from suffering from cold and shock, she was described as being well.

On the return flight to Manston, the pilot, Fg Off. Bates, spotted a swimmer heading for the lilo that they had just left behind, and so they went down again and pulled him out of the water as well. The swimmer had been in the water intending to rescue the young girl, and Flt Lt Crawford later described his efforts as one of the bravest that he had ever seen as there was a very strong tide running at the time. Having landed the girl and the swimmer safely on the beach and reuniting her with her mother, the crew flew out to sea again, and Sgt Hill was finally lowered into the water to rescue the lilo. It was returned to its rightful owner in Pegwell Bay.

There was another dramatic rescue carried out by 22 Squadron on Sunday 26 August when a small fleet of yachts taking part in a race capsized and their crews were thrown into the water off the Isle of Sheppey. The Margate Lifeboat was also launched to support the Southend lifeboat in what was described as gale-force conditions and was at sea for six hours. Five minutes after the helicopter had taken off for Sheppey, a radio report was received that two airbeds had been spotted drifting half a mile off Pegwell Bay. Thinking that there may have been children on the airbeds without lifebelts and that the yachtsmen near the Isle of Sheppey would have them, the pilot changed course for Pegwell Bay.

The crew then received information that the air beds had already been beached and so they resumed their original course for Sheppey. As they neared Shellness Point, the crew observed that there were a number of boats overturned and Sgt Barry Hill was lowered on the winch towards the water. The Southend lifeboat was already on the scene and some boats were still capsizing in the strong wind, but the Whirlwind was running short of fuel.

The winchman managed to pull nine men, a woman, and a dog out of the water, but then landed four of the men, the woman, and dog on a nearby beach before having to return to Manston to refuel. One of who remained in the Whirlwind, a Mr Maurice Fair, was in a very bad way and he had to be given oxygen, so the pilot decided to land at Margate General Hospital. After returning to Manston with the Whirlwind quickly refuelled, and with a fresh crew, it set off again for Sheppey where they searched the area for ninety minutes but no one else was seen in the water, and so it returned to Manston. The Margate lifeboat remained at sea to search for what was thought to be another twenty-eight people but eventually everyone was accounted for.

Flt Lt Hillman of the Air Training Corps HQ arrived at Manston on 28 August to discuss the possibility of setting up a gliding school on the airfield, and he held talks with Wg Cdr Swift and the senior ATC officer. On the same day, Wg Cdr Swift presented what was described as a 'French medal' to FS Smith of 22 Squadron. The award was made for his efforts in rescuing a French sailor from a ship.

It was during September 1962 that the records in the form of the ORB become a little bit erratic, and many of them have either been removed or destroyed. Despite the best efforts of our researcher, Peter Gallagher, he has been unable to find them, and so, from this point onwards, we are forced to use secondary sources, mixed with the ORB's where they have been found.

During September, it was announced that a new civil airline called Air Ferry was to be based at Manston under the control of Wg Cdr Hugh Kennard, who had been involved with Silver City, local aviation, and Ramsgate Airport for several years. The company was to succeed Silver City and had employed a number of its former workers, including Mr R. H. Ilshey, its former chief engineer. Air Ferry was to be equipped with a number of DC-4 Skymasters, a four-engined eighty-seat aircraft, and Wg Cdr Kennard announced that the first one was due to arrive in December.

The wing commander pointed out that nothing was going to happen immediately, and the company was not going to carry out any serious flying until the following March. There would be a slow build up and there was a lot to do, including attending hearings at the Air Transport Licensing Board to apply for route licences. One route that he thought would be very popular was to Ostend, especially for local people who might want a day trip there. He said that Air Ferry was anticipating carrying out regular flight during the summer months to both Ostend and Le Touquet.

In October 1962, RAF Manston was transferred from No. 12 Group, Fighter Command, to 3 Group, Bomber Command. Other changes involved the CTE, which was also transferred from Technical Training Command to Bomber Command. The CTE was expanded, introducing more courses, including one in which civilian policemen were trained to remove injured airmen from ejector seats.

There were further changes to public access across the airfield in November, when a new footpath from Cleve Court to Alland Grange was completed. The clerk of Minster Parish Council had been informed about the footpath in a letter from Wg Cdr Swift, who claimed that the footpath was not unlike a country footpath but there were baffle gates at either end of it to prevent motorcyclists and animals from wandering on to the airfield.

There were still complaints, mainly about access through the gates, and Mr W. T. Bones of Alland Grange Lane claimed that the gates caused a lot of inconvenience and that prams and bicycles had to be lifted over them. A proposal was made by Councillor Edwards that the gates should be removed and that others fitted with a strong spring should replace them. That proposal was passed by Minster Parish Council and forwarded to RAF Manston.

The Queen's Own Buff's Regiment flew into Manston in December when 250 officers and men arrived from RAF Wattisham in thirteen aircraft provided by Transport Command. They were flown in with a mixed fleet of large Blackburn Beverleys and Handley Page Hastings, and as soon as the aircraft came to rest, the troops slid to the ground on a canvas sheet from the Beverleys. The main purpose of the regiment's visit was to take part in an exercise transporting its heavy equipment on board Transport Command aircraft. The unit was part of the British Strategic Reserve, and its purpose was to quickly move to any trouble spot.

In January 1963, figures were produced confirming that 1962 had been an exceedingly busy time for the SAR Flight of 22 Squadron; it had been called out on seventy occasions to deal with yachtsmen and swimmers in difficulties. The busiest month had been in July, when there had been fifteen scrambles to answer emergency calls, including one out of its assigned area to Colchester to help search for a three-year-old girl. Operational figures for all the SAR helicopters in the UK provided by the RAF revealed that 381 sorties had been made in 1962 and a total of 247 lives had been saved. In its first year at Manston, the SAR Flight of 22 Squadron had played a great part in saving many of those.

At the beginning of 1963, RAF Manston had been chosen to take part in a trials programme for the Pyrene Prototype Runway Foamer, commonly known as the 'Foam Carpet' or Foam Landing System. The principal behind the system was that an aircraft could land on the foam and that any sparks caused by friction were smothered and the risk of fire greatly reduced. RAF Manston was already a Master Diversion Airfield, but the Foam Landing System was to make the airfield a popular destination for any pilot who experienced problems with their undercarriage, even if it was sometimes only finger trouble.

Two airlines opposed Air Ferry's plans to establish a route from Manston to Ostend and Le Touquet in April, and not surprisingly, they were the former resident airline at Manston, Silver City, and its parent company, British United. Air Ferry had submitted two applications to operate from 1 March 1963 to 28 February 1970 and, despite the opposition, both were eventually approved but amended to last only until 28 February 1966. Although the case for local demand was purely speculative by Air Ferry, the board had accepted that there was a need for the service and there would not be material duplication.

On 12 March, there was an incident at Manston involving a DC-6 (G-ARMY) from the airline Cunard Eagle, which had taken-off from Manchester on training flight with a crew of six. Two tyres on the starboard main undercarriage had burst and the crew chose to make an emergency landing at Manston. The aircraft's crew burned off excess fuel over the English Channel before making their approach and the aircraft landed safely with the undercarriage remaining intact.

In March 1963, 618 Volunteer Gliding Squadron moved into Manston to give experience of gliding to air cadets and other young people. Volunteer Glider Squadrons were made up of volunteers and commanded by an officer who had been commissioned into the RAF Reserve (Training Branch). On 2 April 1963, No. 1 Air Experience Flight finally moved to Manston on a permanent basis from White Waltham with a small number of de Havilland Chipmunks. The unit was dedicated to giving flying experience to cadets from the Air Training Corps and Combined Cadet Force, and over the next decade, it was to give them and the station's personnel thousands of hours of happy flying.

Cunard Eagle D-C6 G-ARMY at Manston on 12 March 1963 after it had made an emergency landing with two main burst tyres. The aircraft had taken off from Manchester on a training flight. Cunard Eagle later became British Eagle.

The Air Experience Scheme had begun in 1958, and No. 1 had first been formed at Biggin Hill before moving to White Waltahm. Eventually, thirteen AEFs were set up throughout the country to give flying experience to around 3,000 Air Training Corps cadets and another 1,000 from the Combined Cadets Force. They also flew girls from the Girls' Venture Corps and members of the Royal Observer Corps.

At Manston, pilots of the Chipmunks used the callsign 'Alpha' followed by a number that related to each pilot on No. 1 AEF, such as Alpha 51. Whereas the pilots of aircraft with a retractable undercarriage normally called 'On Finals Three Greens to land', as they approached the runway, some of Chipmunk pilots made their own call. There were a few wags who always called 'Alpha 51.... Final approach. Gear down and welded!'

In June, both BEA and British United got together to oppose a decision by the Air Transport Licensing Board to grant a licence to Air Ferry for a route to Verona in Northern Italy. Air Ferry had proposed to operate three flights a week from 15 March 1964 to 30 September 1966. BEA also opposed it on the grounds that it would create wasteful duplication and there was insufficient existing or potential demand to justify the service. The final decision was referred to the minister for aviation.

There was an emergency at Manston one Sunday in June 1963 when an Air Ferry DC-4, which was returning from Basle with seventy passengers, suffered an engine failure. A number of Kent County ambulances stood by on the airfield, but they were not needed, and the aircraft made a safe landing.

AVM Brian Kenyon Burnett inspected the members of the firefighting crew in June after they had won Bomber Command's Fire Fighting Rescue Trophy, on the first occasion that it had entered the competition. The Manston firefighters had won the trophy in the face of fierce competition from other stations and the air vice-marshal inspected the team, accompanied by the station's WO L. W. Saville.

It was a sad occasion in September 1963 when the standard of No. 500 Squadron was consecrated and then finally laid up at All Saints Church in Maidstone. The ceremony was attended by the earl of Avon and Grp Capt. W. K. Le May, who had commanded the squadron in October 1939. Having been awarded the CBE, Le May had been promoted to the rank of group captain in January 1954. The unit, which had been formed at Manston on 16 March 1931 as a RAuxAF squadron, had remained at Manston until September 1938. On its formation, it had been equipped with the Vickers Virginia Mk X, before re-equipping with the Hawker Hart in 1937.

Having been re-equipped again with the Avro Anson in March 1939, shortly before the outbreak of the Second World War, 500 Squadron had been mobilised and began flying patrols over the Channel and the North Sea from its new base at Detling. The squadron's airmen had been awarded three DSOs; twenty-one DFCs and one Bar; one CGM; and nine DFMs. Thirteen airmen had been mentioned in dispatches.

After the war, in July 1948, 500 Squadron had become the first auxiliary squadron to be equipped with jet fighters, the Gloster Meteor F 3. In 1954, after winning the Lord Esther trophy for efficiency two years in succession, the unit was given the Honorary Freedom of Maidstone. It moved to West Malling in May 1946 and remained there until, along with nineteen other auxiliary squadrons, it had finally been disbanded in March 1957. The squadron and its personnel had always kept its connection with Manston where it had been formed. During the old days of the '30s, many airmen from Thanet had learnt to fly with 500 Squadron and it was still fondly remembered among the older generation.

There was another tragic accident on 16 November 1963 when a Chipmunk (WD304) from 1 AEF crashed into the sea some 5 miles north-west of the airfield. The aircraft was being flown by forty-two-year-old Fg Off. Ronald Charles Wace, and his passenger was fifteen-year-old Air Cadet Michael Shepherd. The wreckage of the aircraft and the body of Fg Off. Wace was not recovered until 29 November, when it was taken into Ramsgate Harbour by the Air Ministry vessel *Airmoor*. It had been found approximately 1 mile off North Foreland, but the body of the young cadet was never recovered.

A fifteen-year-old schoolboy who witnessed the incident claimed that he had seen the Chipmunk climb as if it was to do a loop, but then it stopped halfway up before diving into the sea. A *post-mortem* that was carried out by Consultant Pathologist E. K. Spittlehouse found that Fg Off. Mace had suffered no injuries as a result of the crash, but he was suffering from a cerebral haemorrhage that may have impaired his judgement and he may have thought that the aircraft was climbing instead of diving.

Almost a year later, it was revealed that fresh information from the Secretary of State for Air Mr Hugh Fraser had been received about this incident, which suggested that the pilot's brain haemorrhage may not have been the main cause for the Chipmunk to crash. On the day of the accident, Fg Off. Wace had been ordered to fly at a maximum height of 1,000 feet so as not to infringe the low-level cross-Channel route. That height was too low for him to be authorised to perform aerobatics, which was normally 3,000 feet, but a loop was performed in the early part of the flight regardless of this restriction. Immediately after performing the loop, in the first stages of recovery, it was claimed that the pilot had carried out an unauthorised mock attack on another aircraft, during which he had lost control. It was suggested that it was the loss of control after that manoeuvre that caused the aircraft to crash.

It was announced by Wg Cdr Kennard in January 1964 that his company Air Ferry intended to operate a car ferry service from Manston at the start of 1965. The announcement was made at a luncheon at the Royal Aero Club in London, where the wing commander said that the company had built up its staff to 150 people, quite a number of whom had previously worked for Manston's former resident airline, Silver City. A spokesman for Air Ferry at Manston later said that the licence application for the car ferry service was well in hand, but it had been submitted too late for the 1964 season.

The type of aircraft to be used with the potential Air Ferry service was not mentioned, but it would have almost certainly have been the Bristol 170 Freighter. It had begun car ferry services with Silver City from Lympne to Le Touquet in July 1948. The Mk 32 Superfreighter version was powered by two Bristol Hercules 734 engines, and it could carry three cars and twenty passengers.

In March 1964, Wg Cdr William Hoy took over the command of RAF Manston from Wg Cdr Swift, who had served at the station for nearly three years. Born in Edinburgh in 1918, Hoy had won a scholarship to RAF Cranwell and qualified as a pilot in October 1939. After flying Ansons and Hudsons in sweeps over the North Sea, Hoy had joined 420 Flight, flying antiquated Handley Page Harrows over the North of England that dropped aerial mines connected to long pieces of piano wire. It was a desperate measure to attempt to control the activities of the Luftwaffe, especially during night raids over Northern England, but it had very little success.

Having converted to flying the Bristol Beaufighter in late 1941, Hoy had joined 604 Squadron at Middle Wallop, and on the night of 29 July 1942, he had shot down a Heinkel off the coast near Land's End. During the spring of 1943, he had shot down two more and damaged a third, and in July that year, he had been awarded the DFC. After a brief period of rest, Hoy had been given command of 25 Squadron, equipped with the Mosquito, and on 9 July 1944, he had shot down a V-1 flying bomb over the English Channel.

While the backgrounds of some of those officers who served as RAF Manston's CO have not been easy to trace, we know quite a lot about two of them because of their connections with one particular man. The late Flt Lt Bryan Wild, whom I met many years ago while researching for my book *Eyes of the Night*, served with two of them. He had trained in Canada with one of the future COs of RAF Manston, and he later served under another, while flying Mosquitos: Wg Cdr Hoy, CO of 25 Squadron.

Bryan's first flight in a Mosquito was made on 11 October 1944 when he made a twenty-five-minute sortie with Wg Cdr Hoy, who showed him what the aircraft was capable of. On the night of 30 March 1945, Flt Lt Bryan Wild and Wg Cdr Hoy were detailed to fly to Lista on the Norwegian coast to attack any potential targets of opportunity, such as aircraft or shipping. On the return flight, one of the engines on Hoy's Mosquito had ceased up and the chances of getting back home on a single engine seemed bleak.

The wing commander broke R/T silence and asked Bryan to let his family back home know what had happened if he did not make it back. They were 500 miles from base, but Wg Cdr Hoy flew for three hours on a single engine to land safely at Saffron Walden. The sortie had lasted five hours and twenty minutes. Early in September 1945, Bryan Wild was called into the office by Wg Cdr Hoy and asked him if he would like to represent 25 Squadron in the Battle of Britain Flypast that was to take place on 15 September. Led by Wg Cdr Douglas Bader, 300 aircraft were involved in the formation, with eleven of them from 25 Squadron. Thanks to Wg Cdr Hoy, it was one of the proudest moments in Bryan's life.

In 1957, Wg Cdr Hoy had been part of the three-man crew of an English Electric Canberra (WT528), *Aries V*, which established a new record for the time flown between London and Tokyo. The record was set on 25 May and other members of the crew were Flt Lt P. Lagason and Flt Lt J. Denis. The following year, the aircraft and crew went on a tour of RAF stations in the UK, including RAF Manston, although the exact date of the visit there is not known.

There were complaints about low flying over Thanet in March 1964 but not about aircraft flying from Manston for a change, but those carrying out pleasure flights from Ramsgate Airport. Two residents from Sycamore Close in Broadstairs appealed successfully against their rating assessments on the grounds of the noise from low-flying aircraft. Mrs Taylor, one of those involved in the case, agreed that the airport had been there long before the bungalows where she lived had been built, but she said one did not realise the extent of such things until one had lived there. Along with a Mr Austin, she also complained of a lack of facilities in the area, including no convenient bus services with the nearest shops being a twenty-minute walk away.

Canberra WT528 at Manston in 1957, which set a record time for a flight from Tokyo to London in 1956. Wg Cdr Hoy, who commanded RAF Manston between 1964 and 1965, was a member of its crew and is standing on the right.

# 18

# White Foam and White Horses

The first foam landing that was carried out at RAF Manston on 23 May 1964 involved a Vickers Valiant (WZ936) of 543 Squadron, which was based at RAF Wyton in Huntingdonshire. Considering that this was the first foam landing at Manston, it was surprising that there are relatively few details about the incident in the ORB. The foam was kept in two large tankers that were normally parked up in a special bay at the top of the western taxiway, and when they were required, they were towed out on to the runway.

It was the fire section that was in charge of laying down the foam carpet, under supervision from the station commander and senior ATC officer via Pye radio sets. The pattern of each carpet laid depended on the type of aircraft and the kind of problem there was with the undercarriage, such as a single wheel, nose wheel failure, or a complete undercarriage failure. Each emergency was different but normally involved local the emergency services as well as RAF firefighters.

The incident began shortly after the Valiant had taken-off from Wyton, when the captain of WZ936 discovered that there were some problems with retracting the undercarriage. As was the usual practice, the pilot decided to carry out a low 'fly by' of the control tower at RAF Bentwaters, during which the door of the starboard main undercarriage fell off and jammed the wheel. After that, the aircraft was diverted to Manston where it made a complete wheels-up landing on a foam carpet, and although the aircraft was written-off, there were no casualties.

No. 22 Squadron's 'D' Flight was involved in another rescue in June when the 5-ton yacht *Ereina* ran aground on a sandbank about 4 miles off the coast of Margate. There were three men and two women on board the yacht, and the winchman, Sgt Davis, was lowered five times to rescue them from the vessel.

On the civil side, Air Ferry's fleet of aircraft continued to grow, and by 1964, the company had added the third DC-4 and a small number of Vickers Vikings. Air Ferry was a subsidiary company of Leroy Tours, but when that company was taken over by Air Holdings in October 1964, it became an associate company of British United, as Air Holdings was also its parent company. It was at this point, in November 1964, that Wg Cdr Hugh Kennard decided to leave Air Ferry and form his own company, Invicta Airways. It was named after the white horse of Kent, which became the company's logo; this logo appeared on the tail of Invicta's aircraft on a red background.

There was another tragedy at Manston in October when an aircraft that was carrying a mother and her four-month-old baby from Germany to London made an unscheduled landing. The baby was being taken to Great Ormond Street Hospital so that she could be given an emergency operation, but she was taken seriously ill during the flight and, despite the best efforts of the nursing staff on board, she died about an hour before the aircraft landed. The baby's father was a member of the Royal Highland Fusiliers that was serving at Iserlohn in Germany. Also on board the aircraft was a woman suffering from a brain haemorrhage, and along with her husband, she was flown to the Royal Military Hospital at Colchester by a 22 Squadron helicopter.

On 1 January 1965, there was what could have been a potentially catastrophic incident when a helicopter from 22 Squadron was hit by a projectile while returning from a training flight in the Sandwich area. Whirlwind XP351 was examined on its return to Manston and the crew and engineers found what was almost certainly a bullet hole in its airframe, and so the police were immediately informed. The incident was investigated by the Special Investigation Branch of the Military Police who arrived at Manston on the 13th. The SAR flight remained active, and on the 5th, a Whirlwind ferried a TV crew out to the Goodwin Sands to film a vessel that was stranded there.

A conference was held at Manston on the 12th to discuss a proposal that the newly formed Invicta Airways might operate from the station. It was attended by Wg Cdr Reider and Wg Cdr Gibson from HQ Bomber Command and two civil members from the MOD Land Branch.

On 28 January 1965, 618 VGS that had been at the station since March 1963 moved out of Manston and were posted to West Malling. No. 1 AEF remained active and in January flew a total 110 hours and fifteen minutes, giving experience to 251 cadets. That amounted to 319 take-offs and landings. The unit also flew an additional fourteen hours in continuation training. In January, Manston's Aircraft Servicing Flight handled a total of forty-seven aircraft comprising of fifteen different types.

It was reported in the local press in February that Invicta Airways intended to begin flights in March. Invicta received its first two aircraft in February, two Vickers Vikings that it had been bought from Autair International Airlines. Invicta also purchased two DC-4s from British Eagle Airways, which were registered G-ASPM and G-ASPN. The routes to be flown by Invicta included those to Palma, Basle, and Rotterdam, and Air Ferry was planning to operate a car ferry service from Manston in April. It was initially going to operate the Bristol 170 Freighter and replace it later with the newer Aviation Traders Carvair.

Just a few weeks later, in March, it was announced in the local press that there was an Air Ferry 'hitch at Manston'. The company announced that the car ferry service between Manston to Ostend and Le Touquet, which was due to begin on 5 April, had been postponed until further notice due to circumstances beyond its control. For those passengers that had already booked on these services, alternative arrangements had been made and no one would be inconvenienced. Its normal passenger services from Manston were not affected.

No. 22 Squadron's 'D' Flight was in the news again in April when it helped to rescue two schoolboys from the sea near the Beresford Gap near Birchington. The two boys—fourteen-year-old Michael Harrison and fifteen-year-old Roger Balcombe—had set off in a canoe, but when they attempted to turn around near the Gap, the canoe capsized. On this occasion, the helicopter was beaten to the scene by two men who swam out to help rescue the boys.

Roger, who admitted that he was not a strong swimmer, had experienced some difficulty in getting out of the canoe because his trousers had got caught in the boat as it overturned. The two men who swam to help them were Michael King and David Summerfield, who were assisted by a local taxi driver, and he had waded into the water to help the boys. The two boys got safely ashore and the rescue helicopter crew were left with the task of recovering the canoe.

In the same week, a helicopter from 22 Squadron rescued two men who had been trapped by the sea after attempting to climb up an 80-foot cliff and were spotted by the crew while it had been on a SAR training flight. William Welsh of Richmond, London, and James Gadley from Plumstead were pulled aboard the helicopter before other emergency services could react.

It was announced in June that there were plans to develop the former RAF radar station at Sandwich, which had been put under the control of Manston during its closure in 1958. A number of companies were interested in developing the site, including Thanet Signs and Display Ltd and Birchington Fuel Services.

There was an incident on 8 August involving a Vickers Viking (G-AHPL) of Invicta Airways crashed and ended up on its nose after an aborted take-off. Fortunately, none of three crew on board were injured, although their pride might have taken something of a battering. The Viking had first been registered with the Ministry of Civil Aviation in 1946 before joining the fleet of BEA. It had been delivered to Invicta in February 1965 from Claydon Aviation, having previously been leased it to Autair, and after the incident at Manston, it was put into storage before being broken up.

A mock rescue demonstration by Ramsgate lifeboat and a 22 Squadron Whirlwind during Carnival Week 1965 turned into a real-life drama when three swimmers were seen to be in difficulties. Most of those who were gathered around the main beach were probably unaware that it was a genuine rescue as two men were taken aboard the lifeboat and a third was winched up in the helicopter. Two of the men had been swimming by the harbour when they were caught by a strong current, and the winchman who had been dropped on to the lifeboat spotted the third swimmer in difficulty near the east pier.

In September, Manston dealt with an emergency involving a light aircraft, a Miles Gemini twin-engined touring aircraft, which was being flown by a local hotelier, Mr E. C. Brace of the Kimberley Hotel in Westgate. One of the main wheels of the undercarriage had jammed and would not lower, forcing Mr Brace to circle the airfield for over two hours, during which he burned off fuel and attempted to resolve the problem. The wheel remained jammed and he had to make a forced landing on the grass runway, in which he was aided by a strong wind. Along with the pilot, there were three other people on board the Gemini, Dr Brian McAvoy, Mr Roger Bailey, and his wife, and although they were shaken up, nobody was injured.

Wg Cdr Bernard Wills, DFC, took over command of RAF Manston from Wg Cdr Hoy in November 1965. Wills had learnt to fly at No. 12 EFS at Prestwick in October 1940 and was another friend of Bryan Wild (who had later gone on to fly with Wg Cdr Hoy on 25 Squadron). At Prestwick, Wills, who came from the Wirral in Cheshire, was one of three trainees who became known as the 'Three Ws' on the course. The other two were Bryan Wild who came from Bolton and Jimmy Ward from Cambridge. After completing their flying training, the three airmen had sailed to Canada and underwent further training at Moose Jaw as part of the British Commonwealth Air Training Plan.

At Moose Jaw, Canada, Bryan Wild and Bernard Wills were introduced to their flying instructor, Canadian-born Flt Lt Miller, DFC, and they all agreed that they were lucky to have him because he had already been in combat and had four 'kills' to his credit. He was also an expert in aerobatics.

The three 'Ws' all qualified as sergeant pilots and were awarded their flying badges on 21 February 1941, and after arriving back in the UK, Bryan and Bernard were posted to 56 OTU at Sutton Bridge, where their flight commander was Flt Lt Dowding, the son of the AOC of Fighter Command. There they learnt to fly the Hawker Hurricane and were based there for two months, before Bryan volunteered for a new night-fighter flight that was being formed. At that point, the three 'Ws' were split up, with the exception of Jimmy Ward, who reported for duty on 456 Squadron at RAF Valley with Bryan in July 1941.

An RAF airman, a junior technician, at RAF Manston was found guilty in November 1965 of stealing 22 gallons of fuel that he had siphoned off from a Vickers Viking belonging to Invicta Airways. The petrol was valued at £5 17*s* 4*d*. He was also found guilty of stealing an excise licence from a motorcycle that he had altered and put in his own car, along with three large petrol cans that belonged to the Air Ministry. He was fined £5 for stealing the licence plate and another £2 for the petrol cans.

Rather remarkably, despite being found guilty, it was claimed that his character was beyond reproach and his conduct had been previously exemplary. As a result, the court in Margate was told that the airman would be retained by the service,

Invicta Viking G-AHPL sitting on its nose after a mishap while taking off in 1965. The aircraft had three crew on board and was on a training flight.

A Viking stuck in the snow at the end of the main runway. Manston could experience some very bad weather.

although the final decision would be made by CO Wg Cdr Hoy. This particular airman had been found out by chance because of the stolen licence plate, but fuel theft was quite common. All the AVGAS and AVTUR fuels used by the RAF contained a dye that could easily be identified. The Special Investigations Branch of the RAF police regularly arrived on a station unannounced and carried out snap inspections of private vehicles by dipping their petrol tanks.

The second foam landing was made at Manston on 7 February by a RAF de Havilland Dominie (XS712), the military version of the HS.125. There is little detailed information about this incident, but some sources claim that the aircraft made a complete wheels-up landing. It is more likely that it made a normal landing because the Dominie remained in service for many years and was on the strength of 55 (R) Squadron at Cranwell until January 2011 when the remaining six Dominies were put up for sale by the MOD.

It was announced in February 1966 that Invicta Airways was about to launch a regular air service to Ostend from 1 April. There was to be one flight a day, rising to four a day in the summer months, and the route was licenced for passengers and freight. The aim of the flights was not only to allow British holidaymakers to visit Belgium but to facilitate those from Belgium to fly to Kent and visit places of local interest such as the Cinque Ports and Canterbury.

There was another incident involving guns and helicopters in March when three youths were spotted by the crew of a Whirlwind carrying air guns in Pegwell Bay. One of them was seen to point his gun at the helicopter, but it was not known if he actually fired at it. This was the second such incident in just over a year, and after the police had been informed, enquiries were centred around a number of youths known to them, who were living in Ramsgate.

There were two foam landings in March 1966, and both involved English Electric Canberras, the first one being WJ875 on the 5th. This one appears to have been another precautionary landing without the aircraft being damaged because it was later returned to BAC in 1971 and sold to the Argentine Air Force, where it was given the serial B-112. The aircraft, which had been built as a Canberra T.4, had entered service with the RAF late in 1954 and served with the station flight at Wyton before being transferred to 230 and 231 Operational Conversion Units.

On Wednesday 16 March, it was the turn of Canberra B(I)8 XM244, which was being flown by pilot Flt Lt Ron Ledwidge and navigator Martin Fortune. The aircraft was on the strength of 3 Squadron, which was based at Geilenkirchen in Germany, although both of the crew belonged to 14 Squadron, which was based at Wildenrath. The aircraft's port undercarriage had failed to lower due to a faulty hydraulic valve, and Ledwidge had to make a forced landing with just the nose wheel and starboard wheel. A foam carpet, approximately 3,600 feet long and 90 feet wide, was spread along the runway, while the Canberra circled overhead Manston burning off fuel.

After circling for approximately an hour, at 5 p.m., Ledwidge informed the control tower that he was ready to attempt a landing, and as the Canberra touched down, sparks flew from the port side of it. Ledwidge managed to keep the aircraft running straight down the foam strip and a Whirlwind of 22 Squadron hovered close by just in case it was needed to rescue the crew. The cockpit canopy had already been ejected before touchdown and the two crew quickly climbed out uninjured, before the emergency services sprayed more foam over the Canberra.

Despite the damage to the port wing and airframe of XM244, the aircraft was repaired and returned to service with 3 Squadron, and in June 1972, it was finally struck off charge at Laarbruch in Germany the following month. The airframe was later moved to RAF Gütersloh where it became a 'decoy', but it met its end on the station's fire dump in May 1979.

Following General de Gaulle's warning that France was about to withdraw from NATO, rumours began to circulate in March that the USAF was about to return to Manston. A number of high-ranking American officers had recently visited Manston, but a spokesman for the USAF at Ruislip denied any knowledge of such a move, which would have been welcomed by local businesses who had suffered financially since the Americans had moved out in 1958.

A nineteen-year-old cadet from the Air Training Corps was killed while flying a Chipmunk in April, but this time not at Manston. Local airman Cadet Graham Gordon Stewart from Newington Road in Ramsgate was flying a Chipmunk from the College of Air Training at Hamble, near Southampton, but crashed while flying close to Sandown on the Isle of Wight.

The college had been founded in 1960 to train pilots for the two state airlines BEA and BOAC, and it seems that Cadet Stewart had a great future ahead of him, had he survived. The aircraft had spun into the ground and crashed in a field at Adgestone, and the incident was witnessed by his mother who had phoned the emergency services. Despite the fact that petrol was pouring out of the aircraft and there was an immediate danger of an explosion, two local farmworkers, Mr Brian Dobson and Mr Ian Morey, pulled the pilot from the wreckage. College officials flew to Sandown and joined the Air Accident Investigation Board to discover the cause of the accident, and flying instructor Mr Herbert Taplin gave evidence at the coroner's court and the inquest was adjourned for two months.

Adml Sir Kohn Frewin, C-in-C of the Channel, flew into Margate in a Whirlwind helicopter on May. He was greeted on his arrival by the mayor of Margate, Alderman J. W. Walsh. The admiral was in Margate to command a NATO exercise, but it is unclear why he chose to land in Margate instead of Manston where the exercise was being held.

No. 22 Squadron's SAR helicopters were kept busy during the summer of 1966, and in May, described in the press as the 'Angels in Blue', it was called out to rescue a father and son who had been tossed out of their sailing dingy while in Minnis Bay. Mr Raymond May and his son, Michael, from Strood, managed to hang on to the overturned vessel until help arrived. Both were winched to safety by the helicopter crew and landed in a car park on the sea front.

Another rescue made by 22 Squadron crews involved two thirteen-year-old girls and a seventeen-year-old man who were winched from a dingy after getting stranded out at sea in the dark. Graham Salisbury and his sister, Janet, along with her friend, Jean, had gone out during the afternoon. When it got dark and they had not returned, their parents notified the police who then asked for assistance from the SAR crew at Manston. Using a searchlight, the helicopter searched the sea half a mile off the coast of Viking Bay and Louisa Gap for about thirty minutes before they were found. The two girls were winched up first while Mr Salisbury attempted to row ashore, but he had to be winched up as well when he found himself rowing against a strong current.

In May, Manston was visited by AVM Denis Frank Smallwood, Air Officer Commanding 3 Group, who was making his annual inspection of the station. After arriving in the de Havilland Devon of Transport Command, he was escorted to the saluting base by Wg Cdr Wills and took the salute with Fg Off. Hilton leading the guard of honour, which was made up of thirty airmen. The parade took place in brilliant sunshine, and after the formalities were over, the AOC began his inspection of the airfield.

Ramsgate Airport remained open, and in June 1966, it became the home of newly formed Thanet Flying Club. During the same month, Mr Joe Studt, the club's first pupil to gain his private pilot's licence, was presented with his flying certificate and licence by Mr Ted Brace, the club's president, and Chief Flying Instructor Mr Paul Cash.

In July, a Whirlwind of 22 Squadron was called out to *The Londoner*, a steam ferry that was sailing from the Tilbury to Calais. This was to rescue a man who was suspected of suffering from appendicitis. Mr Peter Dick was winched up and taken to Margate Hospital where he was detained for observation.

Sgt Ian Jones, a twenty-four-year-old winchman on 22 Squadron at Manston, was awarded the Air Force Medal in July, and he travelled up to Buckingham Palace to receive it from the queen. It had been awarded to him for risking his life to rescue four Germans, three men and a girl, from a yacht in the English Channel the previous September. The rescue had taken place near Selsey Bill in a force 9 gale when Jones had been on detachment to 22 Squadron at Thorney Island.

In the same week, Sgt Jones announced his engagement to Miss Maria Luisa de Vilhena from Portugal. The son of a squadron leader serving in the RAF and born locally in Birchington, Sgt Jones planned to marry his fiancée in Portugal during October. A short while later, Sgt Jones was invited to the West German Embassy in London and presented with a Life Saving Medal.

Wg Cdr Kennard's Invicta Airways was in trouble with the authorities in August 1966, and a letter was sent to CO Wg Cdr Wills, dated the 26th, that was headed 'RAF Manston—Use By Civil Airlines'. Bomber Command had been taking an interest in the airline's activities since the beginning of the summer, when Mr. W. A. Sweby, from the MOD Land Agency, had visited the station. The letter to the CO, written on 26 August by Grp Capt. William John Stacey, Director of Operations at Bomber Command, demanded that arrangements with Invicta Airways needed to be tightened up.

Not all the rescue operations by 22 Squadrons were successful, and in August, a local yachtsman, fifty-one-year-old Mr Robert Lennox, drowned after being washed overboard while he was making adjustments to the sails. The helicopter, which was accompanied by the Margate lifeboat, was called out to the yacht that was stuck on a sandbank 2 miles off the coast of Margate on a Saturday night. Master Signaller 'Spud' Murphy was lowered on to the boat and managed to push it off the sandbank, and the other occupant of the vessel, Mr Donald Butler, struggled to get the craft safely back to Herne Bay, escorted by the lifeboat. On the Sunday, a full air and sea search failed to find any trace of Mr Lennox, but his body was found off the coast of Herne Bay on Sunday night. An inquest was opened into the incident at Herne Bay the following week.

During the same month, a 15-foot pleasure boat, *Fiesta*, had disappeared off the coast of Margate with three men and a boy on board. The boat had sailed from Westgate late on a Wednesday afternoon in calm sea and excellent visibility on what was its maiden voyage. It was supposed to have been on just a short trip up the coast to Herne Bay. The men on board were twenty-eight-year-old Anthony Roxon, forty-five-year-old Donald Smoker, thirty-year-old Ronald Hamblin, and his twelve-year-old son, Clive. Rescue services, including Manston's SAR helicopter, were alerted when the boat failed to return at 7.30 p.m. Both Ramsgate and Margate lifeboats, along with a 22 Squadron Whirlwind, searched all of Wednesday night into the early hours of Thursday morning but no trace of the boat was found.

There were further rumours that the USAF was about to return to Manston during October, after an American major, who was visiting Thanet, stated that between 3,000 and 5,000 personnel were involved in the move. A staff car bearing the USAF flag had recently been seen at Manston, and it was known that three senior American officers had inspected the base. A colonel in the USAF Information Division did not deny that the air force had shown an interest in Manston and that officials had visited the station, but he claimed that the USAF were continuously looking for new bases in European countries.

Apart from the major's claim that the USAF was about to return, there was other evidence to suggest that the Americans might be back as early as January 1967. During the summer of 1966, a man had visited the offices of the *Isle of Thanet Gazette* and showed staff a letter from an American airman, a friend of his who was living in California. The letter was inquiring about the possibility of accommodation in Thanet as he was expecting to be posted to Manston in the near future. A colonel in the information division dismissed the letter by stating that some airmen may have heard the same rumours as everyone else, and they were just trying to jump the queue.

It appears that 'there was no smoke without fire', and the MOD had been in touch with at least one local resident, a Mr J. W. Holmes of Duncan Road in Ramsgate. Exactly who Mr Holmes was is not known, but it is possible that he was just an ordinary member of the public. A letter to him from a G. J. Gammon stated that, after the withdrawal from France, the USAF had made announcements that they were to move bases in the UK at Mildenhall, Upper Heyford, and Alconbury. The return of the USAF to Manston could not be ruled out, but if it did, it would not necessarily mean there would be any marked increase in military flying.

The former bomb dump at RAF Manston, situated on the left of the Margate Road, was in the news in November when it was put up for sale and the site was proposed as a caravan and camping park. Margate Council turned down the suggestion of acquiring the bomb dump, but in a matter of weeks, it was sold at auction for £9,000 to Mr John Bywater, a veterinary surgeon from Ash. The bomb store that had been used during and after the Battle of Britain comprised of 15½ acres, on which stood three large brick sheds and heavily protected underground stores.

Just a short while later, there was a huge controversy over what the site might be used for and some members of the local councils argued that the area might be developed into an animal experimentation centre. Since the planning application had first been mentioned, several councillors said that their letter boxes had been repeatedly stuffed with pamphlets showing photos of animal experiments taking place. Councillors discussed a recommendation from the planning committee that no objections should be raised, subject to screening. That was approved, but the council then agreed that the surveyor was going to defer the proposal to Kent County Council, and it would make the final decision.

There were still issues to be resolved with Invicta Airways, and in November, the MOD wrote a letter to the secretary of the airline complaining that a number of buildings had been erected on the eastern side of the airfield without permission. These included an engineer's office, an electrician's workshop, an oil drum compound, and the engineer's canteen, and that an electrical and water supply had been connected without authority, along with the drainage system. None of the buildings complied with standards of the RAF, and it was requested that the company get in touch with the MOD's siting office immediately.

AVM John Barraclough, AOC of 19 Group (Coastal Command), arrived at Manston in December to present a bravery award from the Royal Humane Society to another 22 Squadron crewman, forty-three-year-old Master Signaller John Murphy. On 5 March 1966, the winchman had undergone a ninety-minute ordeal to rescue four teenagers that were trapped in mud while they were trying to get their football back. Two of the boys had had their legs entwined and flat boards had to be dropped, which helped other rescuers such as firemen to get them out of the oozing mud. The coastguard had also taken part in the rescue, and one of its members, along with a fireman, also received the award. Murphy, a forty-three-year-old father of two, had served in the RAF for twenty-four years.

19

# A Troubled Year

It was a bad start to 1967 when, on 21 January, an Air Ferry DC-4 (G-ASOG) crashed while it was on the approach to Frankfurt Airport in Germany, killing the two pilots on board. The aircraft, which was based at Manston, had taken-off from Manchester at 2.40 a.m. and was carrying freight on behalf of its parent airline, British United, which comprised of machinery, chemicals, and clothing. The aircraft was completely burnt out and all the cargo on board was lost.

The captain of the aircraft was forty-six-year-old Capt. Frederick Adcock, who lived locally on Minster Road, Ramsgate, and he had a total of 6,600 flying hours experience, including 1,000 hours in command. He had 600 hours' night-flying experience, but there was no evidence to prove that he had ever visited Frankfurt before. Adcock had previously flown for Manston's other resident airline, Invicta, and had only recently moved to Air ferry on 1 January. He had subsequently passed his proficiency check as pilot in command of a DC-4 on 6 January. The co-pilot was twenty-five years old, and he had passed his last proficiency test as co-pilot on the DC-4 on 6 November 1966.

It was later discovered that the two pilots had not set the altimeters to the correct local pressure settings. Both had different QFE and QNH pressure settings on their individual altimeters, as should have been the case, but the wrong ones. The last communication was received from the pilot at 4.11 a.m. and the aircraft crashed at 4.15 a.m. while on an ILS approach to runway 25 right, and at no point did either pilot report that there was a problem.

The undercarriage was down and locked when the aircraft made contact with an oak tree before hitting a number of others, and both wings were snapped off causing approximately 1,000 gallons of fuel to be released, which quickly caught fire. The cause of the crash was thought to have been the incorrect pressure settings, but some days later, a number of pilots reported fluctuations on the ILS glide path. Those complaints were investigated, and it was found that any deviation of the ILS was within the prescribed limits.

Just under a year after Canberra XN244, on 25 January 1967, had unexpectedly arrived at Manston, there was another foam landing at Manston made by a Handley Page Victor (XL189) from Wittering, whose crew were having problems with the undercarriage. Fire crews from both Ramsgate and Margate assisted the station's own firefighters, and an additional foam tender was brought in from Canterbury. As a precaution, the Ramsgate–Canterbury road was closed, but the aircraft made a safe landing on the foam carpet and was soon back in service.

Many years later, on the night of 30 April–1 May 1982, XL189 was involved in the first 'Black Buck' operation to bomb the runway at Port Stanley in the Falkland Islands. Flown by Sqn Ldr Bob Tuxford, XL189 was the last aircraft to pass on fuel to Vulcan XM607, flown by Flt Lt Martins Withers. XL189 landed at Wideawake Airfield in the Ascension Islands after a mission that had lasted fourteen hours and five minutes. The aircraft remained in RAF service until August 1989 when, to the dismay of many people who thought that the aircraft should be preserved, it was scrapped.

During an air show at Manston in June 2013, the authors were privileged to meet Martin Withers and his crew in the mess and talk about the 'Black Buck' sortie back in 1982. As far as we are aware, this was the last time that Vulcan XH588, or any other Vulcan, visited Manston.

It was in February that another debate was sparked off about the plans to build an Animal Research Centre on RAF Manston's former bomb dump, and Anti-Vivisectionist were up in arms. When asked what kind of animals he intended to keep at Manston, Mr Bywater answered 'Anything from a giraffe to a kangaroo. I have been using dogs, monkeys, cattle sheep, pigs and chickens'. He said he could not say exactly what he would do there and that depended on what his customers wanted him to do, but he had done a great deal of work involving Cancer Research. Anti-Vivisectionist Branch Secretary Mrs Phyllis Crook said they would do everything possible to stop that happening.

April was a busy month, and on the 3rd, a Vulcan (XM655) from RAF Cottesmore made a forced landing without the use of the foam carpet. The aircraft had suffered a complete hydraulic failure and had to be towed off the runway by ASF. A working party from RAF Cottesmore arrived to repair the aircraft, and it was put back into service with 9 Squadron. The Vulcan, which was the third last off the production line at Woodford, had been delivered to 9 Squadron in November 1964, but it later became part of the Waddington Wing and served with 44 and 101 Squadrons By the time that the aircraft was put up for disposal in 1983, it was serving with 50 Squadron and it became the first Vulcan to be 'civilianised'. The Vulcan now belongs to Wellesbourne Airfield Trust and carries out regular engine a taxi runs down the runway, but it will never fly again.

On the 14th, an Army Air Corps helicopter, Allouette XN132, visited Manston, and shortly after leaving the airfield on its way back to Middle Wallop, it had to make an emergency landing near Dover. The engine stopped after the fuel pumps failed in flight, and a fuel tanker and work party had to be dispatched to recover the helicopter.

Proposals were made by National Council on Transport in April for an airport to be built on the Goodwin Sands. They were similar to plans proposed in more recent times by Boris Johnson for an airport in the Thames Estuary. The subject of an airport being built on the sands had been mentioned before by the MP for Faversham Mr Terry Boston. The Minister of State for the Board of Trade Mr J. P. Mallalieu had agreed to talks taking place on the issue, and those backing the plan claimed that it would avoid using up scarce land for airport development.

At about the same time, there were plans to build an airport at Foulness, and the airport was to be built on reclaimed land and linked to the mainland by a tunnel or bridge with fast rail connections to London. It was suggested that Ramsgate could be the town chosen as the mainland's rail connection. As usual, the subject of noise became a leading issue.

It was not long, however, before a report commissioned to study the impact of a third London airport on Kent stated that noise from aircraft flying in and out of an airport at Foulness would be much greater than previously thought. The runways would be a lot closer to Kent than previously planned, and it was quite likely that aircraft would be stacked over Thanet and Canterbury. Although no detailed information had been provided by the commission about the stacking of aircraft, it was understood that Manston would be a focal point for aircraft waiting to land. Approximately 37,500 people then lived in the areas in Kent, which would be worst affected, including 22,000 of the Isle of Sheppey.

20

# G-ANCG

On Thursday 20 April 1967, RAF Manston dealt with what was potentially its most dangerous incident when a civil airliner with sixty people on board, made up of fifty-four passengers and six crew, had to make a foam landing. The aircraft was a Bristol Britannia of British Eagle that was registered G-ANCG, and it had had a mixed history. The aircraft had been built in 1959 for BOAC as a Britannia Type 305 and had first flown in November that year.

With the order from BOAC having been cancelled, G-ANCG was then destined to be delivered to Capital Airlines in the USA but then that deal also fell through. It was then about to be purchased by Northwest Airlines and was given the American serial number N6598C. Unfortunately, that order was also cancelled, and it seemed that nobody wanted what had originally been known as *Charlie Golf*.

In December 1959, it was converted to a Britannia Type 308 and was given the temporary registration G-14-2 before finally being delivered to Transcontinental SA Airlines in Argentina and reregistered as LV-PPL. On arrival in Argentina, however, the Britannia was reregistered again as LV-GJC. In October 1961, the aircraft was impounded at New York's Idlewild airport (later known as JFK) for non-payment of landing fees, and the airline stopped trading at about the same time. The Britannia remained impounded at New York until February 1964 when it was bought by British Eagle, and after a lot of work had been carried out, it was ferried to London Heathrow and reregistered again as G-ANCG. The aircraft was converted to carry both passengers and freight and entered service with British Eagle in late 1964.

After entering service with British Eagle, G-ANCG was regularly flown on MOD charters, mainly carrying scientists and freight to Britain's rocket range at Woomera in Australia. The Long-Range Rocket Establishment at Woomera had been established in April 1947 as a joint project between Britain and Australia, and since then, a number of the UK's rocket and missile projects had been tested there. The first missile was launched from there in March 1949, and that was

Bristol Britannia G-ANCG making a foam landing on 20 April 1967. Seconds after this photo was taken, the remaining undercarriage collapsed and the aircraft slid down the runway. (*Collin Wilson*)

followed by others such as the Sylark Rocket, Black Knight, and Europa Rockets. The latter being a modified version of the Blue Streak, a Cold War experimental weapon that nearly became a space rocket. The missile was designed and built by the de Havilland aircraft company and powered by a Rolls-Royce engine.

The flights to Australia were normally flown in conjunction with another British Eagle Britannia, its sister ship G-ANCF, which also had a Manston connection. Many years later, in 1976, G-ANCF was purchased by Invicta Airlines (Invicta International) and was based on the airfield for several years. It is now on static display at Liverpool Airport.

On the day of the incident at Manston, G-ANCG, named *Trojan*, had taken-off from London Heathrow for Kuwait on the first leg of a long flight to Adelaide in Australia when the crew discovered problems retracting and locking undercarriage. It was the starboard main undercarriage that would not lock after take-off, and although the gear was recycled several times, the problem could not be resolved. This was the fortnightly charter flight under contract to the MOD. The aircraft was being flown by Capt. Donald Chubb, but the names of the first officer and navigation officers are not known. The flight engineer was Peter James and the cabin staff included Jan Hansell, Bill Russell, Margaret Day, and Pam Noble.

After take-off, the captain contacted British Eagle operations, 'Eagle Base', over the R/T to discuss the problem, and after investigations had been made and discussions held with the engineering department, it was decided that it could not be resolved while the aircraft was in the air. Two of the passengers on board had actually been involved with the design of the Britannia at Bristol Aircraft Company, but they could not offer any advice either.

This was generally not a good day to be flying in a Britannia, and in Cyprus, another aircraft, Britannia Globe Air's HB-ITB, crashed while trying to land at Nicosia in a thunderstorm. All 117 passengers and nine crew were killed in what was what the worst accident since an All Nippon Airways' Boeing 727 crash in 1966. It was also the fifth highest casualty figure overall involving just a single aircraft. The Swiss-registered Britannia was orbiting to make its third approach when it crashed into a small hillock outside Nicosia, having previously aborted two approaches because of the bad weather and low visibility.

The Globe Air Britannia had taken-off from Bombay at 1.12 p.m. on 19 April with eleven hours and ten minutes of fuel on board destined for Cairo, a distance of 2,698 miles, but it had diverted to Nicosia because of a sandstorm. Its designated diversion airport was Beirut, but for some reason, the captain chose to fly into Cypriot airspace controlled by Nicosia Airport and was overhead the airfield at 11.06 p.m. The Britannia's first approach was made too low and the captain decided to overshoot, making a low pass over the runway before disappearing in low cloud to the north-west.

On its third approach, the aircraft hit the ground 842 feet above sea level while in level flight, with its port wing breaking up on impact before the aircraft hit another hillock where it completely disintegrated. It was never established why the captain had decided land at Nicosia rather than continuing on to Beirut, where the weather was much better. One factor that did come out was that the two pilots were flying in excess of their time limits, which had been exceeded by two hours and forty-seven minutes. Rather remarkably, four people on board did survive, including one member of the cabin crew and three passengers, all of whom were seated in the rear of the aircraft.

Back at Manston, Capt. Chubb, the pilot of *Charlie Golf*, kept a cool head as he made his final approach to the runway at Manston, and from the ground, it appeared that the port main undercarriage and nose wheel were down in their normal position. The starboard undercarriage, however, hung limply in the air, and it was clearly not in its normal position. The landing was a spectacular sight, and after making contact with the foam carpet, the aircraft continued to roll down the runway for some distance before the undercarriage collapsed completely and the aircraft came to a halt.

It was not just passengers that the Britannia was carrying; according to the Manston ORB, classified material was being transferred, which had to be removed from the aircraft and put into storage immediately. There is no mention of where it was stored, but the classified material on rocket and missile development must have been very sensitive. Security on the airfield was a priority anyway, and arrangements had to be made to deal with the large numbers of press and TV crew that arrived, along with hundreds of members of the public, many of them 'ghouls' who had heard about the incident on the news and arrived expecting to see a disaster unfold.

After the Accident Investigation Board had inspected the Britannia to discover what had gone wrong with the hydraulics, the aircraft was eventually removed. It was lifted off the runway with the use of two large cranes and taken away to be scrapped. Several pieces of the aircraft were recovered by the fire section and were put on display there, including the aircraft's registration, G-ANCG.

Grp Capt. Mike Hobson with a Spitfire V at Manston on 7 November 1967. The aircraft was on its way to Germany to celebrate the fiftieth anniversary of 92 Squadron. Wg Cdr Wills, the CO, is standing in the middle with Flt Lt Rushmore on the right.

# 21

# A Personal Experience

RAF Manston closed at the end of March 1999, but because of certain restrictions such as those of space and the missing records, we are not able to give a really detailed account about operations on the airfield. What follows is a history of the station up until the RAF withdrew, mainly using secondary sources and, in this chapter, my (Joe Bamford, author) personal knowledge and experience.

In its role as a Master Diversion Airfield, RAF Manston continued to attract unusual types of aircraft, some of them that would have been more commonly associated with the Second World War. In May 1968, just after the fiftieth anniversary of the RAF, two Heinkel 111s and fifteen Me 109s evoked the memories and fears of many local people when they appeared in the sky above Thanet.

The aircraft were actually Spanish-built versions of the German aircraft that had been built under licence by Hispano, and so technically they were not the real thing. The aircraft had arrived at Manston to be inspected by the Air Registration Board prior to flying on to Duxford, where they took part in the film, *The Battle of Britain*.

I arrived at Manston on 6 November 1968 as a young leading aircraftsman (LAC) straight out of Air Traffic Training School at Shawbury and was put on 'A' watch in the control tower. The shift was run by Cpl 'Robbie' Robinson and Cpl Peter Turner. Being the youngest and least experienced, I was mainly employed on making tea and doing other menial jobs. Peter was later discharged from the RAF and employed on the PBX Telephone Exchange. As will be mentioned later, Peter was later heavily involved in the restoration of Manston Spitfire TB752 in 1979, and then he became one of the first curators/managers of the Spitfire & Hurricane Memorial Building. If anyone deserves the title 'Mr Manston', it is surely Peter.

The control tower had originally been built on three levels, with a fourth added later for Local Aerodrome Control. The meteorological office and radio

A line up of Spanish-built He 111s and Me 109s at Manston in 1968. They had arrived in the UK to take part in the filming of the Battle of Britain.

*Above:* Me 109 (Hispano) lands at Manston to join the other aircraft appearing in the film *The Battle of Britain.*

*Below:* Dan Air Ambassador G-AMAS on the runway after making a wheels-up landing on 30 September 1968. The aircraft had made a touch-and-go landing at Gatwick during a training flight when the right undercarriage wheels failed to retract and the captain decided to divert to Manston. There were only two pilots on board, and the aircraft was written off.

*Above:* Argosy XN854 made a foam landing on 1 November 1968. The aircraft landed safely and flew back to Benson the next day. It was sold to Rolls-Royce in May 1975 and later sold for scrap.

*Left:* Wg Cdr Wills lays a wreath on the war memorial in Manston village. The wing commander was the CO from November 1965 to January 1969. (*Nigel Wills*)

*Above:* A Spitfire from the Battle of Britain Memorial Flight on the main runway at Manston. In the background are the cooling towers of Richborough Power Station, local landmarks that were pulled down in March 2012.

*Below:* A 22 Squadron Whirlwind, XK969, on a medical emergency sortie in 1969. Note the nursing staff from Margate Hospital who were dealing with the case.

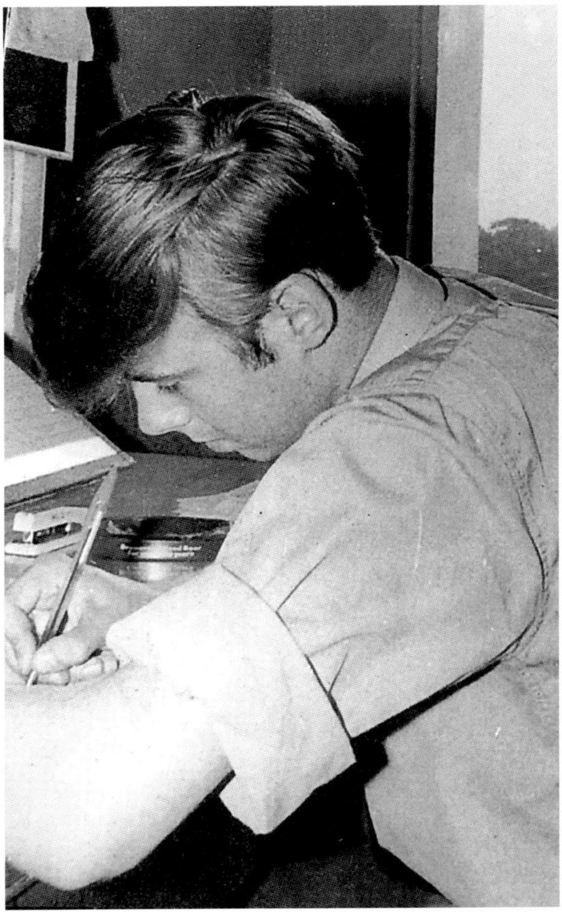

*Above:* An Invicta DC-4 and a Viscount on the ramp at the eastern (civil) side of the airfield in 1969. Buildings of the main camp are in the background.

*Left:* Author Joe Bamford at work, writing out a flight plan in the movements' room on the third floor of the control tower in 1969.

*Right:* The author in the same spot in the control tower in 2016. The dividing wall between the movements' room and the radar room has been removed and it is a totally different place to what I remember of it during the '60s and '70s.

*Below:* The Red Arrows at Manston in 1970. The team, then lead by Sqn Ldr D. Hazell, spent a lot of time at the station that year while the runway at Kemble was being resurfaced. The Red Arrows were then flying the Folland Gnat but re-equipped with the BAe Hawk during the winter of 1979.

Canberra WE168 being pushed into place to join the Spitfire and Javelin as another 'gate guardian' in 1969. The aircraft arrived at Manston *en route* from Germany to Bassingbourne, but it had been damaged when it was blown on to its tail during a storm.

room were on the ground floor along with the toilets (Men Only). On the second floor was the flight planning room, the walls of which were covered in maps of various parts of the world and the airways that covered them. The movements room was on the third floor, part of which was the kitchen and the twenty-line PBX switchboard office. On most other stations, the movements room would have been called the operations room.

At the back of the movements room, sealed off beyond a partition wall, was the radar room, which contained two 787 search radar screens and two precision approach screens. In those days, the radar room had to be blacked out and for the approach room assistant, it was probably the most unpopular place to work. His main role was updating the weather boards every hour with a Chinagraph pen and answering the telephone, mainly to pass on the airfield state and weather to other RAF stations. The radar room also accommodated Kent radar that serviced low-level aircraft flying across the Channel.

In the control tower, we worked a four-watch system that began at 12.30 p.m. and finished at 5 p.m. The following morning, we worked 8 am. until 12.30

p.m., and then again from 5 p.m. straight through until 8 a.m. Normally, only a single airman stayed alert and awake all night while the rest either played cards (normally Clag) or slept down in flight planning. After the night shift, we got two and a half days off, including the day we came off nights before it all began again on an afternoon shift.

The accommodation for single airmen at Manston was in a large 'H'-shaped clock on two levels that had previously served as the sergeants' mess. Rather unusually for this period, each airman had their own room, which contained the usual bed, a small locker, a tall locker, and a few personal possessions. There was central heating, but it often broke down, and much to the dismay of the station's warrant officer, FS Goddard, we used our own electric fires and illegally used the government's electricity.

FS Goddard was the man who most of us tried to avoid because, as he was in charge of discipline, we were often ordered to 'get your hair cut'. He did his best to maintain order, dress, and discipline, but he had little power over individual sections who looked after their own. The SWO often got his own back such as on the occasions of a Battle of Britain parade, when he turned up outside the guardroom with his own barber's set. Those of us who had avoided him all week were forced to sit in the chair he had provided while he trimmed our golden locks and then charged us for the privilege.

Among those whose names I remember who worked in air traffic and with whom I became good friends were Brian Atkinson, Pete Abel, Hughy O'Neil, Mick Cochrane, Pat Welch, and Dennis Todd. Dennis had been a pilot with Burma Airways, but he had to retire as pilot after his vision became impaired. John Scotney, Ron Sadler, and John Pulford were also good friends—Ron and John being corporals. The senior ATC officer was Sqn Ldr John Herrington, a former aircrew signaller. His office was on the third floor and could be accessed through the movements and radar rooms.

At that time, RAF Manston had two gate guardians, Spitfire TB752 and Gloster Javelin XH764, which had been saved by Wg Cdr Wills who had flown the type with 3 Squadron. As I have already mentioned, the Spitfire had arrived at Manston in 1955, while the Javelin had been put on display in July 1968, and in August 1969, they were joined by a Canberra (WE168). It had arrived from Wildenrath along with two others and was destined for Bassingbourn. However, in the early hours of one morning and not having been tied down by ASF, it had been blown on to its tail and was badly damaged. The Canberra had been saved from the fire dump by Wg Cdr Scott, who had taken over from Wg Cdr Wills in January 1968

The Heinkels (Hispanos) that had arrived in the UK to take part in the film *The Battle of Britain* continued to pass through Manston until at least 1970, and on one occasion when I was working in local control, a Spitfire from the Battle of Britain Memorial Flight made a mock attack on one. It was about to land on runway 29 when the pilot must have spotted the Heinkel parked on the eastern side of the airfield near the Invicta dispersals. Without making any radio calls, the pilot pulled up the wheels, overshot, and then proceeded to dive and 'shoot up' the Heinkel. For several minutes, the pilot continued to give a great display attacking the 'enemy' and, being a summer's day, huge crowds of people were out on the airfield and enjoyed the spectacle.

Much to the dismay of the local authorities, 22 Squadron's 'D' Flight was withdrawn from Manston, with its final day of service being 30 March 1969. Despite a campaign to keep the SAR flight at Manston, the RAF refused to reinstate it, and there was talk of the local towns financing their own SAR service.

It was not until April 1971 that the Department of Trade and Industry authorised the Coastguard Service to contract Bristow helicopters to provide the SAR cover, which began in June that year with silver and orange-coloured Whirlwind helicopters. Rather ironically, two of the crew were former members of 22 Squadron.

When I arrived at Manston, Invicta Airways were operating a couple of DC-4s that operated purely cargo flights to various destinations in Europe such as Ostend. However, a small number of its former Viking fleet survived, and they sat on the eastern side of the airfield waiting for the scrap man. Among them was G-AHPL, which had been badly damaged during an incident while taking-off on 2 August 1965 and written off, but its registration was not cancelled until early 1969.

Invicta Airways continued to operate from Manston, and after a brief failed merger with British Midland in June 1969, Hugh Kennard broke away and formed a new company called Invicta Air Cargo. The mainstay of the company continued to be its two DC-4s, G-ASEN and G-ASPM. During the merger with British Midland, Invicta had acquired a small number Vickers Viscounts that it used for passenger flights, and in 1971, the company purchased a number of Vickers Vanguards and resumed passenger flight to various European destinations. The company changed its name again to Invicta International.

In December 1970, 617 Volunteer Gliding School moved into Manston and began operations from the Northern Grass. The gliders were launched by a winch rather than being towed into the air by an aircraft and were mainly flown at weekend. No. 617 VGS replaced 618 VGS, which had pulled out of Manston 1965.

During the late '60s and early '70s, many of those airmen who worked in ATC also worked part time for Invicta Airways, loading and unloading its aircraft and those of the various airlines that it handled. It was in the 1970s, during a national docks strike, that Manston came into its own and dealt with a huge increase in the number of movements. It was not unusual for some of us to work a fifteen-hour night shift in the control tower and then go over to civil side and work another eight hours. Officially, we had to ask permission to perform other work from the CO, Wg Cdr Scott, but nobody ever bothered with that.

Apart from Invicta's aircraft, we handled DC-6s, DC-7s, and Boeing 707s that belonged to a variety of airlines from all over the world. A small number of civil registered C-130 Hercules also regularly visited Manston, including one that belonged to Southern Airlines, which we later heard was an airline operated by the CIA. We were paid 6 shillings and 6 pence an hour in old money—that was hardly a 'king's ransom'.

In May 1971, I was posted out of Manston to RAF Akrotiri in Cyprus. By then, the station was beginning to change anyway and many of my friends had been posted out as well. Even in those days, it was a small air force, and within a short while, I was reunited with some of them, including FS Ray Baker, who was a local controller and my old friend Bill Newman who had worked on ASF. Ray was promoted to the rank of warrant officer, and according to the rumours at the time, he was the youngest warrant officer in the RAF.

Wg Cdr Scott handed over command of the station to Wg Cdr R. A. Jell in July 1971. In March 1951, Wg Cdr Jell (64283) was mentioned in dispatches for distinguished service in Malaya. He had also been awarded the DFC and AFC. Just before he left the station, Scott made the news by grounding eight cadets from a public school for having long hair. They were from a public school in Rochester, and after being inspected, another seventeen cadets whose hair was 'reasonable' were allowed to fly.

In the same month, Rotary Hydraulic Arrestor Gear (RHAG) was installed on the airfield. This was a tensioned hook that stretched across the threshold of the runway to prevent aircraft running off the end. It was first used in January 1972 by a Blackburn Buccaneer that had been diverted from Honington.

In 1973, the foam carpet was used on nine occasions for Canberra WD955, Devon XS766, Basset XS766 (twice), Dan Air Comet G-APYC, Basset XS773, Basset XS773, Canberra XH135, and Beechcraft G-AYPC.

I returned to Manston in November 1973 and missed all the excitement of these emergencies. Many of the old faces had gone and most of the 'old school', those officers and senior NCOs who had served during the war, had retired. I left the RAF in April 1974, got married, and lived locally in Cliffsend. I kept in touch with events at Manston through people like Invicta International flight engineer Collin MaClaren and occasional visits to the Jolly Farmer pub in Manston Village.

In April 1974, Wg Cdr Jell handed over command of Manston to Wg Cdr C. J. Dunscombe. There were only three foam landings in 1974, Victor XA937 and Canberras WJ728 and WH849.

It was in October 1974 that the Bristow Helicopters were replaced by two RAF Wessex of 72 Squadron's 'D' Flight. The Wessex of 72 Squadron were the first of the type to be used for SAR coastguard duties in the UK.

There were three foam landings in 1975, beginning on 29 April with a Canberra T.4 (WT483). The aircraft was repaired and put back into service, and

Lt Cdr John A. Douglas, the chief inspector of the Coast Guard. He visited Manston to inspect the new civilian ASR service provided by Bristow International Helicopters in June 1971.

The Coast Guard commander with the SAR crew from Bristow's Helicopters in July 1971. Whirlwind G-AYTK is in the background.

*Above:* Bristow's SAR standby crew that took over the RAF's role in June 1971, posing in front of their Westland Whirlwind.

*Right:* A member of the Army parachute team, 'The Red Devils', descends to make a very special delivery to the station on 12 October 1971 in the form of a special cover to celebrate the twenty-fifth anniversary of the RAF Education Branch.

The team leader makes the presentation of the special cover to the station's adjutant. It had been flown from Netheravon in a DH.89 Dominie by Fg Off. A. E. Rose, and the parachute drop had been made from 6,000 feet.

An exercise at the fire training school's fire dump in 1971. The aircraft in the background is a Hastings, one of four that were delivered to Manston.

Invicta International Vanguard A-AZRE on the apron outside its operations building, being refuelled, shortly after being delivered in March 1972. The aircraft had previously flown in Canada as CF-TFK. This Vanguard had the company's name 'Invicta International' on the fuselage but others still carried the name 'Invicta Air Cargo'.

Monarch Airlines Britannia G-AOVN on the runway after making an emergency landing on a foam carpet on 13 June 1972, with a suspected nose wheel failure. The aircraft, which had previously belonged to British Eagle, was flying from Luton to Switzerland with 147 people on board.

it ended its days in a museum at Luqa in Malta. On 17 May, G-BCWJ became the only Canadair CL-44 ever to use the foam carpet. The aircraft belonged to Tradewinds, and it was also put back into service and ended its days in April 1978 after its undercarriage had collapsed on landing at Nairobi. A Royal Navy F-4 Phantom made the final foam landing of the year on 6 October 1975. It also survived, and in 1978, it was handed over to the RAF, with which it served on 111 and 43 Squadrons.

Wg Cdr N. T. R. Bulpitt (194399) took over command of the station in February 1976 from Wg Cdr C. J. Dunscombe. No. 72 Squadron's 'D' Flight became 22 Squadron 'E' Flight in June that year, but its personnel and equipment remained the same.

22

# Rebuilding a Gate Guardian

By the late 1970s, Manston's premier gate guardian, Spitfire TB752, was in a bad condition and it had already survived one attempt to have it taken to the breaker's yard. A survey was carried out of the Spitfire and a restoration programme was put into place involving the Medway Aircraft Preservation Branch of the Royal Aeronautical Society. A team of engineers from RAF Abingdon were sent to Manston to take TB752 apart and prepare it for the journey to Rochester Airport where the restoration would take place. On 7 July 1978, the Spitfire was put on to a Queen Mary low loader for its journey up to the Medway. The project leader was Lewis Deal. It would take over a year and hundreds of hours of hard work before a wonderfully restored Spitfire was returned to Manston.

At about the same time as the Spitfire was sent up to Rochester, it was realised that when it returned to Manston, it would be foolish to allow it to be exposed to the elements again. The chairman of Thanet District Council, Councillor John Jones, and the CO, Wg Cdr Collin Campbell, launched an appeal to raise money for a building to permanently house TB752. Wg Cdr Campbell was the CO from March 1978 until August 1980, when he handed over command to Wg Cdr H. H. Skinner. The people of Kent gave generously, and by the time that a decision had been made to begin work on the building in the Autumn of 1980, £17,000 of the estimated £35,000 had already been raised.

During the night of 22 December 1978, RAF Manston was the only airfield in south-east England open and the rest were closed because of foggy conditions. Between 6.10 p.m. and 8.30 p.m., eight civil airliners diverted to Manston and the station's staff were left to deal with over 260 tired and angry passengers. All the station's personnel were called out and eventually the passengers were all put on coaches and driven off to their destination airports.

During 1979, the CO, Wg Cdr Campbell, was contacted by a team of potential aviators who were going to attempt the first man powered flight across the English Channel The team were particularly keen to get the CO's assurance that, should they have to ditch in Channel, 22 Squadron's 'E' Flight would be available to rescue the pilot. The arrangements were made and the MacCready *Gossamer Albatross* made a number of test flights from Manston before moving to Folkestone, where a successful crossing was eventually made on 12 June 1979.

On 15 September 1980, TB752, painted in the markings of 66 Squadron with the letters LZ-F, was handed back to RAF Manston in a ceremony attended by AM Sir Philip Lageson, the AOC of 18 Group, Wg Cdr Campbell, and many local dignitaries. The aircraft had been positioned in its original position, at the front of the sergeants' mess (originally the officers' mess), and for the ceremony, it was flanked by two airmen with rifles, providing a guard of honour. In recognition of the work carried out by the Medway Branch of the Royal Aeronautical Society, the air marshal presented a solid silver Spitfire to Mr Peter Hearne, the president of the Medway branch.

At midnight on 2 October 1980, shortly after the Spitfire had arrived home and after sixteen years of service, RAF Manston's capability to lay a foam carpet was withdrawn. The facility had been used by at least sixty-two aircraft, forty-four military and eighteen civil, and had undoubtably saved many lives and many aircraft. It was claimed by the MOD that the foam laying equipment was both obsolete and worn out and too expensive to replace. The largest foam carpet available was 3,600 feet by 90 feet and used up to 100,000 gallons of foam that cost £3,500, and so in the end, it was all down to cost. The final foam landing was made on 14 August by a Vulcan (XL455) that had a suspected nose wheel failure. XL455 ended its days at an air museum near Flixton in Norfolk.

TB752's final day outside was on 25 January 1981, and the following morning, the Spitfire was pushed inside the Memorial Building, which was still only half built, with the rest of it, including large amounts of glazing, being completed around it. The building was not handed over until May, but even then, certain things, such as the electrics, had to be completed. The Spitfire Memorial Building was officially opened on Saturday 18 June with a large number of VIPs and civic dignitaries present, including AVM John Howe, Commander of the Southern Maritime Region, Wg Cdr Stanford Tuck, and Wg Cdr Hugh Kennard from Invicta International.

Pride of place went to three of the pilots who had first flown TB752 during and after the war: Brian Mason, Danny Smith, and Richard Edwards, who had flown in from Zimbabwe. Also, former Plt Off. Richard Edwards had flown the aircraft with 403 (RCAF) Squadron. Early in 1982, it was decided to change the markings of TB752 to those of 403 (RCAF) Squadron. The Spitfire was given the code letters KH-Z.

The station's role changed in 1982 from being a Master Diversion Airfield to a Military Emergency Diversion Airfield. There was little change to the airfield's operational role, and it remained open and available twenty-four hours a day, 365 days a year. Some sections introduced working on a 9–5 basis, five days a week, but everything else remained much the same.

In July 1982, several pipe mines that had been laid by Canadian sappers in 1940 to combat the threat of a German invasion force landing were found on the grass area on the eastern side (civil side) of the airfield. By this time, Invicta International, which had again re-equipped with a small number of Bristol Britannias (G-ANCF and G-AOVF), had gone into liquidation. Seabourne Express, an air cargo company, had taken over the lease of the civil side and handled aircraft such as Boeing 707s and CL-44s that operated a twice-weekly freight service to Kennedy Airport, New York.

In 1983, former Red Arrows pilot Ted Girdler set up a flying school on the airfield called TG Aviation. It was equipped with a small number of Cessna 152s and a Piper PA-28. Ted was the son of a coal miner from Deal, and he had been inspired as young boy by watching the Chipmunks of No. 1 AEF fly from Manston. Having joined the RAF in the ranks, Ted had worked his way up, and after being commissioned, he served with 111 Squadron and flew the Lightning from RAF Wattisham. After flying with the Red Arrows for three years, Ted left the RAF; after living in the north-east for a while, he moved to Kent, later buying up the assets of Thanet Flying Club and setting up TG Aviation at Manston. Unfortunately, on 18 August 2000, Ted was killed while flying a Czech-built L29 at the Eastbourne Air Show. Ted's legacy, TG Aviation, continued to operate from Manston until 15 May 2014, when the airport closed.

In September 1983, Wg Cdr Jim Ward took over command of Manston from Wg Cdr H. H. Skinner, and he remained at Manston until September 1985, when he was posted to RAF HQ at Rheindahlen in Germany. Ward handed command over to Wg Cdr Tom. J. Hindmarsh in September 1985.

The year 1985 was busy, with 33,734 movements that included thirteen military and seventy-seven civil diversions. Concorde visited the station again in July. No. 1 AEF by then had four Chipmunks on its strength and flew 3,749 cadets on air experience flights. No. 22 Squadron's 'E' Flight, which had taken over SAR duties from 72 Squadron's 'D' Flight in June 1976, had been scrambled 1,166 times and rescued 636 people by the end of the year.

Kent Radar, a civil aviation radar unit, was based in the approach room at Manston; it controlled aircraft flying low level across the Channel to France from airports such as Southend and Lydd. By 1985, it had four controllers working on shifts, and in 1985, it had its busiest year, controlling 25,904 movements across Kent. In January 1986, after serving in 18 Group for nearly twenty-six years, RAF Manston was returned to the control of 11 Group. The handover was officially made in the officers' mess, with AM Fitzpatrick, AOC of 18 Group, and AVM Stear, AOC of 11 Group, in attendance.

In February 1986, Prime Minister Margaret Thatcher and M. Mitterand, the French President, staged through Manston on their way to Canterbury to sign the agreement about the proposed Channel Tunnel. Security was tight, and the

A British Airways Concorde lands at Manston after a pleasure flight up the North Sea, *circa* 1986. (*John Wilson*)

An aerial view of the station when the Hurricane Memorial Building was being built in 1988, next to the Spitfire Memorial Building. The white 'H' block were mainly accommodation blocks and the sergeants' mess. The old parade ground is on the extreme right. Note the Javelin and Canberra flanking the building.

Dame Vera Lynn standing in front of Hurricane BN230 after opening the new section of the Spitfire & Hurricane Memorial Building in 1988. On her right in Wg Cdr Jim Whitson, who had taken over as CO in 1988. On her left is Wg Cdr Tom Hindmarsh, who had commanded the station from 1985 to 1988. (*John Wilson*)

A SR.N4 Hovercraft of Hoverspeed leaves Dover for Calais being chased by a Sea King of 202 SAR Squadron. Hoverspeed had been formed in 1981 after a merger of Hoverlloyd and Seaspeed and operated across the Channel until 2005.

Queen's Colour Squadron provided the guard of honour; the Central Band of the RAF provided the music.

As had occurred during previous years, in 1987, there was an 'Air Day'; on 12 July, the station was opened to the public. It was mentioned in the programme that RAF Manston had recently played host to a group of Russian airmen who had flown in on a giant Antonov 22. The aircraft had arrived to collect three helicopters that had taken part in the World Helicopter Championship, which had been held at Castle Ashby near Bedford.

The CO, Wg Cdr Tom Hindmarsh, played host and the Russians were treated to afternoon tea made up of traditional cream cakes and sandwiches, which were served up on the lawn outside the officers' mess. The Russian airmen remained at Manston for four hours, during which time they visited the Spitfire Memorial Museum where they bought souvenirs to take back home.

The Red Arrows headlined the Air Day, and in 1987, the team was led by thirty-eight-year-old Sqn Ldr Richard Thomas. Among the aircraft participating in the event were a Jaguar GR1 from 2 Squadron, a Tornado GR1, and a Harrier GR.3. Among the civilian aircraft taking part were a British Airways Concorde, pride of the British Airways fleet, and a Pitts Special that was flown by Britain's foremost aerobatic pilot Brian Lecomber. There were also aircraft from USAF, the RCAF, the Danish Air Force, and the Dutch Air Force.

The Lancaster from the BBMF, PA474, carried out a flypast with a Spitfire and Hurricane, and the RAF Falcons provided a display of parachuting. Britain's only airworthy Mosquito, RR299 HT-E, which was then owned by British Aerospace and based at Chester, was displayed; built at Leavesden and delivered to the RAF in 1945, the aircraft had been bought by former RAF night-fighter ace John Cunningham. During the Air Day, the Mosquito was being flown by another former RAF pilot, Mr John Sadler, a British aerospace test pilot.

The 'Great Storm', as it later became known, struck South East England on Friday 16 October 1987, and at Dover, a ferry was blown over and another had to be beached near Folkstone. At Manston, everyone battened down the hatches but there was some damage in the control tower when the air conditioning unit blew in and injured ATC Flt Lt Carol Couchman. The controller, who had arrived at Manston in 1984, was quite badly injured and had to have a number of operations before she returned to duty. Despite her injuries, she remained in the RAF and was to serve at Manston for many more years.

On 22 April 1988, the newly refurbished Hurricane BN230 was wheeled out at Rochester after some 22,000 hours of restoration. Within a short while, the Mk 11c Hurricane was to join Spitfire TB752 on display in the new part and extension of the Spitfire & Hurricane Memorial Building.

There were, and still are, critics who claimed that the Hurricane is just a hybrid because it had previously carried the RAF serial LF751 and had been rebuilt from components taken from two other Hurricanes, Z3687 and PG593. What people tend to forget, however, is that during that war, a lot of aircraft, including Hurricanes, would have been repaired with parts scavenged form other aircraft that were grounded.

While the Hurricane was at Rochester being renovated, parts from the former gate guardian at RAF Biggin Hill, Hurricane LF738, were also used to complete BN230. After its renovation, BN230 carried the marking FT-A and represents a Hurricane from 43 Squadron, the first RAF fighter to fly over Dieppe in August 1942. On that day of the Dieppe Raid, the Hurricane had been flown by Belgium pilot Sqn Ldr DARG Le Roy Du Vivier.

By 10 July 1988, when the next Air Day took place, RAF Manston was under the command of Wg Cdr J. R. Whitson, who had taken over from Wg Cdr Hindmarsh in March. Among those aircraft on static display were an F.111 and F.5 from the USAF, and a Buccaneer, Harrier, Tornado, Jet Provost, and Jetstream from the RAF. Those aircraft taking part in the flying display included a Nimrod, VC10, and Avro Shackleton but, as usual, along with the Battle of Britain's Lancaster, the stars of the display were the Red Arrows.

The Hurricane Memorial Building, which is adjacent to and now part of the Spitfire Memorial Building, was opened by Dame Vera Lynn in October 1988 to house Hurricane BN230. The building cost more than £100,000 and, similar to the appeal that had been made for the Spitfire Memorial Building, most of the money was raised by the people of Thanet. Both buildings are quite unique and were the first to be built to house a RAF station's gate guardian.

On 1 January 1989, the RAF Fire and Rescue Training Squadron amalgamated with the Air Force Department Fire Service Training Establishment to become RAF's Fire Service Central Training Establishment based at Manston. The last course at the former AFDS, 412/88, was completed in December 1988. The merger was described as the end of an era and the 'New Dawn' in firefighting in the form of a fully functional and professional training organisation.

On 6 March 1989, there was a station reorganisation and the officers' commanding the CTE Fire Training School at Manston and Improved United Kingdom Air Defence Ground Environment (IUKADGE) at Sandwich became responsible for their own units. Answering directly to RAF Manston's CO, Wg Cdr Whitson, the senior ATC officer, Sqn Ldr C. Homer, was given overall charge of ATC, the Crash Fire Section, Kent Radar, and Customs. The officer commanding flying/admin, Sqn Ldr D. R. Gasson, assumed command of No. 1 AEF, 617 VGS, and the Supply Flight.

Wg Cdr Gordon C. Milne had been appointed as the CO of the reactivated site at RAF Ash (Former RAF Sandwich) on 2 December 1988. RAF Ash had now been given the title Improved United Kingdom Air Defence Ground Environment Operational Conversion Unit (IUKADGE OCU) and was used as a training unit. Wg Cdr John Gritten, who was appointed as the commandant of the RAF Fire Services Central Training Establishment, was a local man who came from

Westgate and had been educated at Chatham School in Ramsgate. He had been commissioned in 1968 and served in the RAF Regiment in Salalah, Malta, and Gütersloh in Germany.

All the engineering sections were amalgamated into a single squadron under the command of Sqn Ldr Mike Evans. The Engineering Squadron was made up of both the engineers at RAF Manston and the radar unit at RAF Ash. Under the overall command of the OC Engineering was the Engineering Supply Flight, the Handling Flight, the MT Section, Armoury, Communications Centre, and the PBX sections at both Manston and Ash. The long-term plan was for a single officer with the rank of group captain to take overall command of both Manston and Ash.

In February 1990, it was announced that the station's two gate guardians, the Canberra and the Javelin, were to be removed and scrapped. The two aircraft had been on display at Manston for over twenty years, and despite the fact that both the types had only tenuous connections with the station, they were very popular with tourists and had given pleasure to thousands of visitors over the years. The *Isle of Thanet Gazette* stated that the MOD had done a great disservice in seeing the two aircraft as just so many tons of scrap metal and money.

The pilot of a light aircraft that was flying from Ostend to Southend had a lucky escape in March when the engine lost power just off the coast of Ramsgate. Mr David Hudson dealt calmly with the emergency and decided to divert to Manston, but the engine seized up almost immediately and he was forced to ditch into the sea. The forty-eight-year-old pilot managed to free himself before the aircraft slipped beneath the water, and twenty-five minutes later, he was spotted by the crew of a Sea King helicopter from Manston. He was safely winched up into the helicopter and Flt Lt Graham Gow, the Sea King's pilot, told Mr Hudson that he was a very lucky man.

There was another Air Day on Sunday 15 July 1990 to celebrate the fiftieth anniversary of the Battle of Britain, with the gates opening at 8.30 a.m. On the day before the Air Day, thousands of people had packed the seafront at Broadstairs to watch a flypast by a RAF Shackleton to re-enact an 'air raid' on Viking Bay.

The Shackleton was an MR2 from 8 Squadron, which, it was claimed, was the oldest aircraft in the RAF's fleet; it was flown by Flt Lt Roger Reid. Searchlights and pyrotechnics filled the sky to simulate the defences that had been put up during the war. The Shackleton was a descendant of the famous Avro Lancaster bomber, the most famous bomber from the Second World War. Both events were organised by Thanet District Council, and the same evening, the Little Ships returned from the voyage to Dunkirk where they had sailed to celebrate the evacuation of the BEF from the beaches of Dunkirk.

On Sunday, the flying display began at 12.10 p.m. when the C-130 of the RAF parachute display team took-off and completed their drop at 12.30 p.m.

to celebrate the team's twenty-fifth anniversary. It also included the Battle of Britain Memorial Flight, which displayed at 2 p.m., and the Vulcan, which took to the air at 2.30 p.m. The main theme of the Air Day was '50 Years After', and a display by a Spitfire and Hurricane stole the show. The Red Arrows took-off at 4.30 p.m. and began their spectacular twenty-five-minute display before landing again at 5.05 p.m.

The Air Day controller was Wg Cdr Gasson, and an unusual event that he had to commentate on was an attempt to fly a scale model of a Hurricane from the former Luftwaffe airfield at Gravelines across the Channel to Manston. The flight was organised by Thanet Model Flying Club and was an attempt to establish a record for the *Guinness Book of Records*.

Wg Cdr Jim Whitson, the CO, departed RAF Manston in November, when he was posted to the Ministry of Defence and was given a special responsibility for the RAF's role in the Middle East. During his time at Manston, the wing commander had overseen two Air Days that had raised a total of £140,000 for the RAF Benevolent Fund.

The officer who replaced Wg Cdr Whitson as CO was forty-five-year-old Wg Cdr Alastair Montgomery, a former Vulcan pilot who was posted in from RAF Gütersloh where he had served for three years. The wing commander had studied at Edinburgh University and joined the RAF after learning to fly with the university's air squadron.

For many people, Wg Cdr Montgomery's most well-known role was the one he had carried out in 1982 during the Falklands War, when he commanded the Vulcan detachment that had been sent to the Ascension Islands. The first sortie, 'Black Buck 1', was flown by Flt Lt Martin Withers on the night of 30 April–1 May to bomb the runway at Port Stanley. Another six 'Black Buck' operations were flown, and 'Monty', then a squadron leader, took part in several of them.

One of Wg Cdr Montgomery's first job as CO was to see oversee the demolition of the old officers' mess, the original farmhouse that had belonged to Pouce's Farm that had been requisitioned under the Defence of the Realm Act in 1919. The building had a certain reputation for being 'haunted' by a 'white lady', allegedly the ghost of a young woman who had killed herself after being spurned by her intended. The wing commander refused the offer to drive the JCB to begin the destruction of a building that was an integral part of RAF Manston's history.

On 1 February 1991, a funeral service was held in St Catherine's Church in the village of Manston for Sgt Ernest Scott, who had been listed as 'missing, presumed dead', on 27 September 1940. He had been shot down by Maj. Werner Mölders near Maidstone, but his body was not recovered until December 1990 by a salvage unit from RAF Abingdon. The Spitfire had been located by a historical archaeologist group who had discovered the crash site while researching RAF Records at the public records office. After the service, Sgt Scott, who had been a member of 222 Squadron, was buried with full military honours in Margate's

St John's Cemetery, with a twelve-man firing party over his grave and a bugler playing the last post.

It was announced in March 1991 that RAF Manston was to close at night and at weekends, a reduction in hours that would seriously affect the viability of the civil side: Kent International Airport. Just a week or so later, Wg Cdr Montgomery made a statement saying that Manston was to remain open twenty-four hours a day. Mr John Collins, Chief Executive of Kent International Airport, pointed out that his company had a 125-year lease from the MOD to operate the civil side as an airport. He stated that whatever the MOD's plans were, the company would work closely to ensure that civil flights were not affected.

An Air Gambia Boeing 707 was diverted to Manston and made an emergency landing in August after its crew had discovered problems with the hydraulic system; the aircraft was flying from Dublin to Free Town in West Africa with just nine crew on board. A safe landing was made with the landing gear being wound down manually and flaps worked electrically. Fortunately, Manston had a repair facility for a Boeing 707, and after repairs had been carried out, the aircraft departed at 4 a.m. the following morning on a flight to Gambia to collect 175 passengers to fly to back to Gatwick.

There had not been an Air Day in 1991 after the spectacular display in 1990 had caused 25,000 cars to build up in long traffic jam that had been 21 miles long, but Manston's community relations officer, Flt Lt David Stone, announced in October 1991 that the Air Day might return in 1992 and be held in July that year. Flt Lt Stone had taken up the Civil Service appointment as community relations officers after retiring from the RAF as a squadron leader in the supply branch after serving since 1951.

Twelve civil aircraft with hundreds of passengers on board were diverted to Manston (Kent International Airport) on a Friday night in December after fog closed Gatwick Airport. Among them were two aircraft that had been on a day trip to Finland for an early meeting with Father Christmas. A small number of aircraft left Manston the next day bound for Malaga and Geneva, while most departed empty, positioning for the short flight to Gatwick.

It had been stated that a decision on the Air Day would be made before the end of the year. However, it was not until February 1992 that it was finally announced by Wg Cdr Montgomery that the Air Day would take place on 26 July and that the organisers hoped to assemble a host of famous aircraft and aviators, including the Red Arrows, the RAF Falcons, and the BBMF.

Manston-based company Jet Support was announced as the UK's leading aviation maintenance engineers in March 1992. The company had been based at Manston on the civil side that had previously been used by Invicta Airways since 1986 and maintained aircraft from all over the world, but they specialised in the Boeing 707. Jet Support had just completed a contract working on a Nigerian Airways cargo aircraft, which had been handed over at Manston the week before.

Princess Anne flew into Manston on 29 May 1992 to formally open the new £1.8 million combined ranks' mess to be used by the RAF and the Defence Fire Training & Development Centre. There had been fears that the visit might have to be called off because of bad weather, but the Queen's Flight's Wessex touched down safely and on time.

During her tour of the base, she saw a demonstration by an SAR Sea King helicopter of 202 Squadron and was shown firefighting techniques being developed at the station. Princess Anne also visited the Spitfire and Hurricane Memoral Building where she planted a commemorative tree in the garden behind the complex. The princess had last visited Thanet in 1984 when she had gone to Fairfield House School in her role as president of Save the Children. Princess Anne was the first member of the royal family to visit RAF Manston since before the Second World War.

A major operation was put into place in July to deal with the expected volume of traffic that was expected to arrive for the Air Day on the 26th. Four separate routes had been chosen by the police to handle traffic approaching the airfield from London, Canterbury, Dover, and Thanet. Over 60,000 people were expected at the Air Day at which the last-surviving airworthy Vulcan made what was expected to have been its last appearance. The aircraft was then based at RAF Waddington, and on the day, it was flown by Flt Lt Paul Milliken, whose normal role was flying Victor tankers with 55 Squadron.

Other exhibits included a Tornado F3, a Nimrod F.16 from the Royal Danish Air Force, and a C.130 Hercules, which put in an appearance to celebrate the twenty-fifth anniversary of it entering service with the RAF's 36 Squadron during August 1967 at Lyneham. Tickets for the event cost £10 for adults and £5 for children. The entrance fee for a car was £15, but that covered the cost of its passengers.

Princess Anne arrives at Manston on 29 May 1992 and is met by the CO, Wg Cdr Montgomery. The purpose of her visit was to officially open the £1.8 million combined ranks' mess that was also to be used by the Defence Fire Training School. (*Grp Capt. Montgomery*)

The princess meets aircrew from 'C' Flight, 202 Squadron, the SAR unit that had arrived at Manston on 1 September 1988 with its Sea King HAR 3 helicopters. (*Grp Capt. Montgomery*)

Having arrived to officially open the combined ranks' mess, the princess meets staff from the Defence Fire Training & Development Centre (previously the Fire School Central Training Establishment) who shared its facilities. It was announced in July 2019 that the Defence Fire Training facility would move to Gloucestershire and the last course would begin in 2020. (*Grp Capt. Montgomery*)

Outside the Spitfire & Hurricane Memorial Building, Princess Anne helps to plant a tree to commemorate her visit to the station. The building opened on 13 June 1981 and was the first purpose built building in Britain to house a Spitfire. (*Grp Capt. Montgomery*)

Princess Anne is introduced to Mr Peter Turner, who the author (Joe Bamford) served with in ATC at Manston. After leaving the RAF, Peter worked on the PBX at Manston but later became the manager/curator of the Memorial Museum and held that role until 2006. (*Grp Capt. Montgomery*)

*Opposite above:* A group photo with the princess taken in the new combined ranks' mess, with Wg Cdr Montgomery sitting on her right, with his fellow officers posing in front of an iconic painting of the airfield. (*Grp Capt. Montgomery*)

*Opposite below:* A view across the airfield during the Air Day Extravaganza on Sunday 5 September 1993. (*Grp Capt. Montgomery*)

*Above:* Ingrid Montgomery, the CO's wife, takes to the air with a 'bungee' jump. Despite being afraid of heights, she bravely took part and raised a considerable amount of money for local charities. (*Grp Capt. Montgomery*)

*Below:* During the Air Day Extravaganza, a Sea King of 202 Squadron gave a demonstration of how to winch up a casualty. (*Grp Capt. Montgomery*)

23

# An Uncertain Future

Despite a successful Air Day, in November 1992, rumours abounded that RAF Manston was to close within the next five years. It was claimed that the first unit to go would be the SAR helicopter flight, followed by the meteorological office based on the ground floor of the control tower. It was known that RAF bases all over the UK were at risk of closure under a review of the defence budget, and local organisations appealed for some factual information and consultation before any decision was made.

Wg Cdr Montgomery denied suggestions that the RAF was about to pull out but stated that there were ongoing studies taking place at the MOD. He did, however, confirm that 202 Squadron's 'C' Flight would be leaving during the summer of 1994. The rumours about closure might have been a bit premature, but the figure of five years was not far out.

The first Aspro Holiday flight using a Inter European Airways' Boeing 757 took place in November. On a wet and windy Monday morning, the aircraft flew 130 passengers to Larnaca in Cyprus and Aspro's marketing manager, Mr David Hedges, said that the high booking levels had confirmed the company's conviction that Kent International Airport was a convenient location for the people of Thanet. The company, which was based in Cardiff, announced that it would also be starting flights from Manston to Majorca in the spring of 1993.

The death of RAF Manston's former CO, fifty-six-year-old Wg Cdr Jim Ward, was announced in January 1993. He had served at Manston from September 1983 to September 1985 before handing over to Wg Cdr Hindmarsh. Many tributes were paid to Wg Cdr Ward, particularly from his old friend Flt Lt Rocky Stockman, who said that he was a very popular station commander.

Described as one of 'Manston's most tireless workers', Community Relations Officer Flt Lt Dave Stone announced that he was to retire for the second time at the beginning of 1993. Dave had begun his RAF Career at Cardington, but he had later served overseas in Libya, Malaya, and Singapore, as well as lots of station in the UK. Having originally retired from the RAF at the age of fifty-eight with the rank of squadron leader to take on the job at Manston, Dave had dealt with 138 visits to the station, some by high-profile VIPs such as Princess Anne, but he and his wife, Julie, were now looking to retire to travel and follow up his pastime of caravanning.

In March 1993, a decision to close RAF Manston at night had upset a number of local businesses, especially workers at Seabourne Aviation who operated on the civil side of Kent International Airport and feared for their jobs. A spokesman for the MOD was quoted as saying that it had little use for Manston at the moment, but he denied that the station was to close, although he admitted there would be job cuts. An agreement had been made with Seabourne Aviation. Ground Development Manager David Hedges stated that the shorter hours would not affect its operations at all.

A Monarch Airlines A300 was among a small number of aircraft that began to use Manston for crew training purposes in April. Tony Knight from Kent International Airport said that the airfield had been chosen because it was far less congested than other airports in the south-east. Virgin Atlantic was another airline that began to regularly use Manston for crew training on its Boeing 747s.

Thursday 22 May was a terrific day for Manston and Kent International Airport, when a British Airways Concorde visited the station to take passengers on a forty-minute flight up the North Sea, returning via Belgium. Among the passengers were Mrs Jean Thorpe and her seventeen-year-old daughter, Jeanette, who was a student at Thanet College. Jean was disabled and confined to a wheelchair for many years, but she was now able to walk with the aid of crutches. Mrs Thorpe said it had taken her three years to save up the £450 for the flight, but she thought it was well worth it, having flown on the edge of space.

Another passenger, who had won a word search competition that had been organised in conjunction with Goodwood Travel and Kent International Airport, had been given a seat on the flight as first prize. Bill Pratt described his flight on Concorde as 'absolutely out of this world' and asked if he could do it all over again. He said that the cabin staff had looked after the passengers very well and that there had been a planet of Champagne. The lady who he was sitting next to was eighty years old and had never flown before, and he said it was quite an experience for her.

The death of RAF Manston's former CO, eighty-four-year-old Grp Capt. Tom Gleave, was announced in June; he was the man who had commanded the station on two occasions and who had been responsible the station being rebuilt in 1943. During the Battle of Britain as a squadron leader, he had commanded 253 Squadron that was equipped with Hurricanes, and on 30 August 1940, he had claimed five Me 109s destroyed—a claim that was verified. The next day, while flying Hurricane P3115, he had claimed a Ju 88, but he was shot down and badly burnt. Sqn Ldr Gleave was taken to the Queen Victoria Hospital at East

Grinstead where he underwent plastic surgery by Archie McIndoe and became one of his 'guinea pigs'.

Promoted to the rank of wing commander, his first spell commanding Manston was between October 1941 and April 1942 when the airfield was still struggling to recover from the damage inflicted by the Luftwaffe during 1940. In February 1941, he had the unenviable job of ordering the crews of six Swordfish to attack two German battlecruisers that were steaming down the Channel on what was later termed as 'the Channel Dash'. Convinced that they were being sent on a suicide mission, the wing commander stood to attention by the runway as they took-off and saluted each crew.

The 9,000-foot runway that was built in 1943 was attributed to Wg Cdr Gleave after his arguments with the Air Ministry during his second term at Manston between July and September 1942. After leaving Manston, he had joined the planning staff of Operation Overlord and left the RAF in 1953, but for many years, he worked at the historical section of the Cabinet Office. He also wrote his own account called *I Had a Row with a German*. Grp Capt. Gleave was a regular visitor to RAF Manston and had last been at the station on 2 April when he had been the guest of honour during a dinner to celebrate seventy-five years since the formation of the RAF.

In July, RAF Manston was granted the equivalent of the 'Freedom of the City' when the Ramsgate Charter Trustees approved the award of Honorary Townsman Award on the station to mark the long association between the town and the base. There was a parade at the Eastcliff led by Fg Off. Paul Warwick and the mayor, Councillor John Kirby, took the salute. Following the parade, Wg Cdr Montgomery was presented with the Townsman of Ramsgate scrolls. The ceremony also marked the golden anniversary of the Ramsgate/Broadstairs RAF Association Branch and seventy-fifth anniversary of the formation of the RAF.

On Sunday 5 September 1993, there was what was described as a 'RAF Fun Day Extravaganza', which was open to the public from 10 a.m. to 5 p.m. and attracted a crowd of 8,500 people. The station's community relations officer, Flt Lt Carol Couchman, later said that 'It was a good family day which we understand everybody enjoyed'. Among the highlights of the day were displays by the Spitfire, Hurricane, and Lancaster of the Battle of Britain Memorial Flight and the Red Arrows. Other static exhibits included a VC 10, Tornadoes, and a couple of F-16s. An unexpected arrival was a Mosquito that had taking part in the Shepway Air Day and landed at Manston after the pilot experienced technical problems with an engine.

There were lots of other attractions on the airfield, and Wg Cdr Montgomery's wife, Ingrid, took part in a bungee jump even though she was apparently terrified of heights. Proving that her husband was not the only high flyer, she raised £500 for local charities and other money raised on the day also went to local charities such as 'Save A Tear'.

The CO's wife made the news again in October when she officially opened the Merlin Room Cafe in the Spitfire & Hurricane Memorial Building. The plaque should have been unveiled by Caroline Grace who had planned to fly into Manston in her Spitfire, but bad weather made her flight from Duxford impossible and so Ingrid stepped in at the last minute. Wg Cdr Montgomery attended the event along with former Manston CO, Wg Cdr Tom Hindmarsh, and Sqn Ldr Peter Stoneham and Sqn Ldr Bob McCloud. The cafe had actually opened for business at Easter and had already proved popular with the public.

In November 1993, after three years in command of what were crucial years in the station's history, Wg Cdr Montgomery was posted out from Manston. His successor was Wg Cdr David White. After leaving Manston, Wg Cdr Montgomery served at Ramstein in German on nuclear plans and operations until 1994. He was then posted to Strike Command HQ at High Wycombe, where he was promoted to the rank of group captain. He retired in 1997 and became Bursar of King William College on the Isle of Man.

In February 1994, Baroness Cox, a member of the board of Christian Solidarity, flew out of Manston in an Il-76 (RA7642) that was involved in flying relief supplies to help children and other victims of the conflict raging in Armenia and Azerbaijan. On board the aircraft, which was flying to Yerevan, the capital of Armenia, were 3½ tons of supplies, such as food and blankets, and two ambulances that were destined for orphanages in the region. It was 1 a.m. when the aircraft was ready to take-off, and among those who turned out to wish the baroness and her team well was the CO, Wg Cdr David White. She claimed that she was not going with the life-saving cargo as 'Lady Bountiful' or seeking publicity but going into the war zone for the umpteenth time as plain Caroline Cox.

The mayor of Ramsgate, Councillor John Kirby, appealed to Prime Minister John Major in April to save RAF Manston's SAR Flight, 202 Squadron. The flight was due to move to Wattisham in Suffolk during July, but a parliamentary select committee had condemned the move and a local petition had been signed by 6,000 people demanding that the flight should remain at Manston. There were arguments about whether the RNLI supported the move, but it was suggested while the RNLI HQ did not oppose it, local lifeboatmen were totally against it.

Rather ironically, in May, the SAR flight took part in a major operation involving two cargo ships that had collided in the Channel. At 2.35 a.m., Manston's SAR crew had been scrambled to join SAR crews operating out of the flight's future base at Wattisham. A coastguard helicopter from Lee-on-Solent also took part in the rescue operation 20 miles south-west of Beachy Head, to deal with the rescue of the crews of the 30,000-ton *Ming Fortune* and 8,000-ton *Ariake Reefer*. It was 202 Squadron's final major rescue operation and the unit was pulled out of Manston in July 1994.

In June, RAF Manston could boast that it was home to yet another Spitfire that had seen service during the Second World War. The Spitfire IX (MK732), which had previously displayed the markings OU-U, of 485 (New Zealand) Squadron, and was named *Baby Bea*, arrived to spend the summer in the TG Aviation Hangar. It was claimed that the Spitfire, then usually flown by Flt Lt K.J. Macdonald, had shot down a Fw 190 over the beaches of Normandy on 8 June, to claim the first enemy aircraft destroyed on the day.

In September 1944, MK732 had taken part in Operation Market Garden, and it is believed that MK732 is the last-surviving Spitfire that took part in the ill-fated operation. In 1948, MK732 had been exported to Holland and MK732 arrived at Manston in Dutch Air Force colours where it was scheduled to take part in various events to celebrate the fiftieth anniversary of D-Day.

Concorde visited Manston again in June, and there was another prize winner in a competition that had been organised by Kent International Airport in conjunction with the *Isle of Thanet Gazette*. The lucky person on this occasion was forty-year-old Linda Turner from Margate, who had never flown before but arrived at Manston early on Saturday morning looking forward to her first flight, accompanied by her husband, Keith, with her son and daughter. They did not fly with her, however, and after she boarded the aircraft, they returned to the terminal building for lunch. She later described the flight as 'brilliant, absolutely brilliant' as she reluctantly left the aircraft to join her family.

Despite the campaign to save the SAR flight of 202 Squadron, in July, it moved out to Wattisham on what was described in the *Isle of Thanet Gazette* as a 'wave of emotion', with hundreds of local people lining the cliffs as the Sea King carried out its farewell flypast from Minnis Bay to Pegwell Bay at 10 a.m. before returning to Manston in preparation for the move to Suffolk. There was just time for FS Tony 'Rosie' Rose to have one final brew in the crew room before departing from Manston, and while the aircrew would be flying out, the ground crews would be making the long journey by road.

July 1994 was a busy month, and the station organised another Air Fair that took place on Sunday the 24th; not everyone was happy with the event. There was criticism that the Air Fair was a less attractive version of an Air Show and that it had the interest of corporate sponsors and other businessmen than that of the general public. Mr Andy Smith was one such critic who said that he would never visits an air show at Manston again, after having his view of the displays blocked out by rows of hospitality tents and businessmen enjoying themselves. Sqn Ldr Bob McCloud, Deputy CO at Manston, admitted that the display had been smaller than in previous years, but that there had been less personnel available to organise it.

On Friday 29 July 1994, former pilots and ground crew 616 Squadron held a reunion at Manston to celebrate the fiftieth anniversary of the unit being equipped with the Gloster Meteor. The occasion also marked the anniversary of the unit moving to Manston to become the first unit to fly the RAF's first ever jet fighter and the aircraft's half century. One of the few remaining airworthy

Meteors in service, an aircraft that was still being used by Martin Baker for ejector seat trials, flew in to join the veterans. Wg Cdr White joined the veterans as they exchanged stories about their exploits, and a Hawker Hunter, a Spitfire IX, and a Tornado F.3 also flew into Manston.

Manston had its first visit from a giant C-5 Galaxy of the USAF in August, which was to fly relief supplies to Goma in war-torn Zaire. Its 55-ton cargo consisted of pipeline equipment and special biscuits that contained minerals for those suffering from malnutrition. The Galaxy was flown in from Frankfurt by pilots Al Davies and Jim Zeitlar, and it belonged to 436th Airborne Wing. It is understood that the Galaxy was the biggest aircraft ever flown into Manston, and a Boeing 707 had to circle the airfield for some time while it was loaded and prepared for take-off.

During the morning of 24 August, a fire broke out in the engine room of the *Sally Star* after the ship had left Dunkirk for Ramsgate at 3.30 a.m. It was not the first time there had been a fire on the vessel, and a similar incident had taken place in 1988, only eleven days after entering service with the Sally Line. The Dover coastguard, who co-ordinated the rescue, requested an SAR helicopter; a Sea King of 202 Squadron was airborne from Wattisham at 5.50 a.m. to fly to Manston to pick up a fire rescue team. Both the Margate and Ramsgate lifeboats were involved in the rescue operation, and all emergency services in Kent were put on alert.

A Belgian Sea king was also dispatched to the ship, and it arrived on the scene at 6.27 a.m., fifteen minutes before the RAF Sea King. The RAF had claimed that its SAR helicopter could fly anywhere within a 40-mile radius within an hour, but on this occasion, it took seventy-two minutes to reach the *Sally Star*. Pumps and other firefighting equipment were taken on board the ship by firemen from Manston. The captain and nineteen essential members of the crew remained on board, while another eighty-four crew and seventeen lorry drivers took to the lifeboats. Only one member of the crew was injured, and he was flown to Manston by the Belgian Sea King. The *Sally Star* was later safely towed to Dunkirk where she underwent repairs.

There were further reassurances that RAF Manston would remain open in October, but Deputy CO Sqn Ldr Bob McLoud did admit that all the bases in the UK were under threat. He pointed out that the station still housed two training units, No. 1 AEF and 617 Voluntary Gliding School, and it provided important back up to Kent International Airport. 'It is business as usual' was his message to the press.

In January 1995, Manston received five visitors in the form of a detachment of Gazelle helicopters from the Army Air Corps that flew in from Middle Wallop. Rumours abounded as to the purpose of the presence, but Public Relations Officer Flt Lt Carol Couchman said that the detachment was there to practise instrument flying and other exercises and would train at Manston every six weeks.

This was the same Flt Lt Couchman who had been injured during the Great Storm in 1987, and after retiring from the RAF, she had taken over the role of community relations officer at Manston. She also worked with Ramsgate District Guides and Rangers and set up a project to take care of Romanian orphans.

Concorde visited Manston again in June 1995, and one young girl, thirteen-year-old Carly Adkins, was given a special treat when she was allowed a close-up view of the supersonic airliner, having become the junior winner in the *Isle of Thanet Gazette*'s competition. Having recently joined the local Air Training Corps, it was claimed that Carly had become something of a flying addict, but she was also learning to play the Glockenspiel so that she could secure a place in the band. While she was at the airport, Carly also got the opportunity to watch a Russian Il-76 being loaded and take-off.

RAF Manston celebrated VJ-Day on Sunday 13 August with an open day, but even the programme gives little information about the aircraft that were on show, although the front cover did feature Spitfire MK732. The day began with a drumhead service led by the bishop of Dover, and the aim of the event was to remember those who gave us the freedom to live today. The gates opened at 9 a.m. for the service at 11 a.m., and admission cost £1 with free parking.

On 1 April 1995, RAF Manston lost the last long-standing unit to be based on the airfield, when No. 1 Air Experience Flight moved out to St Athan in Wales where it merged with the University of Wales Air Squadron. Having been formed on 8 September 1958 and originally based at White Waltam and West Malling, the unit had been based at Manston for thirty-two years with the de Havilland Chipmunk T.10, having flown an average of 3,500 hours a year and amassing almost a quarter of a million flying hours. After relocation to Wales, No. 1 AEF was re-equipped with the Grob Tutor Mk I.

During August 1995, a campaign was organised by local MP Jonathan Aitken to move the RAF's aerobatic team the Red Arrows from RAF Scampton to Manston when the former was under risk of closure. It was claimed that the flying conditions at Manston were perfect and their presence would boost the local economy, and that it was a strong candidate to be the team's new base. As it happened, RAF Scampton remained open, and at the time of writing, the Red Arrows are still based there.

There was a serious incident at Manston in September when Spitfire MK732, which had been based at Manston since June 1994, made a crash landing after experiencing problems with the undercarriage. The aircraft had taken-off and was heading to Rochester for an air display when the pilot realised that he had a serious malfunction with the left wheel, which had been bent forward. Flt Lt Austin, an air traffic controller, said that the Spitfire returned to Manston and made a safe landing on the grass runway. The aircraft's propeller was bent and there was some other damage to other components, and a crane had to be used to lift it and take it to its hangar.

Concorde was at Manston again in September, and a Margate family, Kevin Henley, his wife, mother, and fifteen-year-old son, were among those who were on the flight. Kevin was another winner in the Kent International Airport/*Isle of Thanet Gazette* competition, whose prize was flight in the world's most famous aircraft. His wife, Amanda, had accompanied her husband to the airport, but she did not believe him when he told her that she was also going on Concorde, until she got the ticket in her hand.

Plans were announced by Wg Cdr White in November 1995 to build a memorial to American airmen who gave their lives in the Second World War. The plans were backed by The Liberator Appeal Group, whose members were Derek Chapman, Bob Massie, Arthur Pay, Eric Aplleton, and author, John Williams. The appeal for funds for the memorial was centred on incidents involving Liberators that crashed locally on 27 April 1944. The aircraft from the 392nd Bomb Group made a belly landing in the sea near Westgate in which four airmen were killed. Later the same day, another Liberator from the 446th Bomb Group crashed at Foreness Point, killing the crew of ten.

The CO, Wg Cdr David White, handed over command of the station in February 1996 to former Tornado navigator Wg Cdr Michael Richardson. Following tradition, the handover involved the passing of the station's wilkinson ceremonial sword. Wg Cdr Richardson had just completed a tour of operations at Strike Command HQ, High Wycombe. Wg Cdr White was posted to the Joint Services Defence College at Greenwich.

Flt Lt Nick Paine, a fighter pilot who had carried out a low-level mock attack on his parent's home in Staple in a Tornado, appeared in court in March. Paine had only recently returned from a tour of duty in Bosnia where the twenty-eight-year-old had been the youngest pilot to fly on operations. The incident had occurred in June 1996 on the occasion of his birthday, when he carried out a single flypast for the annual AOC's inspection. The Tornado screamed over Margate at 1,000 feet before descending to 250 feet towards runway 11 for the run across the airfield. He should than have turned for the coast and flown back to base at Leeming. Instead, he flew directly towards Staple, near Sandwich, where he allegedly terrified a lot of the locals. Paine denied flying an aircraft to cause distress and annoyance, but he was found guilty, fined £500, and given a severe reprimand.

On Friday 26 April, the *Isle of Thanet Gazette* informed its readers that the air show at Manston, one of Thanet's biggest attractions and planned for 28 July, had been cancelled. Flt Lt Marshal, the recently appointed public relations officer, said that the station had been faced with manpower cuts, and its resources were too thinly spread to proceed safely. Certain critical areas of expertise in organisation were needed but were not available, and so the show had to be cancelled.

The Battle of Britain-class locomotive, 34070 *Manston*, was on the move in April after languishing at Richborough Power Station for thirteen years while being rebuilt. The 90-ton steam engine, which had been taken out of service with British Rail in 1967, had close connection with the station and was moved by road to join three other engines at the Great Central Railway in Loughborough. The engine had only been 30 per cent restored, but the only way to complete its overhaul was to move it and it was estimated that it would take another five years before it was back on the track carrying passengers.

On Saturday 1 June, a ball was held at Margate Winter Gardens to celebrate the eightieth anniversary of RAF Manston (RNAS 1916–18). Tickets cost £15 and were available from the council. It was attended by over 300 civic dignitaries, members of the public, and the Air Training Corps. On the Sunday, airmen and officers from Manston paraded through Cliftonville where Wg Cdr Mick Richardson and Council Chairman Margaret Davies took the salute. After the parade, an hour-long service was held in the Winter Gardens, was led by the Reverend Brian Sharp, and music was provided by the band of the RAF from Cranwell and Thanet male voice choir.

Concorde made another two visits to Manston in 1996, in May when one of its passengers was a 100-year-old lady, Mrs Jan Jarman, who was joined on the flight by six of her nine children. On Saturday 28 September, Concorde was back again and carried over 100 local people on another half-hour flight over the North Sea. Mr Alister McBain, a veteran of the Second World War, who had flown forty-five operations as a navigator with Bomber Command, along with a colleague, transported a party of former RAF personnel to Manston in two Rolls-Royce cars. He did not travel himself because he had flown on Concorde before and he said he did it because he thought that the veterans were being neglected.

The closure of RAF Ash was announced in December 1996; the former GCI radar station, which had previously been known as RAF Sandwich, employed a large number of civilians who worked alongside service personnel. The underground station near Woodnesborough had been built after the war and was part of the Air Defence system of the UK, known as ROTOR, which had been replaced by the Linesman/Mediator Air Defence system in 1974. That had resulted in the closure of the bunker at Sandwich, but in 1989, the station had been reactivated as Improved UK Air Defence Ground Environment (IUKADGE).

24

# Countdown to Closure

In March 1997, an official scoreboard from 222 (Natal) Squadron, which had flown Spitfires and was based at Manston on two occasions in 1941 and 1942, was presented to the Spitfire & Hurricane Memorial Building. The scoreboard had been made out of metal from a Messerschmitt that had been shot down over Kent, and it had been a treasured possession of the squadron until it had been disbanded in 1957. The Squadron Association Chairman, Joe Crawshaw, said that he was delighted that the museum had accepted the offer to house it, as it would be seen by many members of the public.

A couple of unusual visitors arrived at Manston in April in the form of two thirty-seven-year-old Alize 1050s of the French Air Force. The type was the French equivalent of the Fairey Gannet, which had been operated by the Royal Navy in the '60s and '70s. The Alize were flown in from Brittany on a courtesy visit by Lt Pascal Carre and Lt Christian Nignucci and remained at Manston overnight.

A sharp-eyed fireman, Derek Williams, prevented a potentially serious incident in May when he spotted a flag hanging from the nose wheel of a Boeing 707 that was taxiing out for take-off. The flag indicated that the locking pin in the nose wheel had not been removed and it could have caused problems with the hydraulics had the crew attempted to raise the undercarriage. Derek was presented a Strike Command Flight Safety Well Done Award and he was presented with the award by Sqn Ldr Jeff Smithson.

The news that RAF Manston would be closed within two years was made public in July when the MOD stated that it had no operational need for the airfield and would withdraw by the end of March 1999. The MOD said that it would hold discussions about the future use of the civil side, Kent International Airport, with Thanet District Council. There were approximately 200 servicemen based at RAF Manston, as well as another 120 civilians, such as drivers and cooks. Armed Forces Minister John Reid stated that he appreciated that the news would not be welcome in the local community, but the withdrawal would not affect the MOD Fire Training School.

The commercial manager of Kent International Airport, Mr David Hedges, said that the news was not unexpected to anyone, and everyone knew that it was just a matter of timing. Roger Gale, MP for Thanet North, said that the closure offered a tremendous opportunity for the area and that he had been discussing the closure with the MOD and Kent International Airport for some time. He also stated that the worst option would be the realisation of the airfield being used as real estate for building, and it was that which he would guard against. A prophetic statement indeed, taking into account events that were to happen many years later.

On 18 July 1997, the Queen Mother visited RAF Manston to unveil a statue dedicated to the memory of Allied aircrew who lost their lives in the Second World War. The life-sized statue stands at the entrance to the Spitfire & Hurricane Memorial Building, and it was sculpted in bronze by Paul Seton, a lecturer at Thanet College. The statue, which had cost £14,000, had been paid for by public donation but organised by the Liberator Appeal Group. The statue was not officially handed over to the museum until Remembrance Day in November, when Sonia Stubbs-Pay, secretary of the appeal, also presented a plaque to Wg Cdr Richardson.

The actual pilot who had flown B-17 *Memphis Belle* during the war, seventy-six-year-old Col. Robert Morgan, visited Manston in August and was given a flight in a Scottish Aviation Bulldog to see the White Cliffs of Dover again. The story of the B-17, which had been the first to complete twenty-five missions, was told in a Hollywood movie made in 1990. Col. Morgan said that he remembered, after returning home from a mission, they had been the greatest sight in the world.

A ninety-year-old woman, Nellie Sollie, was given a flight on Concorde as a birthday present, when the iconic supersonic aircraft paid another visit to Manston in October 1997. The flight, which cost just £250, was paid for by her two daughters, son, and eight grandchildren. She had only flown once before—an internal flight from Gatwick to Newcastle—but she said this was a totally different experience because she was allowed to visit the flight deck and speak to the captain. Nellie, who lived in Finsbury Road, Ramsgate, said she was already making plans to fly on Concorde again for her ninety-fifth birthday.

There was some controversy in December 1997 about aircraft activity at night, which was being blamed on movements at Manston. The operations manager at Kent International Airport, Tony Knight, admitted that he had also heard what sounded like aircraft flying around at 1 a.m., but it had nothing to do with the airport. He claimed that any aircraft flying close by were likely to have been going into Southend Airport and asked those who were complaining to get in touch with the authorities there.

Ugandan-based cargo airline DAS, the largest freight carrier that operated out of Gatwick, stated that is was considering moving into Manston in January 1998. This announcement was made as the MOD was to put the airport up for sale and adverts were about to be placed in property and aviation magazines. The company, Wiggins, Plc, which owned the civil side and the airport, was expected to tender a bid. DAS employed 120 people and operated two DC-10s and two Boeing 707s and had flown a total of 34,000 tons of goods in 1997 and claimed to be Africa's premier cargo airline.

Mr Fisher, the airline's chief accountant said that a move to Manston would generate employment in Thanet and free up valuable slots at Gatwick. Wiggins stated the Manston site had a huge potential and wanted to develop it as a freight centre. It was promising to install new technology such as radar and build a new control tower and landing system.

As time went on, there were many rumours about Manston's future, and it was claimed in March that the airfield might be chosen to be the country's first Euro Air Park. Thanet District Council had commissioned a study into how the 700-acre air base might be used after the RAF had withdrawn. It was suggested that a 'Central Island Vision' could combine the airport with an industrial estate and link the airport with the ports of Ramsgate and Dover. Although Thanet Council had no say in who bought the land, it had already been in touch with Defence Minister John Reid who would make the decision.

By May, Wiggins, Plc, had submitted a bid for the airfield and was awaiting a decision from the MOD. The company already owned the civil side of Manston Airport, which it had purchased in July 1997 and in the same month, the Manston Business Park reopened for business. The 175-acre site on the western side of the airfield, previously known as Kent International Business Park, had closed for restructuring, and it was hoped that it would attract new investment.

Cummins had bought 20 acres of the site where 320 people were manufacturing generators. Wiggins had suggested that the airport could handle more than a million passengers a year and create over 200 jobs. The unemployment rate in Thanet was 9.4 per cent—one of the highest in the country—and it was hoped that the airport could bring further employment in the future.

A decision on the future ownership of Manston had still not been decided by July, and Wiggins stated that it would not pull out of the airfield even if it did not win the bid to buy the whole site. Marketing Manager Nigel Conradi said that the company's 125-year lease on the civil side and airport would not be affected and that tourist flights would continue. He stated that Air Atlanta, an Icelandic Airline, was already planning to move into Manston and operate both passenger and freight service.

It was finally announced in August that the Wiggins group were to be the new owners of Manston Airport, but there were still a few problems to be overcome, such as who was going to provide ATC facilities. Wiggins had approached the Civil Aviation Authority and requested that it provide licensed controllers, but there was not a lot of time left to sort such matters out. The MOD had already been approached by the company and requested that a few key RAF personnel, such as air traffic controllers, be left at Manston until their civil counterparts arrived.

On 13 November 1998, the officer who was to become RAF Manston's final CO took over the station. This was Wg Cdr Peter Kennedy, an officer in the RAF Regiment who was already the CO of the Fire Service Central Training Establishment. He had arrived at Manston in September and taken over the reins of the station from forty-nine-year-old Wg Cdr Michael Richardson who had been at Manston since January 1996. Richardson was posted to Incirlik in Turkey to work with a United Nation's Protection Force. Wg Cdr Kennedy said that his main role at Manston was to ensure a safe transition of the airfield from military to civil ownership.

Prince Philip flew into Manston on Thursday 26 November; the purpose of his visit to Thanet was to unveil a plaque at the North Foreland Lighthouse, which was about to be switched over to an automated system. It was the last lighthouse in the country to become automatic and Prince Philip performed the ceremony in his role as Master of Trinity House. There had been a lighthouse of one kind or another on the site since 1499, to guide ships entering or leaving the Thames Estuary around the Goodwin Sands—the existing structure dated from 1691. The prince, who had travelled from Manston in a Rolls-Royce, told the chairman of Thanet District Council, Margaret Davies, that the automation of North Foreland was the culmination of twenty years' work.

Fred Town, one of a handful of pilots who had flown Manston's Spitfire TB752, died at his home in Canada during November 1998. In 1945, Fred had been a flight lieutenant in the RCAF, when, on 4 May, he had shot down a Heinkel while flying in TB752. Fred was one of only seventeen pilots known to have flown the Spitfire during and after the war, and he had visited RAF Manston on several occasions to see his old plane.

In January 1999, Wiggins claimed that Kent International Airport could play a central role in a network of regional airports after the RAF pulled out of Manston. A spokesman for the company said that it was close to securing a £150 million deal with a financial partner in New York to develop the airport. He went on to say that currently the subject of finance was a sensitive issue, but there would be an announcement about funding during the next couple of weeks.

The transition from a military airfield to a civil one was not without its problems, and in February, more than fifty members of the public protested outside the buildings of Thanet District Council in Margate. Some of them carried banners with slogans, such as 'Wiggins Champagne talk, lemonade money', and demanded a public inquiry into Wiggins's plans for the airport. Head of Wiggins's Airport Group, Tony Freudmann, and chairman of the consultative group, Alister Hunter, agreed to a public meeting to be held at Ramsgate School on 18 February.

## 25

# The Final Days

In March, a second public meeting was held at the Margate Winter Gardens and it was attended by over 600 local people, many of whom attended the meeting because they had not been able to get into the one held at Ramsgate School, where over 1,000 people had turned up. Many of them were concerned about aircraft noise and especially those that might be flying in or out at night, and there were suggestions that grants might be available for double glazing. Another topic discussed was transport and the possibility of a monorail to relive the roads of traffic congestion.

Wiggins announced that it was considering using the name 'London–Manston' to get it recognised internationally, and it was proposing to develop passenger flights to Scotland and North America. Tony Freudmann claimed that in three years' time, Manston would be handling 300,000 passengers (revised from the original 1 million) and 40,000 tons of freight a year. The general feeling of the meeting was one of worry and the lack of control that the people of Thanet would have when the MOD pulled out at the end of the month.

Having been awarded a £50,000 grant from Thanet District Council, Manston Spitfire & Hurricane Memorial Building was able to build a much-needed coach park, the first sod of which was dug by Pat Doyle, Chairman of Thanet's Action Tourism Group. The museum was being visited by 100,000 people a year, and it was hoping to attract even greater numbers by targeting the coach group market. The grant would also go towards a new heating system for the museum to help preserve the two aircraft.

The week before RAF Manston closed, the *Isle of Thanet Gazette* published a brief statement giving its views on the MOD's actions, which was headed, 'RAF Manston gone but not forgotten'. It stated that it was still hard to accept that the historic operations at Manston would be over after the following Wednesday. It went on to say that for the majority of today's local residents, the events of fifty-nine years ago were known only through the history books or on the cinema screen. Their concerns were naturally for the future and what the years ahead might hold. But at the same time, they should never forget the heroic role of RAF crews, 'Without whose selfless efforts there would be no Manston today'.

On the day before RAF Manston closed, I travelled down from Yorkshire with my partner, Janice, and we stayed with our friends Collin and Marion in Cliffsend. Having worked as a flight engineer for Invicta International, flying the Bristol Britannia, Collin knew Manston well, and that night in the Sportsman Inn, we exchanged stories and memories about the old airfield.

Wednesday 31 March 1999 was a bright warm day, and we were up early and drove up to the airfield mid-morning and parked by the Spitfire & Hurricane Memorial Building. There were many other people milling about, but very few seemed to know what was going on and there was talk of the Red Arrows putting in an appearance along with the Battle of Britain Memorial Flight. In the event, neither turned up.

There was an air of anticipation all day as various types of aircraft came and went mainly in the form of fast flypasts by such types as the Tornado, Hercules, Dakota Nimrod, and Canberra. By late afternoon, activity around SHQ began to increase as invited guest and VIPs began to arrive for the final ceremony and there was a very surreal atmosphere around. RAF Manston has many 'ghosts', and I think most of them were present that afternoon to say 'goodbye' to the station that had been their home, some for over eighty years.

Just before 4 p.m., the AOC of 11/18 Group, to which RAF Manston belonged, AVM Brian Burridge, was driven on to the base to join veterans, servicemen, and their families who would take part in the final closing ceremony. No. 11/18 Group had been formed in April 1996 and it was a short-lived amalgamation of Fighter Command and Coastal Command. The AVM had been commissioned in 1967, trained as a pilot, and had flown in the operational role with 206 and 120 Squadrons, mainly flying the Nimrod.

The end of RAF Manston was probably best summed up by the comments of a RAF veteran pilot who attended the closing ceremony, Roger Pierce, who lived in Cliftonville: '… the history here is phenomenal and it's a shame to see part of our national history going'. Former servicemen saluted and a small number of them wept as the time came to lower the ensign.

At exactly 4 p.m., and as Flt Lt Ian Axford-Hawes, who was surrounded by station staff and veterans, requested permission to lower the ensign, Spitfire MK732 performed a flypast. After a blast from a whistle, FS Jim Galloway lowered the ensign, and my own thoughts were about how many times I had raised and lowered it in the past, alone and without ceremony, in my role as the duty airman.

The moving silence was only broken by the noise of the Spitfire's engine as it passed overhead before performing a 'victory roll' as a final salute. It was being flown by Lt-Col. (ret'd) Adriaan Brouwer who had been flying MK732 for two years since retiring from RNLAF. With the ensign having been lowered, eighty-

*Above:* AVM Brian Burridge, AOC 11/18 Group, arrives at RAF Manston for the closing ceremony, 31 March 1999.

*Left:* Just a few moments after 4 p.m. and the flag has been lowered for the last time, although the pennant remains on the flag pole. The crowds on the airfield begins to disperse to watch the Spitfire flypast.

The flag is neatly folded before being handed over to members of the local Royal Air Force Association.

Flown by former Dutch Air Force pilot Adrian Brouwer, Spitfire MK732 pays a final tribute to RAF Manston with a 'Victory Roll'.

A piece of RAF Manston's history in Minster Sidings. The remains of a Ford V8 engine that pumped fuel from the sidings and sent it to airfield to power the FIDO system.

The legacy of RAF Manston's wartime history. Royal Engineers deactivate and recover a pipe mine from an area near the central taxiway in May 2001. In the background is a DC-8 of resident airline MK.

three years of the station's history as a military base came to sudden end. For the crowd of thousands who had gathered to watch, it was a huge anti-climax.

All that remained was for the ensign to be neatly folded before it was presented to Grp Capt. (ret'd) Eric McCabe, Vice-President of the Ramsgate & Broadstairs Royal Air Forces Association. The former group captain, who had served at Manston during the 1930s, said that the ensign would take pride of place in the branch's HQ in Camden Place, Ramsgate. The final tribute was a concert that was held in the Winter Gardens, Margate, where the music was provided by the Central Band of the RAF.

After the RAF had pulled out, Manston (Kent International Airport) remained open until May 2014, and at the time of writing, there are various ongoing campaigns to reopen it. Hopefully at some point in the near future, Manston Airport will be back in action again. There is still a RAF presence in the form of the Defence Fire Training & Development Centre, but even that is threatened with closure.

RAF Manston has always been about more than bricks and mortar and a 9,000-foot runway. The station has always represented the courage, determination, and humility of those who served there through two world wars and beyond—that is why RAF Manston's history will never be forgotten.

# Bibliography

Ayerst, P., *Spirit of the Blue: A Fighter Pilot's Story* (Sutton Publishing, 2005)

Deal, L. E., *Manston Spitfire* (J. M. Preston, 1981)

Finnis, M., *Twilight of the Pistons: Air Ferry—a Manston Airline* (Michaels Bookshop, 2007); *Take-off to Touchdown: The Invicta Airlines Story* (Malcolm Finnis, 2006)

Halley, J. J., *The Squadrons of the Royal Air Force and Commonwealth, 1918–88* (Air-Britain Ltd, 1989)

*Isle of Thanet Gazette*

Stockman, R., *The History of RAF Manston* (RAF Station Manston, 1986)

*The Thanet Times*